ALSO BY JEFFREY TOOBIN

Homegrown: Timothy McVeigh and the Rise of Right-Wing Extremism

True Crimes and Misdemeanors: The Investigation of Donald Trump

American Heiress: The Wild Saga of the Kidnapping, Crimes and Trial of Patty Hearst

The Oath: The Obama White House and the Supreme Court

The Nine: Inside the Secret World of the Supreme Court

Too Close to Call: The Thirty-Six-Day Battle to Decide the 2000 Election

A Vast Conspiracy: The Real Story of the Sex Scandal That Nearly Brought Down a President

The Run of His Life: The People v. O. J. Simpson

Opening Arguments: A Young Lawyer's First Case— United States v. Oliver North

THE PARDON

THE POLITICS OF
OF PRESIDENTIAL MERCY

JEFFREY TOOBIN

Simon & Schuster

NEW YORK   AMSTERDAM/ANTWERP   LONDON
TORONTO   SYDNEY   NEW DELHI

Simon & Schuster
1230 Avenue of the Americas
New York, NY 10020

First Simon & Schuster hardcover edition February 2025

SIMON & SCHUSTER and colophon are registered trademarks
of Simon & Schuster, LLC

For information about special discounts for bulk purchases,
please contact Simon & Schuster Special Sales at 1-866-506-1949
or business@simonandschuster.com.

The Simon & Schuster Speakers Bureau can bring authors to your
live event. For more information or to book an event, contact
the Simon & Schuster Speakers Bureau at 1-866-248-3049
or visit our website at www.simonspeakers.com.

Book text design by Paul Dippolito

Manufactured in the United States of America

1 3 5 7 9 10 8 6 4 2

Library of Congress Cataloging-in-Publication Data is available.

ISBN 978-1-6680-8494-6
ISBN 978-1-6680-8496-0 (ebook)

To Eric Dodd and Noopur Sen

Contents

THE
PARDON

President Ford announces the pardon of Richard Nixon in the Oval Office on September 8, 1974. DAVID HUME KENNERLY/CENTER FOR CREATIVE PHOTOGRAPHY/U OF ARIZONA

PROLOGUE

Daredevil Sunday

EVEL KNIEVEL WAS NEVER A VERY SKILLED DAREDEVIL,
but that was part of his charm. His attempts to vault motorcycles
across long distances, like over rows of cars in the Astrodome or above
the fountains at Caesars Palace, often ended in theatrical crashes. (He
was said to have broken every bone in his body.) But Knievel's show-
manship and bravado, along with his trademark red-white-and-blue
jumpsuit, which was inspired by his friend Liberace, always attracted
attention, and the climax of his career came on Sunday, September
8, 1974. On that day, the nation—the whole nation—was watching to
see if he could pull off his greatest stunt.

Knievel had built what he called the Skycycle X-2, a sort of cross
between a rocket and a motorcycle, which was going to be propelled
off a ramp across a remote stretch of Idaho's Snake River. The goal
was to land safely on the other side, about 1,500 feet away, without
falling 600 feet to the bottom of the canyon. A crowd of 33,000 fans
made the trek to watch the jump in person, and a closed-circuit feed
was beamed to hundreds of theaters for pay-per-view audiences. As
always with Knievel, he promised a spectacle combining life-and-
death drama with camp comedy.

This rubbernecking lark fit the national mood. Just a month earlier, on August 9, President Richard Nixon had resigned, bringing to
an apparent close the grim saga of the Watergate scandal, which had
dominated public life for more than a year. Gone at last was endless
talk of cover-ups and hush money, of White House tapes and indicted

and unindicted co-conspirators. Gone, most specifically, was Nixon himself, who took his endless store of rancor and victimhood to exile in California. People needed a break from all the drama.

In Nixon's place came Gerald R. Ford, who represented a sunny alternative to his scowling predecessor. Ford fit a mid-century archetype of American positivity. He was an open-faced son of the Midwest, an Eagle Scout, a college football star at Michigan, a graduate of Yale Law School, a 33rd-degree Mason, a Rotarian, an Elk, and a veteran of World War II. In a quarter-century in the House of Representatives, he made scores of friends and, it seemed, not a single enemy. At a time when many worried about an imperial presidency, Ford was, the nation learned, a president who toasted his own English muffins in the morning. When he became vice president, just eight months earlier, he had acknowledged that he was "a Ford, not a Lincoln," but at this moment, that sounded more like a boast than a confession. Normal was in; contention was out.

Ford had lived through the final days of the greatest scandal in American political history, and he both reflected and expressed the relief at its conclusion. On the day that he became president, Ford said that "our long national nightmare is over." Three days later, when he first spoke to a joint session of Congress, he said, "I do not want a honeymoon with you. I want a good marriage." Ford already had the first, and it looked like he might have the second, too.

But then, just a few hours before the Knievel vehicle was expected to go skyward on September 8, Ford went to the Oval Office for a hastily scheduled address. The plan for the speech had come together so late the previous evening that, with the primitive technology then available, there was no time to wire the room for live TV transmission. Nor was there time to program a teleprompter, so Ford read from the papers on his desk in remarks that lasted less than ten minutes. Ford started speaking to a single video camera just after 11 a.m.; the recording was broadcast to the nation a few moments later. He concluded with the words of an official proclamation: "Now, therefore, I, Gerald R. Ford, President of the United States, pursuant to the pardon power conferred upon me by Article II, Section 2, of the Constitution, have granted and by these presents do grant a full, free, and absolute pardon unto Richard Nixon for all offenses against the United States which he, Richard Nixon, has committed or may have committed or taken part in during the period from July 20, 1969 through August 9, 1974." In nervousness, perhaps, Ford said *July* when he meant *January*. Then, still on camera, he grasped a ballpoint pen in his left hand and signed the document. "In witness whereof," he ended his speech, "I have hereunto set my hand this eighth day of September, in the year of our Lord nineteen hundred and seventy-four, and of the Independence of the United States of America the one hundred and ninety-ninth."

Before the day was out, Ford's honeymoon was over and the nightmare of Watergate had returned. The Knievel spectacle had a similarly sour denouement. The parachute on the Skycycle deployed prematurely, and the vehicle didn't come close to reaching the other side of the canyon. Instead, it drifted to an ignominious thud on the bank of the Snake River. Knievel was unharmed; his fans, who wanted a more dramatic outcome, one way or the other, were disappointed.

―――――――

In exercising his power to pardon, Ford was employing an anomalous provision of the Constitution. A central principle of the nation's governing document is separation of powers; the underlying theory is that the branches of government can prevent abuses by checking and balancing one another. In the famous words of James Madison in Federalist No. 51, "If men were angels, no government would be necessary. If angels were to govern men, neither external nor internal controls on government would be necessary. In framing a government which is to be administered by men over men, the great difficulty lies in this: you must first enable the government to control the governed; and in the next place oblige it to control itself." There is, however, no check or balance on the president's power to pardon. It is the provision of the Constitution most directly descended from the authority of kings of England.

The history of the pardon power bears out Madison's warning about unchecked powers. Pardons have often led presidents, and sometimes the country, into peril. There is a paradox, too, in presidents' untrammeled authority to grant or withhold pardons. At times, presidents have barely seemed to be in charge of their own pardon powers, because those around them have so successfully manipulated them. In establishing the separation of powers, the Constitution mandates certain processes for the operations of government. For example, laws must be passed by both houses of Congress, and the president can veto them, and those vetoes, in turn, may be overridden by supermajorities in the House and Senate. But the Constitution creates no process for pardons; this absence invites chaos in the executive branch. Presidents improvise their methods for conferring pardons, and this lack of structure invites manipulation and misjudgments.

And this, ultimately, is the story of Gerald Ford's pardon of Richard Nixon. Ford was the most accidental of presidents, the only one ever to take office without winning, or even running in, a national election. Before Ford became president, he spent his brief tenure as vice president attempting to avoid becoming president. His principal duty during that period was to travel the country extolling Nixon's presidency and thus trying to keep Nixon in the Oval Office and himself out of it. Throughout his life, Ford was often given the athlete's accolade—team player—and that was how he behaved until August 9, 1974. To plan for his own presidency would have been to betray his president, so Ford didn't do it. But that meant that when Ford did become president, he was uniquely underprepared, at least as far as Watergate was concerned. Ford was bolstered by his placid temperament and manifest decency, but he had been shielded, and shielded himself, from the precise nature of the issues he would have to address. This was especially true of the remaining challenges of Watergate, which did not disappear, much as Ford wished that they would. In the early days of his presidency, Ford largely depended on the White House staff that he inherited, notably Alexander Haig, who was Nixon's last chief of staff and Ford's first. To understand the pardon, it's necessary to understand the loyalties of those who were advising the new president.

For one of the more straightforward provisions in the Constitution, the pardon power has been the subject of a good deal of litigation over the years, including in the Supreme Court. During the controversy about the Nixon pardon, Ford himself, as well as his most important adviser on the subject, became fixated on a previously obscure Supreme Court decision from 1915. (Indeed, for the rest of his life, Ford carried in his wallet an excerpt from the Court's opinion in that case.) But it's an error—and it was Ford's error here—to believe that the pardon process is fundamentally legal in nature. Above all, pardons are political, not legal, and to be successfully defended, they must be defended in the language of politics. Pardons are the consummate discretionary acts; presidents are never required to issue even a single one. In this way, pardons reveal their roots in the royal prerogative of mercy. There is only one reason why presidents, or kings, issue pardons: because they want to.

For better and worse, pardons operate like X-rays into the souls of presidents. Gerald Ford revealed himself to be earnest, impatient, and overmatched by the dark genius of his predecessor. On his first day in office, Jimmy Carter used a broad clemency to hasten the end of the domestic traumas of the Vietnam War. Early in his presidency, Ronald Reagan used a pair of pardons to announce that he and the Republican Party were finished feeling guilty for the abuses of the Watergate era. In subsequent years, Reagan, George H. W. Bush, and George W. Bush revealed themselves by the pardons they did *not* grant; displays of mercy were in conflict with their tough-on-crime values. Bill Clinton, too, rose to power in the era of mass incarceration, and his own stinginess with pardons reflected that unforgiving moment. At the end of his tenure, in a headlong rush to make up for his harsh record, Clinton embarrassed himself with several unwise pardons. Like George H. W. Bush, Clinton also used clemency to settle scores with the special prosecutor who plagued their administration. Uniquely among modern presidents, Barack Obama moved to reverse some of the effects of mass incarceration, but he did it in a characteristically cautious and limited way. Joe Biden betrayed his principles, went back on his word, and damaged his legacy by pardoning his son.

Still, as with so much else, Donald Trump was, and is, different. The pardons in his first term reflected the characteristics he displayed throughout his presidency; he was transactional, narcissistic, and nearly joyful in provoking the ire of his enemies. Pardons and commutations have rarely figured in presidential elections, but Trump put a promise of clemency at the center of his victorious campaign in 2024. About 1,500 people have been convicted of participating in the riot at the Capitol on January 6, 2021; they were there at Trump's instigation to try to overturn his loss of the 2020 election to Biden. Trump described those who committed crimes at the Capitol as hostages, and he vowed to pardon them. When he does, Trump will again remind us who he is but also tell us something about the country he leads.

CHAPTER 1

Nixon's Lost Insurance

FOR MOST OF RICHARD NIXON'S TENURE AS PRESIDENT, he had an insurance policy against impeachment and removal from office. Its name was Spiro Agnew.

Agnew was a surprising choice when Nixon named him as his running mate at the 1968 Republican convention. At that point, Agnew was not even halfway through his first term as governor of Maryland, and he was virtually unknown in the rest of the country. Despite his obscurity, Agnew did appear to offer some political advantages as Nixon prepared to face Vice President Hubert Humphrey in the fall. Agnew came from the border state region which was expected to be closely contested, and he had made a modest splash by taking a hard line against civil rights and anti–Vietnam War protesters. In particular, Agnew had denounced local Black leaders in Baltimore for not doing more to stem the rioting that followed the assassination of Martin Luther King, earlier in 1968. Agnew's rhetoric fit with Nixon's determination to make law and order a big issue in the campaign, and the governor's contentious relations with civil rights leaders helped Nixon fend off the far-right independent candidacy of George Wallace.

Still, Nixon's political calculations around his vice presidential choice couldn't hide the broader point that Agnew was utterly unfit to be president. Before his brief tenure as governor, Agnew had been county executive in Baltimore County, a job which offered him considerable control over dispensing patronage in a notoriously corrupt state. Agnew had no experience with, or knowledge of, foreign or economic policy. His speeches and off-the-cuff remarks displayed the depth of his ignorance on almost all the issues a president could be expected to face. Once the pair won the election, Nixon began treating Agnew with the kind of casual disdain that Nixon himself endured in his eight years as Dwight Eisenhower's vice president. Nixon originally offered Agnew an office in the West Wing, near the Oval Office, but he quickly made Agnew surrender that space and sent him to the distant reaches of the Old Executive Office Building. (Agnew's office went to Alexander Butterfield, whose duties eventually came to include supervising the White House taping system.)

Initially, Agnew had so little to do as vice president that he spent months presiding over the Senate, a ceremonial role of no substantive importance. Later, Agnew made himself more useful to the administration in a series of speeches in which he attacked the news media for liberal bias. But Nixon himself mostly ignored his vice president. In the run-up to the 1972 race, Nixon almost decided to dump Agnew in favor of his treasury secretary, John Connally, the former Texas governor (and former Democrat). In the end, Nixon kept Agnew on, but the vice president remained a figure of contempt and ridicule among Democrats, who regarded the idea of Agnew's succeeding Nixon as anathema.

When Nixon was reelected, the Watergate story was little more than a blip on the national radar. The burglary of the Democratic National Committee offices in the Watergate complex took place on June 17, 1972. Five men were arrested and charged with attempted burglary and attempted installation of bugging devices. In the immediate aftermath of the arrests, some connections between the burglars and the Nixon White House came to light. But despite the best efforts of George McGovern, the Democratic nominee, and some in the media and in Congress, the story had little resonance for voters, and Nixon won a landslide victory in November.

Still, as Nixon began his second term in 1973, the Watergate scandal, and especially the role of the White House in the cover-up, picked up momentum. A half-century later, the story appears to unfold with an air of inevitability, as if Watergate was somehow always destined to lead to the end of Nixon's presidency. But that's far from true. There had been major and minor scandals for Nixon's thirty-six predecessors as president, and none of them had been forced from office. Only Andrew Johnson had been impeached, but that story was a hundred years old, and history's judgment had been harder on Johnson's adversaries than on his defenders. (One of the heroes of John F. Kennedy's book, *Profiles in Courage*, was the senator whose vote allowed Johnson to avoid conviction in the Senate.) Impeachment had a bad name. Scandals passed. Presidents served out their terms. That's how things worked. There was, in essence, no precedent for Watergate—for the perpetrators or the pursuers. From the crime to the cover-up to the pardon, it was all improvisation.

The story stayed alive in 1973 thanks at first to one of the Watergate burglars, James McCord. He had been convicted for his role, but shortly before he was to be sentenced, in March, McCord told John Sirica, the chief judge of the federal district court in Washington, that higher-ups had been involved. Sirica pressed for answers. At the same time, disclosures in *The Washington Post*, mostly written by Bob Woodward and Carl Bernstein, began to reveal the involvement of Nixon's top aides, H. R. Haldeman and John Ehrlichman, as well as his counsel, John Dean, in a cover-up. On April 30, Nixon requested the resignations of Haldeman and Ehrlichman and fired Dean. He replaced Haldeman as chief of staff with Alexander Haig, an Army general who had been a top aide to Henry Kissinger, then Nixon's secretary of state and national security advisor. In May, a special Senate committee, under the leadership of Sam Ervin, of North Carolina, began holding hearings about Watergate, and the following month, Dean gave dramatic testimony that Nixon himself had been involved in the cover-up about the burglary. In July, Butterfield revealed that there was a taping system inside the White House, which recorded most of the president's meetings. The hearings made for what was known as the "Watergate summer" of 1973.

At the same time as Watergate began dominating the news, a much lower profile investigation was proceeding in Maryland. The U.S. attorney there was looking at corruption in highway paving contracts among current officials in Baltimore County. At first the probe appeared to have nothing to do with Agnew, who hadn't held a county job since 1966. But over the course of 1973, prosecutors learned that cash bribes to Agnew—amounting to about a thousand dollars a week—had continued through his governorship and even when he was vice president. On August 1, Agnew was informed that he was under investigation, and the news broke in the media the following week. From there, the story accelerated quickly. By September, Agnew's lawyers were plea-bargaining with the Justice Department. On October 10, the deal came together. Agnew pleaded nolo contendere—no contest, effectively guilty—to a single count of tax evasion. He would be fined $10,000 but not imprisoned. And he would resign the vice presidency, effective immediately.

Nixon had lost his insurance policy. Agnew was so obviously unqualified to be president that even Democrats preferred to keep Nixon in office. Now, however, Nixon was in a position to name someone to the vice presidency who might turn out to be a plausible president.

———

Nixon was now compelled to become the first president to follow the succession provisions of the Twenty-fifth Amendment to the Constitution, which had been ratified in 1967. Before that time, there had been no way to fill vacancies in the office of vice president. This was why Presidents Harry Truman and Lyndon Johnson, vice presidents who took office upon the deaths of their predecessors, had no vice presidents until they were elected in their own right with running mates. Under the Twenty-fifth Amendment, Nixon could nominate a vice president, who would take office if he was confirmed by a majority vote in both Houses of Congress. Whom would Nixon pick?

The president, a Republican, faced a major constraint. The Democrats possessed substantial majorities in both the House and Senate, so Nixon would have to make a choice that was acceptable to the opposition party. As Nixon later recalled, he initially had three top choices—Connally and two prominent governors, Ronald Reagan, of California, and Nelson Rockefeller, of New York. All three presented problems. Connally had business dealings that raised ethical issues. Reagan and Rockefeller represented the right and left wings of the

Republican Party respectively, and the nominee of either one might split Nixon's party. In addition, all three were likely candidates for president in 1976. As Nixon recalled, "Many of the Democrats were understandably apprehensive at the prospect of the sudden elevation of a strong Republican to a position of such national prominence."[1] Democrats wanted a caretaker vice president, not a putative president.

Nixon had another complication. On October 6, Egypt and Syria launched a surprise attack on Israel in what became known as the Yom Kippur War. During the first week of the war, when Agnew resigned, Israel's very existence was in jeopardy. The president quickly announced that the United States would resupply weapons for Israel; the Soviet Union threatened to retaliate. The world was suddenly menaced by the possibility of world war. Nixon didn't need another major distraction. His staff polled four hundred Republican leaders, who came back supporting Nixon's favored three choices, but a poll of members of Congress produced another name—Jerry Ford. That bipartisan endorsement was especially important because, as Nixon wrote, "they were the ones who would have to approve the man I nominated."[2] So on October 12, just two days after Agnew resigned, Nixon nominated Ford to be his vice president.

———

In nominating Ford, Nixon's political instincts both served and betrayed him. He was right that Ford's relationships in Congress, especially with his fellow House Republicans, meant an easy confirmation process. But Nixon was wrong about something perhaps just as important. Nixon thought that Ford was another insurance policy against impeachment and removal. He regarded Ford as a lightweight whom no one could envision as president. In a conversation with Rockefeller in the Oval Office, which later made its way into the press, Nixon put his hands on the arms of his chair and said with contempt: "Can you imagine Jerry Ford sitting in this chair?"[3]

There was no doubt that Ford, who had just turned sixty, was a stolid, conventional figure. He was no intellectual. First elected from a district centered on his hometown of Grand Rapids in 1948, he was a Republican in a Democratic era. After he became minority leader in 1965, he devoted his career to a single goal: winning control of the House for the Republican Party and becoming Speaker of the House. In this he failed, over and over again. His job, in essence, was to travel around the country recruiting candidates and raising money. He gave as many as 238 speeches in a single year.[4] Focused on his political agenda, Ford neither sponsored important legislation nor conducted any investigations of note. He was a moderate when that was still an important faction in his party; he voted against tax increases and for the Civil Rights and Voting Rights Acts.

Still, ever the good Republican soldier, Ford was willing to take on futile, even embarrassing tasks. In 1970, after the Senate had rejected two of Nixon's nominees to the Supreme Court, Ford tried to help Nixon take revenge by leading an effort to impeach Justice William O. Douglas largely for writing an article for *Evergreen*, a magazine that included nudity. (Ford's initiative went nowhere.) Frustrated with the futility of his quest for a Republican majority in the House, Ford had more or less agreed with his wife, Betty, that he would retire from Congress after winning one more term in 1974. That was before lightning struck in the form of Nixon's summons to the vice presidency.

Like all good politicians, Ford learned to have some fun with his reputation for dumbness. He often quoted Lyndon Johnson's quip: "There's nothing wrong with Jerry Ford except that he played football too long without his helmet." Ford refrained from quoting something else Johnson said: "Jerry Ford is so dumb that he can't fart and chew gum at the same time." And for all Johnson's disdain for Ford's intellect, he knew that Ford was a respected figure in Congress; that was why Johnson named Ford to the Warren Commission, which investigated the assassination of President Kennedy. And, to be sure, Ford wasn't dumb. Rather, he had chosen a political role that capitalized on his best assets—his warmth and conviviality. Ford was a figure of his era in Congress, a time when politicians, especially in the House of Representatives, exchanged barbs on the floor and drinks in back rooms. (Ford's favorite golfing partner was Tip O'Neill, his counterpart as Democratic leader.)

Events conspired to give Ford an even easier ride than expected to confirmation in Congress. After Butterfield disclosed the existence of the White House taping system, Archibald Cox, the Watergate special prosecutor, issued a subpoena to Nixon to obtain the tapes as evidence. On October 12, the same day that Nixon nominated Ford, the United States Court of Appeals for the D.C. Circuit overruled the president's claim of executive privilege and ordered Nixon to produce the tapes. In response, Nixon offered what he called a compromise. He would produce transcripts of the tapes, which would be reviewed for accuracy by Senator John Stennis, of Mississippi, who was notoriously hard of hearing. Cox rejected that proposal, and on Saturday, October 20, Nixon ordered Attorney General Elliot Richardson to fire Cox. Richardson refused and resigned in protest. William Ruckelshaus, the deputy attorney general, also refused, and Nixon fired him. Finally, Robert Bork, the solicitor general and third in line at the Justice Department, agreed to fire Cox. The events created a political firestorm known as the Saturday Night Massacre.

Ford testified on his confirmation before the Senate Judiciary Committee, on November 1, less than two weeks later. Ford had not served in the Senate, but he obviously had many friends there and received abundant professional courtesy from his interlocutors. Members from both parties went out of their way to contrast the reasonable Ford with the embattled incumbent president. Ford was at his folksy best, stating, for example, "Perhaps the worst misgivings I have about the Vice Presidency are that my friends might stop calling me Jerry." His only expression of indignation came when he was asked about a claim in a recent book that he had once been a patient of a New York psychotherapist, Dr. Arnold Hutschnecker. This was still a time when psychiatric treatment was a major taboo for politicians; just two years earlier, Senator Thomas Eagleton had to step down as McGovern's running mate after news broke that he had been treated. To his congressional questioners, Ford asserted, "I'm just disgustingly sane." Manifestly, he was.

Ford's nomination was so uncontroversial that his hearing received only modest attention in the small universe of political news outlets. There was no cable news, no internet, no social media, not even a national newspaper like *USA Today*. Only one network evening news program covered Ford's hearing at all. There was a story in *The New York Times*, and the paper printed excerpts from Ford's testimony, but it didn't include one exchange that later took on considerable significance.

Senator Howard W. Cannon, the Nevada Democrat who was chairman of the committee, asked, "If a President resigns his office before his term expired, would his successor have the power to prevent or to terminate any investigation or criminal prosecution against the former President?"

"Would he have the authority?" Ford replied.

"Yes, would he have the power?"

"I do not think the public would stand for it," Ford said.

Neither man used the word, but Ford was saying—or at least strongly implying—that if he became president, he wouldn't pardon Nixon. And there, for the moment, the issue rested. But the pardon question had been raised, and it turned out the real answer would be a good deal more complicated than this quick exchange suggested. Cannon might well have asked on what basis any president should confer any pardon. What were good reasons—and bad ones? And why, for that matter, did the president have the power to pardon at all?

CHAPTER 2

The Benign Prerogative

WHEN IT COMES TO PARDONS, PRESIDENTS ARE KINGS. NO other provision of the Constitution replicates royal authority with such precision. As Chief Justice John Marshall put it in an opinion from 1833, "As this power had been exercised, from time immemorial, by the executive of that nation whose language is our language, and to whose judicial institutions ours bear a close resemblance; we adopt their principles respecting the operation and effect of a pardon, and look into their books for the rules prescribing the manner in which it is to be used by the person who would avail himself of it." In England, the earliest reference to such authority came under King Ine of Wessex (688–726), when the law stated "be it in the king's doom whether he shall or shall not have life."[1] In these distant years, the pardon existed chiefly as a tool to encourage repentance and reform. For instance, King Cnut (1016–1035) issued a proclamation guaranteeing that "as great mercy as possible shall be shown to him" who "zealously desires to turn from lawlessness to observance of the law."

But even in these early days, the issues arose that haunt the debate over pardons to this day. Who is the real beneficiary of the pardon power? Is it just the recipient, who is relieved of a burden or penalty? Or is it the sovereign himself, who leverages this authority for his own advantage? Almost from the beginning, there were those in Parliament who complained that kings used pardons to reward their friends or to raise money. These protests were generally ineffectual until the seventeenth century, which, not coincidentally, was the period that provided the greatest inspiration to the colonists in America. Parliament began putting certain offenses off-limits for royal pardons, notably those that involved either some kind of self-dealing by the monarch or offenses against Parliament itself. Most notably, if Parliament voted an impeachment, the monarch could not overrule it. As England cemented its hold over the American colonies, the power to pardon generally went to the royal governors who presided there. The controversy went with them.

In the first years after the American Revolution, the pardon power withered. Under the Articles of Confederation, there was no national chief executive and thus no provider of pardons. The structure reflected the general ambivalence at the time about investing so much authority in a single official. In the individual colonies, some governors had the power to pardon but often with a check from the legislature or another independent body. In Delaware, for example, the state constitution provided that "no pardon or reprieve shall be granted, but by a resolve of the house of assembly." To this day, this configuration—the governor may pardon subject to a legislative veto—endures in many states.

Of course, one major reason the Framers abandoned the Articles and wrote a new constitution was to create and empower a national executive, who would be called a president. At the Constitutional Convention in Philadelphia in 1787, the advocacy of Alexander Hamilton and others led the Framers to give the president the power to pardon. But the scope of that power was hotly contested. Roger Sherman of Connecticut proposed that the president have only the right "to grant reprieves until the ensuing session of the Senate, and pardons with consent of the Senate," but that was voted down. In the end, the Framers adopted a proposal close to the English rule. The final version of the relevant portion of Article II, Section 2 reads:

he shall have Power to grant Reprieves and Pardons for Offences against the United States, except in Cases of Impeachment.

Two limitations stand out immediately. First, the power applies only to federal crimes; the president cannot pardon anyone for violations of state law. (Then as now, most crime in the United States is prosecuted by state officials, like the local police, enforcing state law.) Second, the limitation of the president's pardon power preserves the core legislative function of voting impeachments, including of the president. It would be illogical, of course, if the president could use the pardon power to exempt himself from the possibility of being impeached by the House and removed by the Senate; that would render Congress's power to impeach the president a nullity. (Presidential pardons also cannot undo civil judgments.)

As the chief exponent of the Constitution's creation of a strong chief executive, Hamilton embraced the pardon power. In Federalist No. 74, Hamilton described pardons as a check on what would later be called mass incarceration. "Humanity and good policy conspire to dictate, that the benign prerogative of pardoning should be as little as possible fettered or embarrassed," he wrote. "The criminal code of every country partakes so much of necessary severity, that without an easy access to exceptions in favor of unfortunate guilt, justice would wear a countenance too sanguinary and cruel." With characteristic cleverness, Hamilton was in this way flipping an argument against the breadth of presidential power: the pardon existed not to embolden the chief executive but rather to gentle the harsh realities of the criminal law. Hamilton also demonstrated considerable prescience in asserting that pardons could help presidents address broader political problems, not just rectify single injustices. He wrote, "there are often critical moments, when a well-timed offer of pardon to the insurgents or rebels may restore the tranquillity of the commonwealth."

As Hamilton predicted, presidents needed the pardon power almost immediately, to address early threats to the peace of the Republic. In 1791, Congress and President Washington imposed a new excise tax on whiskey. Farmers in the West—that is, Pennsylvania—felt wronged by the new levy, and thousands protested, some violently, in what became known as the Whiskey Rebellion. Washington sent a major force to put down the rebels, who mostly surrendered without a fight. Still, several were prosecuted for treason. In the end, though, Washington thought mercy was better than martyrdom for the rebels, and he pardoned all those convicted.

In 1798, Congress passed, and President John Adams signed, a series of laws known as the Alien and Sedition Acts. The laws included
a series of restrictions on political speech that Adams's opponents
argued were unconstitutional under the First Amendment (as they
surely would be found today). There were several prosecutions of Adams's opponents under the laws. Outrage over the Acts contributed
to Thomas Jefferson's victory over Adams in the election of 1800, and
President Jefferson promptly pardoned all those convicted under the
laws that he and his supporters despised.

The motivations behind these first two important groups of pardons differed. For Washington, it was magnanimity; for Jefferson,
vindication. But for both presidents, the pardons were political acts,
aimed to advance the larger goals of each man's administration.
Their successors have offered various rationales for the high-profile
pardons of their terms, often labeling them merciful gestures. But the
better prism for these presidential decrees—always—has been politics. Pardons are manifestations of the presidential id—actions un-
constrained by even the possibility of check or balance. For better or
worse, the unilateral nature of the power means that a pardon reveals
a president's truest self.

———————

Even more than Washington and the Whiskey Rebellion, or Jefferson
with the Alien and Sedition Acts, the Civil War forced Abraham Lincoln to confront the issue that Hamilton anticipated: how to use the
pardon to address the gravest crisis in American history. In the nineteenth century, the penalty for treason was death, and thousands,
if not millions, of Southerners were arguably guilty of it during the
Civil War. Criminal prosecutions on such a scale were both infeasible
and unwise. The situation raised a classic dilemma for presidential
mercy. How should the president bestow enough forgiveness to help
restore the Union, while at the same time impose an appropriate cost
for a massive, region-wide betrayal?

By this point, the pardon power had broken down into four categories, which remain to this day. Collectively, these are often referred
to as the presidential powers of *clemency*.

A *pardon* is the broadest exercise of presidential mercy. It treats a conviction as if it never occurred and frees the recipient from any of its continuing consequences, like a limitation on voting, owning a firearm, or serving in office. (Today, restoration of the right to own a firearm is a principal motivation for many seekers of pardons, even long after they have been released from custody.)

A *commutation* ends a punishment—a prison term or a fine—but the recipient retains the status of a convicted criminal.

A *reprieve* merely delays the imposition of a punishment. Reprieves were never common and long ago fell into disuse.

An *amnesty* differs from a pardon in that it applies to a whole class of persons or communities rather than to individuals. It also differs from a pardon in that it is granted regardless of whether there is proof of the recipients' guilt. Amnesties can also impose conditions on those who receive them.[2]

Lincoln's approach reflected the spirit of his Second Inaugural Address: "with malice toward none with charity for all." As far as the Union Army was concerned, Lincoln was famously reluctant to allow executions of deserters, and he pardoned any number of the soldiers under his own control.[3] The South presented a more complex problem. There were simply too many rebels to identify and pardon one by one, so Lincoln offered a series of amnesties to Southerners in 1863 and 1864 if they would take oaths of loyalty to the Union. All but high government and military officials from the South were eligible. Those who took the oath could get their property back (except enslaved people). Thousands took him up on the offer. The generosity of Lincoln's amnesty concerned many Radical Republicans, who wanted stronger action against the rebels.

After Lincoln's assassination, on April 15, 1865, just six days after the South surrendered, President Andrew Johnson appeared to take an even harder line than his predecessor on granting relief to the former rebels. His first orders restricted the number of Southerners eligible for Lincoln's amnesty. But in short order, Johnson revealed his true nature as a slaveholding Southerner. After restricting the amnesty for ordinary Southerners, he coddled the leaders of the Confederacy by granting them pardons. For Radical Republicans, Johnson's crowning outrage came in 1868, when he pardoned the Confederate president, Jefferson Davis.

Before Lincoln's death, his allies among the Radical Republicans tolerated his attempts toward reconciliation with the South. But the Radicals reviled Johnson, whom they regarded as a rebel sympathizer, or worse. So, after Lincoln and Johnson used amnesties and pardons to protect the rebels, the Radicals tried at least to prevent leading Southerners from returning to power. To this end, the Radicals crafted Section 3 of the Fourteenth Amendment, which was ratified in 1868. That provision barred from high federal office any person who "shall have engaged in insurrection or rebellion." (Under this provision, two states barred Donald Trump from the presidential ballot in 2024 because of his connection to the events at the Capitol on January 6, 2021. However, the Supreme Court, in a unanimous decision later in 2024, overturned the states' judgments and returned Trump to the ballot.)

In a series of cases during and after the Civil War, the Supreme Court upheld the president's broad authority under the pardon clause of Article II and dealt Congress out of the process. The pardon power belonged to the president alone. In 1866, the Court ordered an Arkansas lawyer and ex-Confederate, who had received a presidential pardon, to be allowed to return to law practice. In his opinion in *Ex parte Garland*, Justice Stephen Field spelled out the wide scope of the president's authority. "This power of the President is not subject to legislative control," he wrote. "Congress can neither limit the effect of his pardon nor exclude from its exercise any class of offenders. The benign prerogative of mercy reposed in him cannot be fettered by any legislative restrictions."

Moreover, according to Field, "The power thus conferred is unlimited, with the exception [of impeachment]. It extends to every offence known to the law, and may be exercised at any time after its commission, either before legal proceedings are taken or during their pendency or after conviction and judgment." There are two important implications of this part of the ruling. First, a pardon can only excuse crimes committed in the past. In other words, a pardon cannot be a license to violate the law in the future. Second, the president can issue a pardon to cover conduct that is not yet the subject of criminal charges. This precedent, then, is the reason that Ford could pardon Nixon before he was indicted and guarantee that he never would be.

———

Lincoln's amnesty, and the expansion of the federal government as a whole during the Civil War, had an impact on the processing of pardon requests. Previously, the whole matter was handled on an ad hoc basis, as the president and his staff acted on pardons as best they could. But in 1865, Congress created what is now called the Office of the Pardon Attorney (OPA) in the Department of Justice. As always, the ultimate responsibility for pardons would remain with the president, but the pardon attorney existed, at least at first, to create intelligible and fair standards and procedures.

The Office of the Pardon Attorney remains a part of the federal bureaucracy, with a current roster of about forty attorney and non-attorney staff members. In recent years, the head of the office has been a career official, not a political appointee. The standards for recommendations by the pardon attorney have long been publicly available. According to Justice Department regulations, applicants should wait at least five years after conviction or release from confinement (whichever is later) to seek a pardon. OPA will then consider the applicant's post-conviction conduct, character, and reputation; examine the seriousness and relative recentness of the offense; and the applicant's remorse and atonement for his or her crime. Notably, too, the OPA will seek out the recommendation of the federal prosecutors who brought the case against the applicant. In all, the OPA has long been a cautious and slow-moving part of the Justice Department bureaucracy.

But the nineteenth-century change in the federal bureaucracy also had a less obvious effect. The existence of the OPA essentially bifurcated the pardon process. All presidents have relied on the pardon attorney to greater or lesser extents, but no president is obliged to agree with OPA recommendations or even to consult OPA at all. In addition to acting on the OPA recommendations, each president has also operated as his own pardon attorney, weighing pardon requests that come directly to the White House or to the president himself. This is their right under the Constitution, but the pardons outside the OPA process have always been the most controversial. These White House pardons, as opposed to those screened by the Department of Justice, have raised the same kinds of issues relating to the abuse of power that were familiar to king and Parliament hundreds of years ago.

———————

After the Reconstruction era, the presidential pardon entered a period of placid acceptance. Each president pardoned several hundred people, though that number grew with the overall population, and few of the grants drew much attention. In an era before the development of parole and other systems for limiting incarceration, presidents took active roles in ameliorating the harsh effects of long sentences. Often, the requests for pardons and commutations came from federal judges who felt that the laws had required them to impose unduly harsh sentences.[4] Rutherford B. Hayes granted more than one thousand acts of clemency, including to twenty-four murderers on death row.[5] The records from the nineteenth century are imperfect, but some of the recipients appear to have been elderly ex-convicts who wanted to get their affairs in order before their deaths. Members of Congress often petitioned the president to cut breaks for favorite constituents. At a time when the population of the United States was less than a third of what it is now, and when the federal prison population was less than 10 percent of what it is now, hundreds of acts of clemency had a significant impact. As one scholar of the late nineteenth and early twentieth century observed, "Pardoning throughout this period was a regular part of the housekeeping business of the presidency. Pardons were granted frequently and generously at regular intervals over the course of each President's term, with no slow starts and no bunching of grants at the end."[6] (William Henry Harrison and James Garfield, who both served briefly, are the only presidents to have issued no pardons.)

The most surprising pardon took place during the brief and uneventful presidency of Warren Harding.[7] In the election of 1920, Harding and Calvin Coolidge defeated the Democratic ticket of

James M. Cox and Franklin Roosevelt handily in the Electoral College and 16 million to 9 million in the popular vote. Eugene V. Debs, the Socialist Party candidate, received 914,000 write-in votes, or 3.41 percent of the total, even though he was in a federal prison in Atlanta on Election Day. (This was Debs's fifth run for president; in 1912, he received 901,000 votes, or 5.99 percent of the total.)

By the time Harding was inaugurated, in March 1921, Debs was sixty-six years old and in poor health and at risk of dying in prison. He was serving a ten-year sentence for violating the Espionage Act by giving a speech at a picnic in Canton, Ohio, denouncing American involvement in World War I. Speeches like Debs's would eventually be protected by the First Amendment, as the Supreme Court came to adopt the dissenting opinions of Justices Louis Brandeis and Oliver Wendell Holmes from this era.[8] But that deliverance would come too late for Debs himself. Harding's own politics could scarcely have differed more from Debs's worldview, but the president worried that Debs might die a martyr, so he arranged for the prisoner to take a train, on his own, from Atlanta to Washington to meet with the attorney general, Harry Daugherty. The pair had an animated talk about government, religion, and socialism, and then Debs returned himself to prison.

Then, two days before Christmas in 1921, Harding commuted Debs's sentence to time served, along with the sentences of twenty-three other political prisoners, including members of the Industrial Workers of the World (the "Wobblies"). On December 26, Harding welcomed Debs to the White House, telling him, "Well, I've heard so damned much about you, Mr. Debs, that I am now glad to meet you personally."

As Gerald Ford would discover a half-century later, not all acts of clemency ended so happily.

Vice President Ford seated next to his aide Robert Hartmann on Air Force Two. DAVID HUME KENNERLY/CENTER FOR CREATIVE PHOTOGRAPHY/U OF ARIZONA

CHAPTER 3

The VP's Job

ANY AIRPLANE CARRYING THE VICE PRESIDENT IS DESIG-
nated Air Force Two, but all VPs have one plane designated for their
exclusive use. When Ford was sworn in as vice president on December 6, 1973, he was assigned a twenty-year-old propeller-powered Air
Force Convair C-131. The fuselage was narrow, the exterior dented,
the engines noisy; it twitched in the air. Its maximum speed was less
than 300 mph, and it could fly only 1,500 miles without refueling.
Long after he left office, Ford called it "that horrible airplane."[1]

The government's executive fleet included modern jets which
were twice as wide, twice as fast, and could go twice as far on a tank
of gas. But Alexander Haig, the White House chief of staff, who made
such decisions, thought Ford was adequately served by the aging prop
plane. And Ford wasn't the kind to complain in a new job. On the
other hand, Robert Hartmann, Ford's chief of staff, was.

In the eight months of Ford's vice presidency, and the following
month until the pardon, Hartmann was a key figure, though he is
largely forgotten today. Born in 1917, Hartmann as a teenager went
to work as a copy boy at the *Los Angeles Times*, graduated from Stan-
ford, returned to the *Times* as a reporter, and then served four years in
the Navy as a press officer and military censor during World War II.
He then worked at the *Times* for two decades, an era when the newspaper was in a sturdy and enduring alliance with the Republican
Party. As the Washington bureau chief, Hartmann cultivated close
ties with Republican politicians, including Jerry Ford. Hartmann

"was a Republican and proud of it," Ford later wrote. "Most Washington reporters insist they're 'independent' when, in fact, they are liberal Democrats. Bob stood out in that crowd and I admired him for it."[2] In 1966, Hartmann went to work for Representative Ford as a speechwriter and ultimately chief of his legislative staff.

Ford and Hartmann were an odd couple. Ford was genial, open, and easygoing. Hartmann was suspicious, surly, and frequently angry, especially when he was drinking. Dick Cheney, who later joined Ford's presidential staff, recalled of Hartmann in an oral history interview, "The stewards used to keep score. He never knew this, but they'd keep track of how many drinks they served him. He was a big martini man. At the end of one of these counts, I'd just get a piece of paper with a little number on it, and that was Hartmann's consumption for that day. It was big time."[3] Based on the number of reported martinis, Cheney could adjust his behavior around Hartmann or avoid him entirely.

Like the best speechwriters, Hartmann had a gift for putting Ford's own thoughts into more graceful form. "I found that Ford was not inarticulate," Hartmann recalled. "He was very intelligent, but almost tone-deaf to a felicitous combination of words."[4] Ford understood his own limitations and decided to put up with Hartmann's. As Ford later wrote, "He was always snapping at people and he was a terrible administrator himself. But I could—and did—overlook these faults because Bob was shrewd and he possessed good political judgment. In addition, he could write an excellent speech, one that suited my style."[5] In the small confines of a congressional office, especially one in the minority, where there were few responsibilities for governing, Ford and Hartmann, both pipe smokers, had the time to chat at length. Since Ford's major assignment was to travel and talk up the Republican Party, Hartmann was, as his communications adviser, invaluable.

That changed in the White House. Ford named Hartmann his chief of staff, which the vice president quickly came to regret. "A dreadful mistake," Ford later called it.[6] The administrative problems that Ford saw in his congressional office were magnified with a bigger staff, and higher stakes, in the vice presidency. In short order,

Ford layered in another staff member to handle the bureaucracy, but Hartmann remained Ford's chief political adviser. In Congress, that had mostly meant figuring out how to joust with the Democratic majority, but in the White House, Hartmann fixated on a different set of rivals—Nixon's staff. Hartmann dubbed Nixon's enablers "the Praetorian Guard," after the Roman officials who surrounded and protected the emperor. With characteristic dyspepsia, Hartmann called this group "an arrogant, elite guard of political adolescents who nearly wrecked the Republican Party."[7] Chief among Hartmann's villains was Haig. And assigning Ford a shabby airplane was the least of Haig's crimes. Through Hartmann's title changed as Ford moved from vice president to president, his influence endured. Hartmann didn't win every bureaucratic battle, but Ford heard him out on every issue, up to and including the pardon of Richard Nixon.

In a way, the conflict between Nixon's and Ford's staffs was just an exaggerated version of the tension that exists in every administration. The president's people, with a measure of condescension, believe the vice president's job, above all, is to serve the president; the vice president's staffers want their boss to have an independent political identity. Here, the conflict was exacerbated because Nixon was facing an existential threat to his job, and Ford, his putative replacement, had never been elected to anything except congressman from the 5th District of Michigan. Resentments on both sides were inevitable, and immediate. Over the eight months of Ford's vice presidency and then the one month until the pardon, the conflicts between Nixon's and Ford's staffs, and especially between Haig and Hartmann, would play out with singular importance.

Ford had an odd, and revealing, introduction to Haig in his role as Nixon's chief of staff. When Nixon called Ford to tell him that he was going to nominate him as vice president, the conversation went this way: "Jerry, General Haig has some good news to tell you." Then he put Haig on the phone to deliver the message.[8] Nixon always preferred to work through subordinates, and after Haig replaced Haldeman in May 1973, the general was Nixon's preferred vehicle. Indeed, by the time Ford arrived, in December, Haig was operating as a kind of deputy president. Nixon continued to work with Henry Kissinger on foreign policy, but for most other matters, Haig spoke for him, including to Ford and especially to Hartmann. In short order, Haig took Hartmann's measure and didn't like what he found. "His habitual manner was caustic, aggressive, rude," Haig wrote of Hartmann, "he seemed never to have gotten over being an outsider, and he appeared to think like one."[9] Much later, Haig made his contempt for Hartmann even clearer in an interview with the journalist James Cannon. "The Secret Service reported to me that Bob would get drunk in the office, take off his clothes, and chase his secretary around the desk," Haig said.[10] (This apparently did not happen.)

Nixon miscalculated when he thought the public would regard Ford as a patently unfit president—that is, as the second coming of Spiro Agnew. Ford's confirmation hearings in Congress were more like love fests, and he won confirmation 92 to 3 in the Senate and 387 to 35 in the House. Those totals demonstrated that Ford was already seen as a far less divisive figure than Nixon and in many ways a more appealing one. Those around Nixon—the Praetorian Guard—saw Ford as a threat as much as an ally.

Preoccupied in his first days with assembling a staff, Ford also had another priority: preserving his annual December ski vacation with Betty and their four children to their condo in Vail. (During his confirmation hearings, he had charmed his inquisitors by detailing his financial struggle, which included cashing in his congressional pension, to afford the modest chalet.) After a short detour to Spain for the funeral of the prime minister—a classic vice presidential duty—Ford made it to the slopes on December 22.

———

The question remained: what was Ford supposed to *do* as vice president?

The answer, it quickly became apparent, was pretty much what Agnew had done—and what Nixon had done under Eisenhower in the 1950s. Nixon gave Ford virtually no access to the decision-making process in the White House. In one of their rare meetings in the Oval Office, Nixon talked for more than an hour and a half without asking Ford anything. Instead, Ford was expected to travel around the country defending Nixon and revving up the Republican base for the 1974 midterms. Ford quickly found out that he had his work cut out for him. As his confirmation vote illustrated, he still had a reservoir of personal support in the Capitol. But the Republican brand was in trouble with the voters. On February 18, 1974, there was a special election to fill the congressional seat based in Grand Rapids that Ford had held since 1949 and that Republicans had controlled for sixty-two years. The Democrat won a narrow victory.

Still, Ford took to his assignment with enthusiasm and energy. According to the calculations of his biographer Richard Norton Smith, in Ford's first six months as vice president, he traveled 80,000 miles, visiting 30 states and making 375 speeches and appearances. In May 1974 alone, he was on the road for 28 days, most of them 16 hours long. At one point, the reporters who accompanied him sent Ford a three-word memo, "Subject: Complete Exhaustion."[11]

Even as Ford traveled the country defending Nixon, Hartmann wanted Ford to maintain a measure of independence from the White House, especially since Nixon's political situation was deteriorating and Congress was about to consider impeachment. Hartmann interjected himself into the larger White House speechwriting operation for Ford and struggled to put some distance between his patron and Nixon. In this Hartmann failed from the start. "These guys figured the Vice President for an empty-headed neophyte who knew little or nothing about what was going on," Hartmann later wrote. "They also intended to integrate his supporting staff so completely with the White House that it would be impossible for him to assert even the little independence Agnew had managed for five years."[12]

Characteristically, Ford handled the situation with more finesse than his bumptious aide, but the vice president saw many of the same problems. He felt the condescension from Nixon's staff. He couldn't get the office space, even the office furniture, that he wanted in the Old Executive Office Building. (Unlike Agnew, Ford was never even offered an office in the West Wing.) When Ford read the speeches Nixon's speechwriters had prepared for him, he spoke in their language of harsh partisanship. In remarks to the Farm Bureau Federation in Atlantic City, he heard himself lashing out at "a few extreme partisans . . . bent on stretching out the ordeal of Watergate for their own purposes." He went on to accuse the AFL-CIO union leadership, with whom he'd had cordial relations, of trying "to crush the President and his philosophy."[13] Ford was embarrassed but he did it anyway. In the new year, Nixon and the Senate Watergate Committee were still fighting over access to the White House tapes. Ford went on *Meet the Press* and suggested that some sort of "compromise" might be appropriate. The word came back to him that he was only to proffer full-fledged support for Nixon's hard line. "White House Disowns Ford's View on Tapes," ran the headline in the next day's *Washington Post*.[14]

By temperament, Ford remained a team player, but he could see that Nixon's political peril was deepening. His own position was becoming incoherent, even to himself. "On the one hand, I was chiding Nixon for failing to turn over all the evidence; on the other, I was saying that his attitude was proper," he later recalled. "By the nature of the office I held, I was in an impossible situation. I couldn't abandon Nixon, because that would make it appear that I was trying to position myself to become President. Nor could I get too close to him, because if I did I'd risk being sucked into the whirlpool myself."[15]

In the end, Ford decided that the prudent course for him was to withdraw from the day-to-day struggles over Watergate. Ford's personality was nothing like Nixon's, and the vice president went out of his way to draw attention to the contrast. For example, he frequently made himself available to reporters, which was very different from how Nixon handled himself. In his eight months as vice president, Ford held fifty-two press conferences, gave eighty-five formal interviews, and had countless informal chats with reporters.[16] But in those conversations, Ford went out of his way not to make any news. Once, though, in a gesture to take the focus off himself, he told *U.S. News & World Report*—almost categorically—that if he succeeded to the presidency, he would not run on his own in 1976. (This was consistent with his earlier agreement with Betty that he would not run again for his House seat in 1976.)

In all, then, the vice presidency was a pleasing interlude—and, it seemed, a likely capstone—in Ford's career in public service. The political environment was tough, and the bureaucratic standoffs with Nixon's staff enervating, but Ford himself liked being vice president. Few people, it seemed, held Nixon's problems against Ford. He received warm welcomes on his travels. The Fords didn't have to move from their modest home at 514 Crown View Drive in Alexandria, Virginia. (The government had settled on a residence for the vice president on the grounds of the Naval Observatory in Washington, but it wasn't yet ready for occupancy.) For the first time in her life, Betty Ford became a public figure, especially after she voiced support for abortion rights in an interview with Barbara Walters. At the time, the Secret Service protected only the vice president himself, not his family, so Betty and their four children came and went as they pleased. There was one brief scare. On February 4, 1974, Patricia Hearst, the newspaper heiress, was kidnapped from her home in Berkeley, California, by a radical group that called itself the Symbionese Liberation Army. In an early communiqué, the SLA threatened also to kidnap Susan Ford, the sixteen-year-old daughter of the Fords, who was then in boarding school in Virginia. As a result, for a brief period, the Secret Service also tailed Susan, which irritated the teenager to no end. But the threat passed.[17]

Mostly, Ford waited. He made a point of never asking Nixon about his own involvement in Watergate. He took Nixon's lawyers' claims at face value. He used his speeches to tout the administration's achievements in other areas, especially foreign policy. Ford began building a relationship with Henry Kissinger, the secretary of state and national security advisor. (With his keen eye for the ebb and flow of power, Kissinger cultivated Ford.) To an unusual extent for a politician, Ford was a spectator to his own fate. His future as a footnote—or as a president of the United States—would depend on something over which he had no control: the evidence in the Watergate scandal.

CHAPTER 4

"A Total Pardon"

IN SIMPLE TERMS, "WATERGATE," AS THE BROADER SCAN-
dal became known, was born on January 27, 1972, in a meeting in the
office of John Mitchell, then the attorney general. Mitchell was about
to step down from that job and assume leadership of Nixon's reelection campaign. But before he left the Justice Department, he hosted
a meeting with G. Gordon Liddy, a former FBI agent who was now
the top lawyer for the campaign. (The formal name of the campaign
was the Committee for the Re-election of the President, but it became
better known by the imperishable acronym, CREEP.) John Dean, a
former aide to Mitchell who was now the White House counsel, also
attended. The purpose of the meeting was for Liddy to propose a
"campaign intelligence" program, which he code-named Operation
Gemstone. As Dean later described the plan to Nixon (in a meeting
captured on the White House tapes), "Liddy laid out a million-dollar
plan that was the most incredible thing I have ever laid my eyes on. All
in codes, and involved black bag operations, kidnapping, providing
prostitutes to weaken the opposition, bugging, mugging teams." Despite the clear illegality (and madness) of Liddy's initial plan, Mitchell
told him only to scale it back, and he later approved the project.

The Watergate break-in was a product of Liddy's Gemstone initiative. The June 17, 1972, incursion was actually the second one at the
offices of the Democratic National Committee in the Watergate complex; the first one, in late May, had been a successful attempt to plant
wiretapping equipment. The second, when the five burglars were

caught, was to repair the microphones. To a surprising extent, after all these years, there remains considerable mystery about the break-in itself. Who ordered it? What were the burglars looking for? Why did they decide to tap the phones of the DNC, which was not a major center of campaign activity at the time? Despite decades of study by journalists and historians, those questions remain without clear answers.[1]

There was no evidence that Nixon (or Dean) knew of the plans for the break-in in advance, but Dean recognized immediately that the break-in had been a product of Liddy's Gemstone plan. Dean's top priority became distancing the White House from it—that is, conducting a cover-up. This was going to be difficult. One of the burglars had an envelope in his possession with a check from the account of E. Howard Hunt, a former CIA agent and sometime novelist who had recently left the White House staff, where his duties included serving as Liddy's contact. (The check from Hunt was for $6.36 payable to the Lakewood Country Club, which was near his home in Maryland. Hunt had asked the burglar to mail the check to the club from Florida to maintain the fiction that he lived out of state and so qualified for a lower membership rate.) James McCord, another burglar, ran internal security for CREEP. Scrambling to destroy evidence, Dean emptied the safe in Hunt's White House office and put aside any material that might tie the White House to the break-in.

In private, shortly after the break-in, Nixon told Charles Colson, another White House aide, that the reaction should be to "stonewall it"—ignore the whole matter, with the assumption that the press and public would lose interest. To that end, the public White House response was to dismiss Watergate as a matter of no consequence. Ron Ziegler, the White House press secretary, famously dismissed the event as "a third-rate burglary attempt."

But Nixon and his top aides, including Mitchell, Dean, H. R. Haldeman, the White House chief of staff, and John Ehrlichman, the top domestic policy adviser, knew that the facts were otherwise. They knew that there were many links between the burglars and the White House, and they struggled to cover up those ties, especially before the 1972 election.

The use of presidential pardons turned out to be a central part of that story. As it turned out, Nixon did not wind up granting pardons to any Watergate figures during this period, but he and his aides dangled them as a way of keeping their troops in line. This effort by Nixon's team would have struck a chord with the seventeenth-century parliamentarians who sought to limit the king's pardon power in England. They knew that sovereigns only sometimes dispensed pardons as instruments of mercy, but just as often used them as instruments to preserve and expand their own power.

After the arrests on June 17, 1972, the FBI took over the investigation. On June 23, Nixon instructed Haldeman to tell the CIA to instruct the FBI to back off the Watergate investigation on spurious national security grounds. (When the tape of this conversation was released in the summer of 1974, it became known as the smoking gun, and it prompted Nixon's resignation.) But in the summer of 1972, Nixon did not succeed in fully shutting down the FBI's Watergate investigation. So, Nixon and his aides explored a different tack—persuading the break-in defendants not to cooperate with the investigation.

How? On July 19, Nixon proposed to his aide Charles Colson that he would pardon all five burglars, as well as their supervisors, Hunt and Liddy, who were also charged with supervising the break-in.[2] Nixon suggested a package deal for what he called "both sides." The previous week, six members of the Vietnam Veterans Against the War were indicted in Florida for planning violence against the Republican National Convention, which was to begin in August, in Miami. Nixon's idea was to issue pardons of the Watergate seven and the group eventually known as the Gainesville Eight simultaneously after the election.

"There's bound to be . . . the Vietnam Veterans Against the War conspiracy . . . By God, be sure they have some of those guys with charges still hanging on after the election," Nixon said, according to the White House tapes.

"I see this morning they grabbed some," Colson said.

"Huh?" said Nixon.

"They grabbed some this morning," Colson said.

"Some . . . Now, if you can keep some of them alive and others arise . . . Then we've got to pardon the whole kit and caboodle after the election," Nixon said. This idea of ideologically balanced pardons would recur throughout the Watergate story, including during the Ford presidency. Other presidents had the same idea, too, to use ideologically balanced sets of pardons as a kind of cover for unpopular acts of clemency. But there was never any evidence that the public is fooled by this kind of political legerdemain.

The extraordinary cynicism of Nixon's idea for the Gainesville Eight and the Watergate seven (the five burglars, plus Liddy and Hunt) became even clearer two weeks later, on August 1. Nixon asked Haldeman if the White House was "doing our best to be sure" that the Gainesville Eight were "kept under indictment or—whatever it is—they are charged until after the election, on the other side. . . . The strategy is . . . you've got to pardon everybody." In other words, Nixon was trying to make sure that the Gainesville defendants remained locked up, solely so he could pardon them alongside the Watergate defendants after the election. Also in this conversation, Nixon talked about the payment of hush money to several of the defendants, who were demanding cash to remain silent.

Nixon won in a landslide in November, but that didn't solve the problem of what to do about the Watergate defendants, especially as their trial approached in January 1973. Dean, as White House counsel, was coordinating the cover-up at this point, and he was promising cash and pardons in return for continued silence. Liddy was weighing pleading guilty in advance of the trial, and Dean offered him a menu of benefits if he did. "First, you'll receive $30,000 per annum. Second, you'll receive a pardon within two years. Third, you'll be sent to Danbury," a relatively comfortable federal prison in Connecticut at the time.[3]

"You said 'pardon,'" Liddy responded. "You know the difference between a 'pardon' and a 'commutation'?"

"I do," Dean responded, "and it's a pardon."

Howard Hunt was an especially troublesome defendant for the White House to keep under control. Hunt was supporting a large family while awaiting trial in the break-in. Then, shortly before he was to go on trial, his wife died in a plane crash at O'Hare Airport in Chicago. Hunt and Colson were college classmates at Brown, and Nixon assured his aide Colson that his friend would get a pardon. "Don't worry about Hunt," Nixon said. But, the president added, the other burglars "must not expect a pardon at the same time."

As the scandal heated up in 1973, Nixon continued to see pardons as weapons to use for his political survival. When Judge Sirica was imposing long prison sentences for the Watergate burglars, in order to force them to testify, Nixon proposed responding in kind. "If Sirica can sit there and use the threat of a sentence, why can't we use the promise of clemency?" On later tapes uncovered by Professor Timothy Naftali, Nixon even suggested that he could somehow justify pardons to the Watergate defendants as part of the Bicentennial celebration. Haldeman thought Christmas pardons would be easier to justify.[4]

Alexander Hamilton defended the creation of an unfettered pardon power in the hands of a president as an instrument of mercy, to prevent "justice" from wearing "a countenance too sanguinary and cruel." But that idea was based on an optimistic assumption about the kind of person who would occupy the office of president; Richard Nixon was not that person. In weighing all of these potential pardons to Watergate figures, Nixon was motivated by self-interest rather than any kind of altruism or generosity. That, too, was a consequence of how the Framers established the president's power to pardon.

––––––––––

The specter of Watergate continued to haunt Dean. The hush money plan was falling apart. The demands for cash from the defendants, especially Hunt, were endless. In a March 21, 1973, meeting in the Oval Office, Dean laid out the problem for Nixon: "There's no doubt about the seriousness of the problem we've got. We have a cancer— within, close to the Presidency, that's growing. It's growing daily. It's compounding, it grows geometrically now because it compounds itself. That'll be clear as I explain some of the details, because (1) we're being blackmailed; (2) people are going to start perjuring themselves very quickly that have not had to perjure themselves to protect other people and the like." He told Nixon that he and Haldeman had used $350,000 in cash that had been left over from the campaign for hush money, because "we decided that there was no price too high to pay to let this thing blow up in front of the election."

In that meeting, which was also recorded on the White House tapes, Dean told Nixon that he had "worked on a theory of containment" regarding the scandal, but that was becoming untenable. Hunt was demanding both a pardon and more money, or he was going to turn on Ehrlichman and others in the White House. "Hunt's now demanding clemency or he's going to blow," Dean said. "And, politically, it'd be impossible for, you know, you to do it." Nixon agreed: "That's right." Dean continued, "I'm not sure that you'll ever be able to deliver on clemency. It may be just too hot."

But even if a pardon was politically impossible, at least for the time being, Dean said hush money could still keep Hunt quiet, if they could continue to find the money. The cash had run out, and Dean didn't know how to get more. "It'll cost money. It's dangerous," Dean said. "People around here are not pros at this sort of thing. This is the sort of thing Mafia people can do: washing money, getting clean money, and things like that. We just don't know about those things, because we are not criminals and not used to dealing in that business."

"That's right," Nixon answered.

Dean told Nixon that all of his closest aides, including Mitchell, Haldeman, and Ehrlichman, were implicated in the scandal, and it would cost a fortune to keep everyone else quiet.

"I would say these people are going to cost a million dollars over the next two years," Dean said.

"We could get that," Nixon replied.

"Uh, huh," said Dean.

"If you need the money, I mean, you could get the money," Nixon said. "What I mean is, you could get a million dollars. And you could get it in cash. I know where it could be gotten."

The March 21 meeting ended with an assignment for Dean to write a report about where things stood with Watergate. "I want you all to stonewall it," Nixon told Dean, "let them plead the Fifth Amendment, cover up or anything else if it'll save it—save the plan. That's the whole point." But as soon as Dean returned to his office, he received more bad news. McCord, the burglar, told Judge Sirica that hush money had been paid to some of the other defendants, and the White House had pressured him and the others to lie about the involvement of higher-ups. As Dean retreated to Camp David to write his report, he felt his options narrowing. An honest report would incriminate him as well as several other White House aides. Dean knew that starting almost from the day of the break-in eight months earlier, Nixon and his top aides had been scheming to deceive the FBI, as well as the public, about the connections between the burglars and the reelection committee. Dean himself had been at the center of that illegal effort, but it had also involved his superiors in the White House, including Mitchell, Haldeman, Ehrlichman, and the president himself. In light of his own junior status in this group, Dean recognized that the others would find Dean the convenient scapegoat for the entire Watergate cover-up.

So, in early April, Dean resolved to switch sides. He hired a lawyer and began secretly meeting with prosecutors in Washington. As a final act as White House counsel, on April 15, he told Nixon that he had met with the U.S. attorney. "Mr. President, I hope someday you'll know I was being loyal to you when I did this," Dean said. "I, uh, felt it was the only way to end the cover-up."[5]

With Dean starting to cooperate with prosecutors, Nixon recognized the danger to his top aides—and, ultimately, himself. So, Nixon raised the prospect of pardons for senior officials as well as for the original Watergate defendants. If his top aides were going to protect him, Nixon recognized that they needed the protection of pardons, too. Even Haldeman recognized the impropriety of Nixon's dangling pardons in this way, as in this exchange on May 18:

> Nixon: "I don't give a shit what comes out on you or John [Ehrlichman] or even that poor, damn dumb [former Attorney General] John Mitchell, there is going to be a total pardon."
>
> Haldeman: "Don't even say that."
>
> Nixon: "You know it. You know it and I know it. Forget you ever heard it."

With the scandal growing, Nixon felt he had no choice but to clean house, so he fired Dean and secured the resignations of Haldeman and Ehrlichman. He also accepted the resignation of Richard Kleindienst, who had succeeded Mitchell at the Justice Department. This turned out to be especially consequential, because Nixon appointed as the new attorney general the man who was currently serving as his secretary of defense, Elliot Richardson. A Massachusetts Brahmin, Richardson was a Republican but also a former prosecutor with a starchy sense of rectitude. In other words, Richardson came from a different world than Nixon's inner circle. Democrats in the Senate extracted a promise from Nixon as a price for their votes to confirm Richardson. For the continuing criminal investigation of Watergate, Richardson would have to appoint a special prosecutor, who would have his own staff and a measure of independence from the rest of the Justice Department. For that role, Richardson hired an old friend from Massachusetts, Archibald Cox, a professor at Harvard Law School who had been solicitor general under President Kennedy.

The choice horrified Nixon, who had a longstanding rivalry with the Kennedys. (While it's never been entirely clear why Liddy and Hunt ordered the bugging of the DNC offices at the Watergate, one theory was that it was to gain intelligence about Senator Ted Kennedy, who was then a putative Nixon rival in 1972.) Cox's appointment, and the aggressive investigation he was sure to lead, doomed Nixon's hope to put Watergate behind him.

Now officially separated from the White House, Dean also agreed to testify before the Senate Watergate Committee, chaired by Senator Sam Ervin, of North Carolina, which began hearings in May. On June 24, 1973, Dean took his place at the witness table in the Kennedy Caucus Room in the Russell Senate Office Building. Broadcast live on all three major networks and public television—there was no cable or internet—Dean's testimony became an iconic moment in the history of the decade. Poised and preppy (a term that was a decade away from wide use), with his striking blond wife, Maureen, seated behind him, Dean recalled in extraordinary detail his conversations with Nixon and others about their efforts to contain the scandal. The weeks of testimony that followed kept Watergate at the top of the news, especially on July 16, when Alexander Butterfield publicly revealed the existence of the White House taping system.

From there, the story accelerated. Both the Senate committee and Cox's investigators sought the tapes. In October, when Cox defied Nixon's order to cease his quest for the tapes, the Saturday Night Massacre followed, with the departures of Richardson and Ruckelshaus and Bork's agreement to fire Cox. (A decade later, President Reagan nominated Bork to the Supreme Court. Bork's capitulation to Nixon was one reason why the Senate failed to confirm him as a justice.) Amid this crisis and the Yom Kippur War, barely registering amid the cascade of news, Agnew resigned and Nixon nominated Ford as his replacement.

––––––––––

So, this was the state of play in Watergate when Ford took office as vice president at the end of 1973. The scandal was rolling forward, but it did not yet seem to threaten Nixon's presidency. Democrats in the House of Representatives were preparing to open impeachment hearings in the Judiciary Committee in the new year, but they probably didn't have the votes for an actual impeachment either in the committee or in the full House. Dean had transfixed the nation with his testimony, but it was debatable whether he had implicated Nixon in actual crimes. It was shocking to hear of any president discussing such seedy topics as hush money in the sacred precincts of the Oval Office, but it would be tough to base a criminal case, or an impeachment, on Dean's testimony alone. (Around this time, Nixon mused to his aides in the Oval Office, "Do you think the people of the United States are gonna impeach a President because of *John Dean*?") Crucially, at this point, the tapes had not yet been released to the public. For this reason, Nixon's supporters could still dismiss Dean as a liar. The investigation of the scandal was at this point largely bogged down in fights in the courts over access to the tapes.

In response, Ford played it safe as the new vice president. With fateful consequences, Ford contented himself with a kind of intentional ignorance. After Nixon's lawyers spanked him for his endorsement of a "compromise" on the tapes, he withdrew from that debate.

Ford declined offers from Nixon to examine for himself the evidence in the scandal. "I didn't want to look at the evidence and have to pass judgment either exonerating or convicting him," he later recalled. "Once I listened to the tapes or read the transcripts, I'd be sucked into the whirlpool of claims and counterclaims, and that was something I had to avoid."[6] Ford was also careful to avoid doing anything that made it look like he was preparing to take over as president, even though he knew that was at least a possibility. "Yet this was something I couldn't address publicly. I had to be very careful not to let it affect my behavior in any way and I couldn't afford to mention it to anyone—my family, my staff and certainly the press."[7] In other words, Ford knew less than an attentive newspaper reader about Watergate and little more than when he was a congressman about being president. It was a risky way to welcome 1974.

CHAPTER 5

To Charge *Le Grand Fromage*

THE CONSEQUENCES OF FORD'S WILLFUL WITHDRAWAL—
his failures to learn about the evidence in Watergate and to prepare to
be president—grew more perilous with each day. There were no signs
of a benign conclusion to Watergate. Nixon hoped that firing Cox
would both stifle the prosecutor's effort to obtain the White House
tapes and slow the overall pace of the investigation. The opposite occurred. Public outrage about the Saturday Night Massacre only deepened Nixon's political crisis.

There was also a less obvious aftermath. In the days after the
Massacre, Nixon was despondent and drinking to excess. At times,
he was simply unavailable to govern. That included a moment when,
in the continuing crisis of the Yom Kippur War, the Soviet Union
threatened to send troops to the Middle East. In response, Haig and
the cabinet decided unilaterally to put U.S. nuclear forces on a global
alert. Without consulting the president, they raised the threat level
from a peacetime DEFCON 5 to DEFCON 3. (DEFCON 1 is thermo-
nuclear war.)[1] Haig's unprecedented usurpation of a core presidential
function began a period when the chief of staff functioned as the deputy president. Haig's role would remain this way through the rest of
Nixon's presidency and into Ford's, with major implications for every
White House decision, including, ultimately, Ford's pardon of Nixon.

Haig put his power right to work. In light of the outrage in response to the Massacre, he recognized that Nixon would have to keep
the Watergate Special Prosecution Force intact, which meant that it

needed a new leader. Again acting on his own, Haig quickly settled on Leon Jaworski. Nixon made the announcement of the new prosecutor, and he said pointedly that Jaworski's job was to "bring Watergate to an expeditious conclusion." But would he?

The lawyers of the Watergate Special Prosecution Force were now calling themselves "Archie's Orphans." Cox had built his team from scratch and earned tremendous loyalty from his prosecutors and investigators. In Jaworski, the "orphans" expected a Nixon puppet more than an independent prosecutor. To them, Jaworski looked like a corporate shill—a prominent Texas lawyer and former president of the American Bar Association who prospered off the largesse of big business clients. Above all, the theory went, if Nixon and Haig liked Jaworski enough to select him for this role, how independent could he really be? After Haig sent an Air Force plane to Houston for Jaworski, and he arrived in the prosecutors' offices on November 5, 1973, he received a frosty reception. "To say that we had little confidence in our new boss," two of Cox's prosecutors later wrote, "would be putting it mildly."[2]

They sold Jaworski short. His background could scarcely have differed more from the aristocratic Cox's—and from the Ivy Leaguers whom Cox had recruited for his team. Jaworski had a hardscrabble upbringing outside Waco, Texas, where his father, an itinerate evangelical preacher, supported the family by charging five dollars a service. Leon graduated from nearby Baylor and its law school at eighteen and became the youngest-ever member of the Texas bar in 1924, at nineteen.[3] He soon started Fulbright & Jaworski, which quickly rose to be one of the largest law firms in Texas and then in the United States. During World War II, Jaworski volunteered for the Army and then prosecuted German war crimes. He earned the rank of colonel and appreciated being addressed by that title for the rest of his life. He returned to Texas where he entered the orbit of Lyndon Johnson, whom he represented in litigation that allowed Johnson to run for both senator and vice president in 1960. The new special prosecutor was a figure of the establishment, not a boat-rocker, but a man of integrity.

Jaworski began earning the trust of his staff. For one thing, he didn't bring a single lawyer or employee with him from Texas, not even his secretary. He adopted Cox's staff as a group. And just as everyone called his predecessor "Archie," Jaworski asked to be called "Leon," even though he generally preferred "Colonel." More importantly, Jaworski disappointed Nixon and continued Cox's efforts to extract the tapes from the White House. Nixon's lawyers refused to produce all of the tapes, citing executive privilege and national security, but they did turn over some of them. Nixon had hired a new lead defense attorney on Watergate matters—James St. Clair, a respected litigator from the Boston firm of Hale & Dorr. But in an illustration of the wide range of Haig's responsibilities in the White House, Haig was the one who took over negotiations with Jaworski about access to the tapes. Every time Jaworski asked for more tapes, Haig asked him not to ask for any more; each time, Jaworski refused to make this promise. The negotiations slowed down the delivery of any tapes, and some of them Haig refused to produce at all.[4]

Still, one Saturday in December 1973, Jaworski was in his office when Haig called and said the first group of tapes were ready to be picked up. Carl Feldbaum, one of the newer lawyers on the staff, also happened to be there, and Jaworski told him to make the ten-minute walk to the White House and pick up the tapes. As always, even on a Saturday, Jaworski was wearing a suit, but Feldbaum, dressed for a party that night, was wearing bell-bottoms, in the fashion of the era. He felt a little awkward visiting the White House in such clothes, and he drew nasty stares from the tourists he leapfrogged in the line for admission. Feldbaum eventually found himself in front of Fred Buzhardt, the White House counsel, with nine tapes on the table in front of him. These were the originals, and, it turned out, some of the most important artifacts in American history; Feldbaum was struck by the informality of the turnover. The tapes were loose, with stickers attached noting the date and time. He asked the grim-faced Buzhardt for a box, which was produced. The two lawyers then scrawled a handwritten receipt to commemorate the delivery.

Feldbaum took the tapes back to his office, secured a tape recorder, and summoned some of the other lawyers who happened to be there that day. They first cued up the recording of the March 21,

1973, meeting where John Dean warned Nixon and Haldeman about the "cancer" on the presidency. The lawyers had all heard Dean's description of that conversation during his testimony before the Senate Watergate Committee; after hearing the tape, the lawyers were dazzled by the precision of Dean's recollections. Feldbaum then brought the tape recorder into Jaworski's office so he could hear the March 21 conversation for himself. Jaworski listened without expression. When Feldbaum returned to his colleagues, they all wondered what Jaworski thought of the tape. "I have no fucking idea," Feldbaum told them.

In fact, the March 21 tape moved Jaworski profoundly. One exchange in particular drew his attention. After Dean told Nixon that Watergate was a "cancer" on the presidency, Haldeman joined the meeting in the Oval Office. The three men were discussing ways to avoid having White House officials, including Haldeman, testify before the Senate Watergate Committee. They kicked around an alternative idea of Haldeman testifying before a special grand jury, which could be controlled by their allies in the Justice Department. Dean said it was possible to take the Fifth Amendment in a grand jury.

Nixon: "That's right. That's right."

Haldeman: "You can say you forgot, too, can't you?"

Nixon: "That's right."

Dean: "But you can't . . . you're in a very high risk perjury situation."

Nixon: "That's right. Just be damned sure you say. 'I don't remember.' 'I can't recall.' I can't give any honest . . . an answer that I can't recall. But that's it."

Nixon's voice, especially its staccato urgency, haunted Jaworski. "I was badly shaken, so shaken that I didn't want anyone to notice it," Jaworski later recalled. "I closed the door. I needed to be alone." He went on, "One thought kept coming back, hammering its way through the others. The President of the United States had without doubt engaged in highly improper practices, in what appeared to be criminal practices. . . . I had not come to Washington expecting this. I had expected to find all sorts of wrongdoing by his aides . . . but it had never occurred to me that the President was in the driver's seat. . . . The President—a lawyer—suggested that Haldeman could be coached about how to testify untruthfully and yet not commit perjury. It amounted to subornation of perjury."[5] "Subornation," or encouragement, of perjury is a crime itself.

This was an early turning point for Jaworski. Back in Houston, he hadn't followed Watergate closely, and though nominally a Democrat, he was generally sympathetic to Nixon's politics. But the tape—Nixon's own voice—demonstrated that the president was deeply involved in at least the impropriety, if not the illegality, of Watergate and its aftermath. Jaworski was still the cautious corporate lawyer that he had been when he arrived in Washington, but he now understood why Cox's "orphans" were so fired up about their work.

The main task for the group at this point was to craft an indictment based on the cover-up. To that end, the members of the White House task force under Jaworski produced a 128-page memo outlining the prospective defendants, evidence, and charges. Only eight copies were produced, to reduce the chance for leaks.[6] The lawyers decided that the payment of hush money would be at the center of the case, and Dean would be the star witness. (Dean had pleaded guilty to conspiracy to obstruct justice and was cooperating with prosecutors.) The theory of the case was that the break-in emerged from Gemstone, the campaign intelligence operation that Gordon Liddy proposed to Mitchell before the 1972 election. Even in scaled-back form, Gemstone's operations included the two break-ins at the Watergate, which were choreographed by Howard Hunt, from inside the White House.

Once the burglars were caught on June 17, 1972, the cover-up began. Mitchell demanded that the Gemstone planning papers be burned, and they were. Dean directed that Hunt's White House safe be opened and its incriminating contents hidden. Haldeman and Ehrlichman met with top CIA officials and asked them to intervene with the Justice Department and demand that the Watergate investigation be curtailed in the interest of national security. (The CIA officials refused to do so.) Haldeman and Ehrlichman also told the FBI in interviews that all they knew about Watergate was what they read in the newspapers. Haldeman approved the transfer of $350,000 in leftover CREEP funds to pay hush money to the burglars, as well as to Hunt. Hunt's persistent demands for more cash were discussed in depth on the March 21 tape. (Prosecutors learned that $75,000 went to Hunt on the very night of that White House meeting. Hunt had been especially demanding for money after his wife's death in the plane crash, as he was raising their children by himself.)

The prosecution memo also addressed the culpability of the president, and it concluded that Nixon, too, could be a defendant: "The evidence before the Grand Jury clearly demonstrates that President Nixon knew prior to March 21, 1973, about the existence of a conspiracy to obstruct justice on the part of his closest White House aides and high officials of his Re-election Committee, and that on March 21, when the President learned many of the material details of the cover-up and the potential criminal liability of those involved, he joined the conspiracy."[7] And now it wasn't necessary to take Dean's word for what happened in the Oval Office on March 21; it was all on tape.

It looked like a strong case against the White House aides, and it was bolstered every time the prosecutors extracted more tapes from the White House. The legal fights to access more tapes continued. But as the time for the indictment approached, Jaworski's lawyers became concerned, then obsessed, with another issue. Could they also indict President Nixon? Indeed, in light of the evidence they had amassed, how could they *not* indict Nixon?

———

It was—and remains—one of the most consequential questions in constitutional law: can a sitting president be indicted?

The issue had arisen even before Richardson appointed Cox as special prosecutor. When the Watergate investigation was still under under the control of the local United States attorney in Washington, he assigned a young lawyer (and future federal judge) named Paul

Friedman to research the question. Friedman's memo suggested that prosecutors refrain from indicting a sitting president and instead allow the House of Representatives to consider impeachment before any criminal proceedings were instigated. But this brief memo apparently never circulated outside the Washington courthouse, and it certainly didn't purport to represent the official policy of the Justice Department. That was up to the attorney general.

Elliot Richardson understood the stakes. While he was still attorney general, before he was forced out in the Saturday Night Massacre, Richardson quietly asked one of his top aides to address the question. At the time, Richardson had not been told specifically that Cox and the Watergate prosecutors were weighing an indictment of Nixon, but the AG was enough of a prosecutor himself to know that they had to be considering the possibility. So, he put the question to Roger G. Dixon Jr., whom Richardson had recruited from a law professorship at George Washington University to serve as the assistant attorney general in charge of the Office of Legal Counsel. That made him the department's top interpreter of constitutional law.

On September 24, 1973, Dixon replied in a memo which has become one of the most cited—and controversial—internal documents in Justice Department history. Dixon began by noting that the question of whether a sitting president can be indicted "has been debated ever since the earliest days of the Republic."[8] He said that the text of the Constitution did not directly address the issue. Article II said the Congress could impeach the president, and Article I, Section 3 defined the limits of that power:

> Judgment in Cases of Impeachment shall not extend further than to removal from Office, and disqualification to hold and enjoy any Office of honor, Trust or Profit under the United States: but the Party convicted shall nevertheless be liable and subject to Indictment, Trial, Judgment and Punishment, according to Law.

In other words, Congress could not use its impeachment power to throw a president in prison, but an impeached president could still

be charged with a crime. And charging a president with a crime following an impeachment would not subject him to double jeopardy,
which was prohibited by the Fifth Amendment. Dixon noted that
in three different Federalist Papers (Nos. 65, 69, and 77), Alexander
Hamilton said a former president could be prosecuted. (For example,
in No. 65, "After having been sentenced to a perpetual ostracism [by
impeachment], he will still be liable to prosecution and punishment
in the ordinary course of law.") But as for whether a *sitting* president
could be indicted, the Constitution, and Hamilton, were silent.

To Dixon, the guidance from the Constitution was ambiguous.
For example, he noted that the Constitution did specifically protect
sitting members of Congress from criminal prosecution under the
Speech or Debate Clause; but the absence of such a provision for
presidents didn't mean that the protection shouldn't exist. Likewise,
Dixon found no firm direction from the principles of separation of
powers, concluding that "it cannot be said either that the courts have
the same jurisdiction over the President as if he were an ordinary citizen or that the President is absolutely immune from the jurisdiction
of the courts in regard to any kind of claim." To be sure, practical
problems in the trial of a sitting president would abound. "Undoubt-
edly, the consideration of assuring a fair criminal trial for a President
while in office would be extremely difficult," Dixon wrote. "It might
be impossible to impanel a neutral jury."

In the end, Dixon recognized that the law did not provide a clear
answer about whether a sitting president could be indicted. Ultimately, for the Department of Justice, the resolution was a matter of
choice and of discretion. But that ambiguity didn't prevent Dixon
from reaching a firm conclusion. The logistical obstacles for such a
case were bad enough. He wrote, "It could be argued that a President's
status in a criminal case would be repugnant to his office of Chief Executive, which includes the power to oversee prosecutions. In other
words, just as a person cannot be a judge in his own case, he cannot
be a prosecutor and a defendant at the same time." Dixon noted, too,
that the president always possessed the pardon power, though he did
not address the issue of whether the Constitution allowed a president
to pardon himself.

And then, for a bureaucratic document, Dixon's memo turned almost lyrical: "A necessity to defend a criminal trial and to attend court in connection with it, however, would interfere with a President's unique duties, most of which cannot be performed by anyone else." It would simply be wrong for the Department of Justice to remove a president from the obligations only he can perform and force him to sit in a courtroom. "In view of the unique aspects of the Office of the President, criminal proceedings against a President in office should not go beyond a point where they could result in so serious a physical interference with the President's performance of his official duties that it would amount to an incapacitation." Such a prosecution would injure the public, not just the president: "The President is the symbolic head of the Nation. To wound him by a criminal proceeding is to hamstring the operation of the whole governmental apparatus, both in foreign and domestic affairs." So, Dixon concluded, even though the Constitution did not forbid the indictment of a sitting president, it should be the policy of the Department of Justice to refrain from bringing any such case.

Dixon's conclusion has largely stood the test of time, even as prosecutors in later scandals questioned whether it should be followed. Cox and later Jaworski commissioned their own legal research on the question of whether a sitting president could be indicted, and they concluded he could be. Likewise, there were members of the staff of both Ken Starr, in his investigation of Bill Clinton, and Robert Mueller, in his probe of Donald Trump, who believed that the policy was wrong and that presidents should be charged. There is much appeal to the notion that the Oval Office should not serve as a shelter for a criminal; no person, after all, is above the law. But under our Constitution, the president is more than an individual. He is himself a branch of government. His responsibilities, especially in the nuclear age, are simply too important and extensive to subject him to the ordeal of sitting in the dock of a courtroom, much less serving a prison sentence. The availability of impeachment operates as a meaningful enough check on the fitness of the president to serve, so that prosecution can wait until he is out of office. It was not until the investigations of Donald Trump in 2023 and 2024 that anyone would even suggest that *former* presidents were also immune from prosecution.

————————

Unlike Cox, who favored long group discussions among many prosecutors, Jaworski preferred to get opinions from his staff in writing, ruminate in his office, and then make a decision. That's how it worked with the decision whether to indict Nixon. Jaworski assigned Philip Lacovara, his top legal adviser, and a deputy, Richard Weinberg, to replow the ground from the Dixon memo, and they came out roughly the same way as Dixon. There was no constitutional or other legal bar to indicting Nixon while he was in office, but for reasons of "propriety," it was better not to do so.

The more aggressive (and younger) members of the team dissented. They were the ones closest to the evidence and most outraged about the behavior of the man they called, in a kind of half-joke, half-code, "*le grand fromage.*" They wrote their own memo to Jaworski arguing for an indictment. Carl Feldbaum, George Frampton, Gerald Goldman, and Peter Reint went to the heart of the conflict: "No principles are more firmly rooted in our traditions, or more at stake in the decision facing this office and the Grand Jury, than that there shall be equal justice for all and that no man in this country is so high that he is above the law. For us or the grand jury to shirk from an appropriate expression of our honest assessment of the evidence of the President's guilt would not only be a departure from our responsibilities but a dangerous precedent damaging to the rule of law." With some prescience, the quartet added: "Another possible consequence is an increased likelihood of wrong-doing by a future President who need not fear the strictures of the criminal law as a limitation on the exercise of his immense power."

In a reflection of how exposure to Nixon's behavior, especially on the tapes, had radicalized the fundamentally cautious Jaworski, he was torn on the issue. But in the end, he decided the safer course was to omit Nixon from the indictment that the grand jury voted on March 1, 1974. Mitchell, Haldeman, Ehrlichman, Charles Colson, and three lesser-known aides were charged with conspiracy to obstruct justice and a handful of other crimes. Never in American history had so many close and trusted advisers to a president been charged with crimes, much less together in the same enterprise. Inside the prosecutors' offices, however, the moment smacked of anticlimax, because of the one individual who wasn't named. This disappointment was leavened, however, by Jaworski's decision to provide all the assistance that the law allowed to the impeachment investigation in the House of Representatives. The hearings in the Judiciary Committee would begin in May.

the Army at the tail end of World War II, and went to law school upon his return. In 1962, he ran and won as a Democrat in his home congressional district. A zealous advocate for a strong national defense and a loyal member of Harry Byrd's conservative Democratic Party machine, Marsh increasingly fell out of step with his Democratic colleagues. For this reason, and notwithstanding their other political differences, Marsh became a close friend of Ford's when they were both in the House. (This was also a time when friendships across the aisle were a great deal more common than they are today.) In 1970, Marsh was disgusted enough with his party to drop his reelection bid. In response to the nomination of George McGovern in 1972, Marsh joined Democrats for Nixon. In 1973, Nixon named Marsh the chief congressional liaison for the Pentagon.

In light of their friendship, and Marsh's expertise, Ford brought Marsh on as his vice presidential national security advisor. He quickly joined Bob Hartmann as Ford's top two aides. Hartmann and Marsh were temperamental opposites; Hartmann was brash and confrontational; Marsh reserved and contemplative. But they formed a bond in their affection for Ford, and they spent most days by the vice president's side in the far reaches of the OEOB, well separated from the locus of power in the Nixon White House. As with Agnew, Nixon thought Ford should be little seen and rarely heard, at least in the West Wing. That was fine with Ford's two advisers as well. Watergate was consuming the White House. "It was kind of dangerous," Marsh recalled. "You want to stay out of those things because you didn't know who was involved and what would eventually happen."

But Ford went beyond simply staying away from Watergate—he wouldn't talk about it, even with his closest aides. "We had an understanding—Ford, Hartmann and myself," Marsh said. "We would never discuss the status of the Watergate proceedings because all three of us felt that if we started doing it, invariably it would get out and be leaked, and that would be the worst position for Ford to be in. By us taking that position, every member of the Vice President's staff was put on notice: 'This is off-limits. You're not to talk about it because Ford doesn't talk about it.'" This reasoning was peculiar. If Ford, Hartmann, and Marsh were so concerned about leaks, they

CHAPTER 6

Both Sides of West Exec

WEST EXECUTIVE AVENUE IS THE MOST EXCLUSIVE PARK-
ing lot in Washington and perhaps the world. "West Exec," as it's
known, runs less than a quarter-mile, between the White House and
the Old Executive Office Building. The Secret Service controls access
to the street, which is mostly used for parking by top aides to the
president. (Less exalted staffers have to park in more remote parts of
the eighteen-acre White House complex.) West Exec serves as a symbolic barrier as well. The president and his closest aides work in the
West Wing, which is attached to the White House building itself. The
OEOB (which was renamed for Dwight Eisenhower in 2002) houses
hundreds of staffers whose immediate presence the president deems
unnecessary. For connoisseurs of power in Washington, West Exec
separates the Promised Land from purgatory.

When Jack Marsh went to work for Vice President Ford early in
1974, he quickly discovered that the roadway between the two buildings was "just about as wide as the Potomac River instead of a street."
In the West Wing, Nixon and the people around him were increasingly obsessed with the possibility of impeachment; in the OEOB,
Ford and his staff couldn't stay far enough away from the subject.
(Nixon himself maintained a hideaway office in Room 180 of the
OEOB, but the hideaway part was the point; it was a place where he
didn't want to see people.)

Marsh's career followed a similar trajectory to Ford's, though he
was a few years younger. He grew up in central Virginia, enlisted in

could have addressed that problem by not leaking. Instead, Ford decided to cut himself off from the information he needed most—about whether he would become president and what to do if he did. And since Congress was now actually considering impeachment, the consequences of Ford's self-imposed isolation grew more significant.

————————

The Saturday Night Massacre in October 1973 had generated the first significant momentum for impeachment, which Nixon sought to reverse with a televised press conference on November 17. Hoping to talk about anything but Watergate, the president did manage to draw several questions about the energy crisis; the oil-producing nations in the Arab world had embargoed oil exports in connection with the Yom Kippur War. But there were still questions about Watergate, including one about his own tax returns, which had become a peripheral issue in the far-flung scandal. In response, Nixon provided one of the defining sound bites of the era: "People have got to know whether or not their president is a crook. Well, I am not a crook."

Congress was unpersuaded, and the sentiment was ominously bipartisan. The following month, Peter Rodino, the chairman of the House Judiciary Committee, and Edward Hutchinson, the ranking Republican, decided to join forces and together hire a lead investigator for an impeachment inquiry. Unlike the Senate Watergate Committee, which had dueling Democratic and Republican staffs, Rodino and Hutchinson collaborated, and they chose a consensus candidate—John Doar, a Wisconsin Republican who had been a courageous civil rights attorney in the Kennedy and Johnson administrations. Doar's task was to organize the investigation, and the assignment was especially challenging. The Senate committee, under Sam Ervin, had investigated what happened in Watergate, but the job for the House Judiciary Committee was very different. Those members had to decide what to do about it—whether to remove the president from office. At the beginning of 1974, when Doar began work, no living person had any experience with the subject. It wasn't even clear what the standard for impeachment was. As one of his first acts, Doar tried to find out.

The final wording of the impeachment provision in the Constitution emerged from a brief debate among some of the greatest of the Framers, on September 8, 1787, in Philadelphia. The working draft of the document allowed Congress to remove the president only for bribery and treason, but George Mason, fearing an unduly powerful chief executive, proposed that "maladministration" be added as another ground for impeachment. His fellow Virginian James Madison objected, because "so vague a term will be equivalent to a tenure during pleasure of the Senate." In other words, Madison warned, if the standard for impeachment were "maladministration," the Senate would be within its rights to remove the president at any time. Gouverneur Morris added a similar point, noting that "an election every four years will prevent maladministration." As an alternative, Mason offered to add instead a phrase that had been used in English law as early as 1386—"high Crimes and Misdemeanors."

Today, the word "misdemeanor" suggests a minor offense, but the Framers had a different understanding. In eighteenth-century England, high misdemeanors referred to offenses against the state, as opposed to those against property or other people. Thus, from the start, impeachment was meant to police those who abused the powers of their office. As Charles Cotesworth Pinckney said in the debate over the ratification of the Constitution in South Carolina, impeachment was for those who "betray their public trust."

Madison prevailed in the debate in Philadelphia, and "Treason, Bribery, or other high Crimes and Misdemeanors" has defined the standard for impeachment of presidents, vice presidents, and "civil officers," such as federal judges, through all of American constitutional history. (The remaining provisions are straightforward. If the House passes an impeachment of a president by a simple majority, the matter moves to the Senate for a trial, presided over by the chief justice of the United States. A vote by two-thirds of the Senate is required for removal from office.)

For all its august beginnings, however, the early history of impeachment unfolded largely by negative example. The two most celebrated instances were fiascoes. In 1805, Justice Samuel Chase, a Federalist serving on the Supreme Court, was impeached on politically motivated charges of judicial bias raised by his Jeffersonian adversaries; he was then acquitted, by a narrow margin, in the Senate. The low point in impeachment history took place in 1868, when a bitter Reconstruction era political battle nearly drove President Andrew Johnson from office. Radical Republicans, who controlled the House and despised Johnson, had passed, over his veto, a plainly unconstitutional restriction on the president's power to fire his cabinet. Johnson tested the law by firing his secretary of war, Edwin M. Stanton, and the House responded by voting to impeach the president. Johnson avoided conviction in the Senate by one vote. By 1974, there had been a total of only twelve impeachments—nine judges, one cabinet member, one senator, and one president.

After the Chase and Johnson debacles, the impeachment process largely fell into disuse, except for the occasional removal of judges, so when John Doar started the 1974 House inquiry, he tried to tease out useful strands in the history of impeachment. He recruited the Yale historian C. Vann Woodward to lead a study of misconduct by all the presidents before Nixon. (As one of his assistants in the project, Woodward recruited a recent graduate of Yale Law School named Hillary Rodham.) The Woodward study was dry and straightforward, and it summarized largely forgotten scandals. In 1792, during George Washington's first term, an assistant secretary of the treasury stole roughly $250,000 in public funds (a very large sum in those days). In 1964, Lyndon Johnson's special assistant Walter Jenkins was arrested on morals charges along with another man in a public restroom in Washington. Woodward's report left open the question: if those matters weren't impeachable, what was? What did "high Crimes and Misdemeanors" actually mean?

That issue went to Joseph A. Woods Jr., an Oakland, California, lawyer who was a law school classmate of Doar's. The Woods team defined impeachment broadly, asserting that not all crimes were impeachable offenses but that not all impeachable offense were crimes, either. This was a controversial point at the time—that impeachable offenses need not also be crimes—but that came to be generally accepted as the correct view. For example, it would be no crime for a president to move to a foreign country and refuse to return—or to take a vow of silence in the United States—but, just as surely, such conduct would be grounds for impeachment. The decisive factor is conduct that fatally compromises the ability to do the job as president. As Woods's report stated, impeachment is a "remedy addressed to serious offenses against the system of government," and impeachable offenses are "constitutional wrongs that subvert the structure of government, or undermine the integrity of office and even the Constitution itself."

These definitions were adequate as far as they went, but they didn't offer much practical guidance to the members of the House of Representatives, who might actually have to vote on the issue. Woods chose to omit what was then (and remains) the most famous definition of impeachable offenses, which had been uttered by none other than Gerald R. Ford. On April 15, 1970, Representative Ford took to the well of the House to speak in favor of the impeachment of Justice William O. Douglas. "An impeachable offense," Ford said, "is whatever a majority of the House of Representatives considers it to be in a given moment in history." The effort to evict Douglas quickly fizzled, and Ford's remark drew scorn from scholars over the years, but it did capture the inherently political nature of all impeachment controversies. And though Doar and his staff never specifically said so, they more or less adopted Ford's formulation. They left the political judgment up to the politicians. The members of the Judiciary Committee would decide for themselves what constituted an impeachable offense.

Of all people, then, Vice President Gerald Ford should have understood what was happening. Years before Watergate, Ford recognized that impeachment was less about parsing the constitutional text than reading the political winds. And those winds were running ever more strongly against Nixon. In early 1974, the White House was engaging in a series of complicated legal battles over the tapes. Nixon's lawyers produced some tapes, but they were also fighting off demands for more tapes from Jaworski's prosecutors, from Judge Sirica, and from the impeachment investigators at the House Judiciary

Committee. Ford had never discussed Watergate with Nixon in any depth, but the president had assured him that he was not involved in the cover-up, and that the tapes, if they were released, would vindicate him. But if that were true, why didn't Nixon release the tapes? Ford never pressed Nixon on the issue, nor did he explore the contents of the tapes himself or ask anyone else to do so. To an extent that sometimes astonished those around him, the vice president was a trusting man. Ford simply chose to believe Nixon.

Loyalty was a key value to Ford, as was his determination to be a team player. He was on Nixon's team, and he was going to stay there. His aides, especially Hartmann, saw some short-term political advantage to that approach. Above all, Hartmann thought, Ford should not appear to be trying to push Nixon aside and elevate himself into the presidency. But this presented Ford with a dilemma about what he should do and say as he traveled around the country as vice president. Ford at least had to acknowledge the unfolding scandal and not pretend he was oblivious to it. So, with advice from Hartmann, as Ford hit the road in 1974, he came up with a new approach. He would draw a distinction between Nixon, the national Republican Party, and Ford's chosen scapegoat for Watergate—the Committee for the Re-election of the President, CREEP.

"Never again must Americans allow an arrogant elite guard of political adolescents like CRP to by-pass the regular party organizations and dictate the terms of a national election," he said in a speech to a Republican audience in Chicago. "The fatal defect of CRP was that it made its own rules and thus made its own ruin. It . . . ran roughshod over the seasoned political judgment and experience of the party organization in the fifty states. . . . If there are any more cliques of ambitious amateurs who want to run political campaigns, let the Democrats have them next time." (Ford, like most Republicans at the time, chose to use the anodyne acronym CRP rather than the more evocative CREEP.)

Ford's argument about the 1972 campaign was, to put it mildly, a stretch, especially as far as Nixon himself was concerned. There was no evidence that Nixon's presidential campaign was somehow imposed on him against his will or without his knowledge. It was led by John Mitchell, who was not only Nixon's own attorney general but also his longtime friend and former law partner. Even after Haldeman and Ehrlichman resigned from the White House, Nixon called them "two of the finest public servants it had been my privilege to know." National Republicans had no complaints about the Nixon campaign when it was winning forty-nine states against George McGovern in 1972. Still, as Republicans searched for some way to address Watergate in anticipation of the 1974 midterms, the GOP faithful welcomed Ford's effort at collective exoneration and blame-shifting.

The broader political currents were clear. Nixon saw them, even if Ford chose to look away. Pondering his fate in the Judiciary Committee, Nixon was grimly realistic, doubting that he could find a majority to vote against impeachment and thus kill it.[1] "One only had to be able to count to know that the House Judiciary Committee was a stacked deck," Nixon wrote later.[2] The committee had twenty-one Democrats and seventeen Republicans. In Nixon's view, eighteen Democrats were sure to vote against him, "despite their pieties about objectivity." Perhaps he could get the three Southern Democrats, who often voted with him on policy issues. But Nixon was sure of only eleven Republicans, because the others were liberals or "facing difficult re-election campaigns." Overall, Nixon concluded, his chances of victory in the committee were "extremely remote."

CHAPTER 7

Expletive Deleted

NIXON HAD MORE ON HIS MIND IN EARLY 1974 THAN JUST the votes on the House Judiciary Committee. Far more than Vice President Ford, President Nixon realized the seriousness of the threat presented by Watergate. Sitting alone in his study in the Old Executive Office Building, Nixon would often scribble out his thoughts and plans on a yellow legal pad. With these doodles, he created a kind of aspirational Nixon, which bore only some resemblance to the actual one on the tapes. That Nixon was racist, antisemitic, and (according to many of the Watergate prosecutors) felonious. The Nixon of his own imagination was steely, high-minded, and almost apolitical, concerned only about the long-term good of the nation. This Nixon resembled his hero Churchill, whom he cited sixteen times in his memoirs. Shortly after the new year, Nixon wrote to himself:

Decision to fight:

Resign sets precedent—admits guilt

Lets down friends

Fight now only makes possible fight for future as man of principle.

Only substance, not politics, must affect this decision.

He wrote out his goals:

Above all else: Dignity, command, faith, head high, no fear, build a new spirit, drive, act like a President, act like a winner. Opponents are savage destroyers, haters. Time to use full power of the President to fight overwhelming forces arrayed against us.

But both Nixons, the real and imaginary ones, were realistic about his fate. The president knew that if the case against him came down to his word against John Dean's, he would almost certainly survive. But the tapes changed everything, and even the ones that had already been released were terribly damaging to him. Later, in his memoir, he referred to "the enemy within: the tapes." As 1974 began, his lawyers were fighting to stop more releases, but there was no guarantee that they would succeed. No one, not even Nixon, could be sure what was on the unreleased tapes. Recalling his thinking in this period, Nixon wrote, "The ones I reviewed were bad enough: now what might be on the others haunted us all?"[1]

———

At the remove of five decades, with all the intervening technological change, it's tempting to think of the "White House tapes" as a single entity or at least a collection of digital files. But the truth in 1974 was very different.

Presidents since Franklin Roosevelt had engaged in some taping of White House conversations, but Nixon was the first to undertake a broad, systematic effort. After experimenting with the use of a human note-taker in most meetings, Nixon and Haldeman decided to install a taping system in the White House. It became operational in the Oval Office and Cabinet Room on February 16, 1971. Later, Nixon's phones, as well as his lodge at Camp David, were added. Only two of Haldeman's staffers, Alexander Butterfield and Lawrence Higby, as well as a handful of Secret Service agents, were aware of the system. In all but the Cabinet Room, where Butterfield controlled the on-off switch, the system was voice-activated; it automatically recorded everything that was said.[2] (The system was shut down on July 13, 1973, the day that Butterfield revealed its existence to a staffer of the Senate Watergate Committee; Butterfield testified in public about the taping system three days later.)

Even by the standards of the day, the technology of the taping system was precarious. The recordings were produced on nine Sony TC-800B reel-to-reel machines using a very thin 0.5 mil tape at the extremely slow speed of 15/16 inches per second. The Secret Service technicians set the slow speed so that they wouldn't have to change the reels frequently, but that compromised the quality of the recordings. There were seven hidden microphones in the Oval Office, and they were connected to recorders in a hidden locker in the basement of the West Wing. At one point, not long after the system was installed, Haldeman asked Nixon if he wanted the tapes transcribed. The president said no; he wanted them to remain private, most likely for his use in writing his memoirs after his presidency. When the system was shut down, it had recorded about four thousand hours of material. At the time Butterfield revealed their existence to the public, only Nixon and Haldeman had ever listened to any of the tapes; no one had listened to the vast majority of them.

Once the existence of the tapes became known, they became the focus of obsessive attention from Nixon's pursuers. The first task, then, was for someone on the White House staff to identify them, catalogue them, listen to them, transcribe them, and evaluate their importance. The job went to Fred Buzhardt. Though he was just fifty years old, the task nearly killed him—literally.

Buzhardt was a small-town lawyer from South Carolina who became a protégé of Senator Strom Thurmond. Buzhardt had been general counsel of the Department of Defense for three years when Haig brought him to the White House in mid-1973, largely to handle Watergate matters. A former West Point contemporary of Haig's, Buzhardt was quiet and discreet, and Nixon deputized him as the point person on the tapes. Buzhardt was a sepulchral presence at the White House, a chain-smoker of unfiltered Camels despite a heart condition. As a colleague wrote of him, Buzhardt was "hunched over and skinny as a split rail, his face pinched by bad dentures and a consequently restricted diet of soft foods."[3] Known (behind his back) as the Buzzard, he had, with the tapes, the most thankless of all thankless tasks.

The tapes themselves were a mess, thrown haphazardly together in the West Wing basement. Some were mislabeled or had no labels.

Some were missing. But the problem with locating the tapes paled next to the difficulties of listening to them. Buzhardt and Rose Mary Woods, the president's longtime secretary, were responsible for transcribing them—an experience he called "sheer torture." As Buzhardt described the process to a colleague, "The voice-activated recording system was frequently started by the rustling of papers or the rattling of a coffee cup. The placement of the microphones, whether a person spoke with his head up or down, whether he had a higher- or lower-pitched voice, all served to render their words distinct or indistinct."[4] Worse yet, Nixon and his aides often spoke over one another, and they communicated in mumbled sentence fragments and grunts of approval or disapproval.

The process was agonizing. Woods told a friend that for the first tape she transcribed, it took more than twenty-five hours to get a one-hour conversation on paper. (Of course, all of these transcripts were produced by typewriters on paper, which made the correction process lengthy and arduous.) Woods also had to keep up with her other secretarial duties, which led to the moment which earned her a kind of unwelcome immortality. Woods prepared transcripts for the first round of tapes that Nixon agreed to provide to the Watergate investigators, including one of the most important, a conversation between Nixon and Haldeman on June 20, 1972, just three days after the arrests at the Watergate. Woods said she was distracted by a phone call and wound up deleting eighteen-and-a-half minutes from the tape. When Nixon's lawyers reported the gap to Judge Sirica (and the public), the reaction was ridicule and disbelief. Jaworski's team retained a team of experts to analyze the gap and found that the deletions were the product of five separate, seemingly intentional, erasures, but they couldn't prove who did it. (The leading suspects were Woods and Nixon himself.)

Buzhardt, who, like most lawyers of his generation, didn't know how to type, spent nearly as long as Woods did on each taped conversation. Over and over again, Buzhardt hit play and rewind and scribbled on yellow legal pads. The process of trying to decipher the words and names on the tapes was so painful for Buzhardt that he said he could physically endure it for only an hour at a time—and he was working fifteen- to nineteen-hour days.[5] Even if Woods and Buzhardt were inclined to delegate some of the work with the tapes (which they weren't), Nixon initially prohibited anyone else from handling the originals.

Jaworski's prosecutors were at the head of the line demanding the tapes, and Judge Sirica, who would preside over the Watergate cover-up trial of Nixon's top aides, was their eager ally. Jaworski differed from Cox in how he dealt with the White House. Cox always saw Nixon's people as adversaries, but Jaworski had confidence in his skills as a negotiator, and he thought he could make progress with Haig. So, the two men met frequently, and Jaworski didn't always fill in his subordinates about what was said, which unnerved the young zealots. These meetings produced a few tapes for the prosecutors, but the talks ultimately stalled. Jaworski went ahead with the cover-up indictment on March 1, 1974, but his team pushed him to keep pressing for the tapes. The tapes might incriminate or exculpate the defendants (and Nixon), but the prosecutors felt an obligation to hear them before the case went to trial.

Frustrated by Haig's failure to deliver more tapes, Jaworski decided to escalate his fight with the White House. Customarily, the main tool of prosecutors in a criminal investigation is the grand jury subpoena, which yields evidence that can be used initially to determine whether to bring charges and then in any subsequent trial. But after an indictment is filed, it's less common but still permissible for a judge to issue a trial subpoena, which is aimed at producing evidence to be used in the trial that follows. In response to a request from Jaworski, Judge Sirica on April 18 issued a trial subpoena to the White House for sixty-four missing tapes. To a certain extent, the prosecutors were flying blind in terms of which tapes to seek. Even with Dean's help, they didn't know what was discussed at each meeting. At the last minute, they decided to add a demand for the Oval Office conversation on June 23, 1972, six days after the break-in. It was a fateful choice.

In response to the trial subpoena, Nixon tried to flip his usual script of defiance. He would comply, sort of. Nixon decided that he would release to the public transcripts of forty-six tapes, but not the tapes themselves. He included some, but not all, of the conversations sought by Jaworski and the impeachment investigators in the Judiciary Committee. This set off a flurry of new work at the White House, expanding the circle of people involved in the process. A group of White House secretaries was recruited to prepare the transcripts, and these drafts were reviewed by Buzhardt and James St. Clair, the Boston lawyer brought in to handle Watergate. The final check was by Diane Sawyer, a young aide to Ron Ziegler, the press secretary.[6] In a speech to the nation on April 29, Nixon appeared in front of a stack of blue notebooks embossed with the presidential seal that allegedly contained the transcripts; in fact, the notebooks were props that did not include the transcripts, which amounted to 1,200 pages. In the speech, Nixon announced a preemptive vindication: the tapes "will, at last, once and for all, show that what I knew and what I did with regard to the Watergate break-in and cover-up were just as I have described them to you from the very beginning." Nixon all but explicitly said these disclosures would conclude his cooperation with the Watergate investigators, both in Jaworski's office and in the Judiciary Committee: "To anyone who reads his way through this mass of materials I have provided, it will be totally, abundantly clear that as far as the President's role with regard to Watergate is concerned, the entire story is there."

In keeping with the consistently misbegotten nature of Nixon's defense, the release of the transcripts made his situation worse. In his speech, he predicted the transcripts "will embarrass me and those with whom I have talked—which they will—and not just because they will become the subject of speculation and even ridicule—which they will." He was right about that much. The tawdry nature of the exchanges with his aides, and their obsession with political advantage, diminished any remaining aura of rectitude for Nixon. Even the expurgations provided public amusement. The transcripts frequently included the notation "[expletive deleted]," which became a national catchphrase.

More to the point, the transcripts satisfied none of his pursuers, especially Jaworski's team. They knew they could not trust the accuracy of the transcripts (which turned out to be dreadful), or the outright omissions, both in individual exchanges and entire conversations. Because Jaworski was prohibited from testing the accuracy of the transcripts, they were useless as evidence in the courtroom. He needed the tapes themselves. The question was how to get them.

Haig knew that Jaworski had one great point of leverage over the president: Jaworski could resign in protest over Nixon's failure to produce the tapes. Haig recognized that the public would see such an action by Jaworski as a sort of Saturday Night Massacre redux. The political firestorm from the departure of a second special prosecutor might well force Nixon out of office. Jaworski recognized the potential of this strategy, but there was a problem with it, too. Jaworski didn't want to resign. He was as competitive as any lawyer, and he had staked his reputation on the success of the Watergate cover-up prosecution. He didn't want to leave before the trial.

The obvious approach for Jaworski was to keep fighting in court to get access to the tapes. But the passage of time presented a problem. It was now May 1974. Judge Sirica had ruled in Jaworski's favor on the tapes, but Nixon's lawyers had appealed to the D.C. Circuit. The losing side there would surely appeal to the Supreme Court, which was scheduled to close for its customary summer recess on June 17. (It would not return until the first Monday in October.) With the cover-up trial scheduled to begin on September 9 (later moved to October 1), there was no way that Jaworski could get decisions out of both the appeals court and the Supreme Court—and get the tapes—in time.

So Jaworski decided to take a gamble. His lawyers would try to take advantage of a rule that allows a case to bypass the appeals court if it is of such "imperative public importance as to require immediate settlement."[7] The Court had only granted such a request twice since World War II, the last time in 1952, in a landmark case about President Truman's seizure of the nation's steel mills. Nixon's lawyers objected fiercely, arguing that there was no reason to take Jaworski's demand for the tapes out of the usual calendar of cases. It's a truism of law practice that procedure often dictates substance; issues of briefing and schedule often serve as proxies for how judges feel about the merits of cases. So, Jaworski's team was especially pleased when the Supreme Court on May 31 granted the motion for expedited consideration and scheduled argument in *United States v. Nixon* for July 8—right in the middle of the justices' treasured summer break.

The Supreme Court's action in 1974 offers a revealing contrast to an analogous application fifty years later. Jack Smith, the special counsel investigating former president Trump, obtained an indictment of Trump charging him with the use of unlawful means on January 6, 2021, to overturn the results of the 2020 election. As in 1974, the trial judge in 2024 ruled in the prosecutor's favor on a legal motion to dismiss the case. Also, as in 1974, the president's lawyers appealed to the D.C. Circuit, which would delay the case, here until after the 2024 presidential election. Like Jaworski, Smith asked the Supreme Court to bypass the appeals court and hear the case right away. "When the government sought certiorari before judgment in *United States v. Nixon*, a case presenting similarly consequential issues of presidential privilege, the Court granted the petition and resolved the constitutional question expeditiously so that trial could begin as scheduled," Smith wrote in his brief. The Supreme Court should expedite matters again "to ensure that it can provide the expeditious resolution that this case warrants, just as it did in *United States v. Nixon*."

But the Supreme Court's response in 2024 was the opposite of what it was in 1974. Without comment, the justices declined Smith's request for expedition and put his case on the regular calendar. By doing so, even before reaching the merits of the case, they effectively ruled in Trump's favor, by making it all but impossible for Smith to try his January 6 case before the 2024 presidential election. Jaworski, in contrast, got the schedule he needed to stay on course. Both the Supreme Court of 1974 and the one in 2024 had majorities of justices appointed by Republican presidents, but the later Court was more partisan and thus more willing to assist a Republican president.

Still, in the summer of 1974, the special prosecutor had to persuade the justices that he was right on the law—and that Nixon had to turn over the tapes.

CHAPTER 8

Supreme Stakes

SINCE THE DAWN OF THE REPUBLIC, THE SUPREME COURT has sought to define the limits of presidential power. In 1803, in *Marbury v. Madison*, the Court established the principle that the justices themselves had the ultimate authority over the actions of presidents, because "It is emphatically the province and duty of the judicial department to say what the law is." In *Youngstown Sheet & Tube Company v. Sawyer*, the case the Court heard on an expedited basis in 1952, the justices held that the president did not have the right to seize control of most of the country's steel mills without specific authorization from Congress. In the summer of 1974, the Court addressed a similarly weighty matter: whether the president was obliged to comply with a subpoena for tapes of his own conversations in the White House for use in a pending criminal trial.

The powers of the presidency range from nearly absolute to barely existent. The pardon power belongs in the former category. As William Howard Taft wrote shortly after he left the presidency, "The duty involved in the pardoning power is a most difficult one to perform, because it is so completely within the discretion of the Executive and is lacking so in rules or limitations of its exercise. The only rule he can follow is that he shall not exercise it against the public interest."[1] A few years later, in 1925, after Taft became chief justice, he ratified this expansive view of the pardon power on behalf of the Court, writing, "When the words to grant pardons were used in the Constitution, they conveyed to the mind the authority as exercised by the English crown, or by its representatives in the colonies." If Congress objected to the president's use of his pardon power, Taft said the legislators had only one tool at their disposal: "a resort to impeachment rather than to a narrow and strained construction of the general powers of the President."

The case of *United States v. Nixon* turned on a more tenuous claim of presidential power: "executive privilege," which is not even mentioned in the Constitution. In fact, as of 1974, the Supreme Court had never even considered a doctrine by that name. By constitutional standards, the claim was new and untested. During the Eisenhower administration, the president declined to produce some records for Senator Joseph McCarthy on the ground that he had "uncontrolled discretion" to withhold information from Congress. But no court, much less the Supreme Court, had ratified that claim.

The argument in Jaworski's brief to the Supreme Court was straightforward. "First, the President, like all executive officials as well as the humblest private citizens, is subject to the rule of law," he wrote. "Second, in the full and impartial administration of justice, the public has a right to every man's evidence." The prosecutor had an additional advantage in asserting this claim. As part of the indictment in the cover-up case, the Watergate grand jury had named Nixon an "unindicted co-conspirator." This meant that the grand jurors believed Nixon was part of the charged conspiracy to obstruct justice, even if they did not add his name as a defendant in the indictment. Jaworski had agreed to describe Nixon this way in part as a sop to members of his staff and grand jurors who wanted to indict Nixon along with the other cover-up defendants.

There was also a technical legal reason for this classification of Nixon as a co-conspirator, relating to the rules against hearsay evidence. Under the ordinary rules of hearsay, the words of an outsider like Nixon would not be admissible against the cover-up defendants. But the law allows hearsay statements if they are uttered by co-conspirators. This was especially important in the cover-up case because Jaworski's team planned on using Nixon's words on the tapes as evidence against the other conspirators. So, Jaworski argued, even if executive privilege existed in certain circumstances, it was not justified in this one: "The qualified executive privilege for confidential intra-governmental deliberations, designed to promote the candid interchange between officials and their aides, exists only to protect the legitimate functioning of government," he wrote. "Thus, the privilege must give way where, as here, it has been abused."

There was an additional, if unspoken, political advantage to this argument. Like Cox, Jaworski knew that he was in a political battle with Nixon as well as a legal one. Labeling his adversary an "unindicted co-conspirator" left an indelible stain on Nixon's reputation and legacy. Civil libertarians have long challenged the practice of prosecutors using that term because it's highly prejudicial and there is no mechanism to challenge or refute it in court. Whatever the motivations behind its use, "unindicted co-conspirator" joined "expletive deleted" as one of the rhetorical legacies of Watergate and one that did lasting harm to Nixon.

In addition to the "co-conspirator" hearsay issue, Nixon had other problems with his legal position. Nixon had hurt his case before the Supreme Court with his earlier accommodations of congressional inquiries. To prove he had nothing to hide, the president had failed to raise an executive privilege objection to the testimony of many of his closest advisers during the hearings of the Senate Watergate Committee. Several of these witnesses, including Dean, Haldeman, and Ehrlichman, were on the tapes Jaworski was now seeking. If Nixon wanted to do all that he could to get the Supreme Court to protect those conversations under subpoena, he should have objected from the start.

Still, Nixon had powerful arguments before the Supreme Court. Notwithstanding the absence of Supreme Court precedent on "executive privilege," the general idea of a need for confidentiality was likely to appeal to the justices, who zealously protected their own deliberations from outside attention. Nixon himself gave a cogent explanation for the need for such a doctrine in his speech announcing the release of the tape transcripts. "The principle of confidentiality is absolutely essential to the conduct of the Presidency," he said. "Brutal candor is necessary in discussing how to bring warring factions to the peace table or how to move necessary legislation through the

Congress." This was a point likely to have intuitive, as well as legal, appeal for the justices.

What was more, the simultaneous impeachment investigation created a complication for Jaworski. Nixon's lawyers said Jaworski was essentially serving as a stalking horse for the congressional impeachment investigation. "Court process is being used as a discovery tool for the impeachment proceedings—proceedings which the Constitution clearly assigns to the Congress, not the courts." Worse yet, Jaworski was trying to get information—the tapes—that Congress had sought through the courts and failed to obtain. Because Jaworski had already shared some of the results of his investigation with the Judiciary Committee, Nixon's lawyers said that allowing the prosecutor access to the tapes "would be to produce evidence for the Congress that the Congress could not obtain by its own procedures." Finally, Nixon recognized the political damage he had suffered by being named an unindicted co-conspirator. His lawyers' brief denounced that label as "unsubstantiated, unprecedented and clearly unconstitutional." It was none of those things, but at least the brief offered the Nixon team a chance to protest.

Meeting the short filing deadlines for the briefs in the Supreme Court created another crash assignment for the lawyers on both sides. Thanks to the team that Cox had assembled, Jaworski's prosecutors managed the process without much trouble. As usual, much of the burden on the president's side fell on Buzhardt, who was already overwhelmed and exhausted by his assignment with the tapes. On June 14, just before the briefs were due, he had a massive heart attack at his home in suburban Virginia. (St. Clair finished the brief and argued the case.) Buzhardt survived, but never fully recovered. Back home in South Carolina, he died of another heart attack in 1978 at the age of fifty-four.

————————

As the battle over the tapes inched toward the Supreme Court in the spring and summer of 1974, Richard Nixon had a secret. Haig had been keeping the president abreast of his negotiations with Jaworski over the tapes. Before their talks broke down altogether, leading to the fight in the Supreme Court, the pair discussed various compromise proposals which involved the disclosure of some tapes but not others. During those negotiations, Haig suggested to Nixon that he familiarize himself with the tapes. It had been years since the conversations took place. There was no way he could remember everything that was said.

So, late on the Sunday night of May 5, after Nixon returned from a weekend at Camp David, he went to his study and cued up the tape of his conversation with Haldeman on June 23, 1972. At that point, it had been less than a week since the break-in, and the investigation by the FBI was just beginning. The first ties between the burglars and CREEP were starting to come to light. The president and Haldeman knew that if Bureau agents continued to probe further, the connections to the White House would become more obvious and ominous. From the beginning, Nixon had said publicly that he had not interfered in the FBI investigation in any way. The June 23 tape said exactly the opposite.

On that early summer morning in 1973, Haldeman told Nixon, "On the investigation, you know, the Democratic break-in thing, we're back to the problem area because the FBI is not under control. . . . Their investigation is now leading into some productive areas. . . . And, and it goes in some directions we don't want it to go."

Haldeman then raised the question of how to get the FBI to stop an investigation that would create problems for the White House. "The way to handle this now is for us to have [Vernon] Walters [deputy director of the CIA] call Pat Gray [acting director of the FBI] and just say, 'Stay the hell out of this . . . this is ah, business here we don't want you to go any further on it.'" Gray and his subordinate Mark Felt would then tell his subordinates at the Bureau, "'We've got the signal from across the river, to put the hold on this.'" (CIA headquarters was across the Potomac River in Virginia.)

How, then, to get the CIA to tell the FBI to halt its investigation? "The only way to do that is from White House instructions," Haldeman said, "and it's got to be to [CIA director Richard] Helms. . . . And the proposal would be that Ehrlichman and I call them in."

"All right, fine," Nixon said. Then the president began telling

Haldeman what to say to the CIA. This "will uncover a lot of things. You open a scab there's a hell of lot of things, and that we feel that it would be very detrimental to let this thing go any further." Nixon warmed to the idea of bringing in the CIA: "You call them in. Good deal! Play it tough. That's the way they play it, and that's the way we are going to play it."[2]

For good reason, the June 23 tape, after it was made public, became known as "the smoking gun." Nixon approved a plan to use the CIA to tell the FBI to stop its investigation of the Watergate burglary, not because of any legitimate national security reasons, but because it would lead to political embarrassment for the White House. In his memoir, Nixon acknowledged, "I had indicated in all my public statements that the sole motive for calling in the CIA had been national security. But there was no doubt now that we had been talking about political implications that morning."[3] Nixon was savvy enough to recognize the implications of public disclosure of this tape. From that night in May, when he first heard the tape, Nixon knew that he was doomed if the June 23 tape came to light.

––––––––

The case of *United States v. Nixon* raised a sartorial question as well as a legal one. At the time, it was customary for the solicitor general and other lawyers representing the government to wear what was known in bygone days as "morning clothes"—black frock coat with a long tail, gray ascot, black vest, and striped pants. But now, in this case of the prosecutor vs. the president, who was "the government"? Some on Jaworski's staff wanted him to wear the traditional outfit as a symbol of his status as the real representative of the people of the United States. But Jaworski demurred. "If you keep it up," the Texan told his subordinates, "I'll show up in cowboy boots and jeans."[4] So, on July 8, 1974, Jaworski wore a business suit to the Supreme Court, as did James St. Clair, who would be arguing on behalf of President Nixon.

It was already 90 degrees when the lawyers mounted the famous steps of the Court, in advance of the argument at 10 a.m. Spectators had been camped out in front of the Supreme Court for two days, in hopes of securing a seat in the courtroom. The occasion was unprecedented—a case that skipped the appellate court to land in front of the justices in the middle of their summer vacation, with the fate of the president on the line. The tension in the courtroom was extraordinary as Jaworski took first to the lectern.

The special prosecutor failed to rise to the occasion. Jaworski began with a ponderous summary of the procedural history of the case and droned on from there. It had been a long time since Jaworski tried many cases and argued appeals, and the rust showed. The liberals on the Court tried to help him along. William Douglas, the cantankerous progressive who had been a Nixon antagonist for decades, said, "We start with a constitution that does not contain the words 'executive privilege,' is that right?" Jaworski agreed, and the gist of the questions suggested the Court was leaning his way. That continued during St. Clair's turn, as when Lewis Powell, one of three Nixon appointees on the Court, asked, "Mr. St. Clair, what public interest is there in preserving secrecy with respect to criminal conspiracy?"

"The answer, sir, is that a criminal conspiracy is criminal only after it's proven to be criminal," St. Clair said. But that wasn't the way the law of unindicted co-conspirators worked. It was up to the prosecution to designate the conspirators, and St. Clair had no response to that basic aspect of the law.

Philip Lacovara, Jaworski's in-house counsel, presented the final argument, and he came closer to matching the moment. It was true, he acknowledged, that there was an impeachment proceeding underway, but that was irrelevant to the issue before the Court. "This is a trial of tremendous national importance," he said. "This is an independent, separate constitutional process that is underway, and a traditional, ordinary, prosaic remedy—a subpoena—has been utilized to obtain evidence for that trial." Lacovara's point was straightforward. This was an important case, but the ordinary rules for all trials should apply. No trial, like no man, was above the law. And with that, the justices retired behind their burgundy curtain to discuss and decide.

Jaworski surprised his staff with his reaction. He appeared to experience a clinical depression.[5] In part, he was wounded by the harsh reaction in the press to the quality of his argument. Also, after nine months as special prosecutor, he was lonely in Washington and ready to return to Houston. As he waited for the Supreme Court's decision, he retreated to his suite at the Jefferson Hotel and rarely appeared in the team's offices, just five blocks away. He had not brought any colleagues with him to Washington, and he had kept on all the lawyers who once referred to themselves as "Archie's Orphans." Almost to a person, they had developed a respect for Jaworski—for his judgment and his courage, even if they didn't agree with every decision he made. The prosecutors made pilgrimages to the Jefferson, hoping to lure him back to the office. Carl Feldbaum, his tapes impresario, came by twice a day, bringing letters and telegrams of support that had arrived for him.

It was true that Jaworski missed home and grieved his bad press, but there was something else eating at him. Much as he had built mutual esteem with the young firebrands on his staff, he was not one of them. He had done his part. He had obtained the indictment in the cover-up case and pushed the tapes issue all the way to the Supreme Court. But Jaworski didn't want to do more. He still respected the presidency, if not this president, and he didn't want to be the one who brought him down. Jaworski believed in the constitutional process, and if Congress wanted to impeach and remove Nixon, that was up to the people's representatives. But Jaworski didn't think that he, or any prosecutor, should be the instrument of Nixon's demise. Jaworski didn't want to prosecute Nixon, and what's more, he didn't think the president should be prosecuted. Secretly but insistently, Jaworski tried to make sure Nixon never would be. Jaworski's reluctance to bring a case against Nixon was the background music, which was sometimes ignored, as the issue of a pardon came to the fore.

CHAPTER 9

The Vise Closes

IN THIS GREATEST POLITICAL CRISIS OF HIS LIFE, RICHARD Nixon became more like himself. As his pursuers drew closer, and his options narrower, and as he waited for the Supreme Court to decide the fate of the tapes, the president became more aggrieved, more isolated, and more paranoid. But face-to-face Nixon was also strangely conflict-averse, so his approach in the middle of 1974 was to withdraw—physically. He avoided the White House. He traveled overseas. He bunkered down in his vacation homes on opposite sides of the country. He tried to hide from the problem that wouldn't go away.

For a politician, Nixon was a paradoxical figure. He was immensely, even historically, successful as a candidate. He appeared on a national ticket five times, a number matched only by Franklin D. Roosevelt. (Like FDR, Nixon won four of five.) In 1972, Nixon triumphed in arguably the greatest presidential landslide in American history, winning more than 60 percent of the vote and losing only Massachusetts and the District of Columbia. Yet, at the same time, Nixon was nothing like most successful politicians. He was not gregarious, like FDR, Bill Clinton, and the two George Bushes, or charming like JFK or Barack Obama. Nixon was, rather, withdrawn, shy, fundamentally antisocial. He preferred to be alone most of the time, which was why he spent so much time in his hideaway in the Old Executive Office Building. Even those most devoted to him saw the strangeness of his personality. No one spent more time with Nixon, or was more devoted to him, than Haldeman, who traveled with him during the 1960 presidential campaign and stayed by his side for much of the next thirteen years. But in private, Haldeman referred to his boss with such sarcastic nicknames as Leader of the Free World, Milhous (Nixon's middle name, which he detested), and Thelma's husband (after Pat Nixon's discarded first name). Haldeman was sure that, even after all that time, Nixon never knew how many children Haldeman had. Behind his back, his aides would mock how he shoved White House trinkets—tie clips, pens, cuff links—at visitors without looking at them.[1] His social skills were practically nonexistent.

As the Watergate crisis deepened, Nixon clung to the one part of the presidency that he could still control—foreign policy. By the middle of 1974, he had real accomplishments in this realm. Nixon had opened a relationship with China and achieved a measure of stability—détente—with the Soviet Union. After the Yom Kippur War, he had guaranteed Israel's survival and brokered a tense but holding peace. Belatedly, but finally, he had ended American military involvement in the Vietnam War. On his overseas trips, the president could receive the kind of welcome that was no longer available to him in the fifty states. So, as the walls closed in, Nixon fled Washington.

On June 10, he left for Austria, en route to the Middle East. On Air Force One, Nixon's left leg became swollen to twice the size of his right. The White House doctor diagnosed phlebitis, an inflammation of a vein. The danger was that a clot might form, break loose, and reach Nixon's lungs, causing a fatal embolism.[2] The doctor instructed Nixon to wrap his leg four times a day and stay off his feet. Nixon ignored him. Instead, when Nixon arrived in Cairo, he joined with President Anwar al-Sadat in an open-topped car for a motorcade that passed in front of a million people. As Sadat and Nixon stood and waved for more than an hour, the throng chanted, "Nik-son! Nikson!" Despite the pain and the triple-digit heat, Nixon enjoyed showing off that Watergate had not diminished his appeal in the broader world.

From Egypt, Nixon went on to Saudi Arabia, Syria, Israel, Jordan, and Portugal, before returning to Washington on June 19. Just five days later, the president headed to Brussels for a meeting with NATO allies and then on to the Soviet Union for a week-long summit with Leonid Brezhnev in Moscow and several more locations. The trips were longer on symbolism than accomplishments, but Nixon still reveled in them. When he landed at an Air Force base in Maine, on July 3, Vice President Ford, ever loyal in public as well as private, led the welcoming delegation, saying the world was now "a little safer and a little saner" thanks to Nixon's trip.[3] Nixon had been gone from Washington for eighteen of the previous twenty-three days, and then he continued to stay away.

From Maine, Air Force One flew to Florida, where Nixon had a compound in Key Biscayne, known as the Winter White House. He also had a home in San Clemente, on the Pacific Coast about midway between Los Angeles and San Diego, which he called "La Casa Pacifica," or the Western White House. In his first term alone, Nixon spent about 150 days in Key Biscayne and 200 days in San Clemente, nearly a full year.[4] In both places, for the most part, his only companions were Bebe Rebozo, a Miami bank owner who lived next door in Florida, and Robert Abplanalp, who became rich by inventing the modern spray nozzle on aerosol cans. (Abplanalp and a few friends built Nixon, for his exclusive use, a three-hole golf course on the twenty-six-acre grounds of the Western White House.) In addition to a home near Key Biscayne, Abplanalp also owned a small private island off the Florida coast. For even greater isolation, Nixon would often retreat there. (During his presidency, Nixon also spent 160 days in the quasi-isolation of Camp David, the presidential retreat in Maryland.)[5]

After spending the Independence Day weekend in Florida, he returned briefly to Washington, where he was when *United States v. Nixon* was argued on July 8, and then four days later he went west to San Clemente for two weeks. The mood there was grim. His daughter Tricia and her husband, Ed Cox, came along, and they were traumatized by, of all things, the state of Nixon's private golf course. "Wasted, neglected, ugly, dead. The golf course of 'Friends' of the President is no more," Tricia wrote in her diary. "The sight is sickening, not because it is a sickening sight, but because of what it signifies. Deserted. Killed. The golf course. The man for whom it was created."[6]

On July 13, Ford paid his only visit to La Casa Pacifica for a rare conversation between the president and vice president. Ostensibly, the purpose of the meeting was to talk about Nixon's plan to address inflation, which had spiked following the Arab oil embargo. Nixon and Ford had known each other since they began serving in Congress together in the 1940s, and each considered the other a good professional friend, though hardly an intimate. But as with everyone else, Nixon pushed his vice president away, as he suffered through Watergate alone. (At one point, Nixon wrote Ford a handwritten note of appreciation for his public support. As Ford noted in his memoir, "'Dear Gerry,' he began, misspelling my name.")[7]

The two men talked about the economy in the house overlooking the Pacific, and Ford later wrote, "I cannot pick out a date and say, 'This is when he started to lose his grip,' but it was clear to me that he wasn't as strong either mentally or physically as he was before. I had a growing sense of his frustration, his resentment and his lack of a calm, deliberate approach to the problems of government. He complained bitterly how he was being mistreated by Congress and the press. His resolve to stay and fight seemed to be weakening."[8] Nixon's diary entry at that time reflected his fading prospects. "I intend to live the next week without dying the death of a thousand cuts. This has been my philosophy throughout my political life. Cowards die a thousand deaths, brave men die only once."[9]

There is no record that Ford shared his dour view of Nixon's state of mind with any of his advisers at this point, and he continued his unqualified support for the president in public. But the news kept getting worse. On July 24, while Nixon was still in San Clemente, the Supreme Court issued its ruling about the tapes.

When the Court scheduled a session for that morning, there was no doubt what was coming. There was only one case to be decided. Chief Justice Warren Burger spoke for the Court, which was unanimous, 8 to 0. (William Rehnquist, then an associate justice, recused himself because of his service in the Nixon administration.) Burger's opinion swept aside all of Nixon's arguments. Even though Jaworski was part of the executive branch, he had the right to sue the president, the leader of the executive branch, for compliance with the trial subpoena. The tapes were relevant evidence in the cover-up case against Nixon's advisers. Executive privilege did not shield Nixon from complying with the subpoena.

The previous night, Nixon had been up until 2:30 a.m. working on a speech about inflation, so he was still asleep in San Clemente when Haig, who was staying nearby, woke him with a call at 9 a.m.[10] "How are things going?" Nixon asked.

"In a strained voice," Nixon recalled, Haig said, "'Well, it's pretty rough, Mr. President. I didn't want to wake you until we had the complete text, but the Supreme Court decision came down this morning.'"

"'Unanimous?' I guessed.

"'Unanimous. There's no air in it at all,' he said.

"'Not at all?' I asked.

"'It's as tight as a drum.'"

On the day of the decision, Fred Buzhardt, Nixon's White House counsel, who was back in Washington, called Haig in San Clemente with an idea.[11] Buzhardt had listened to more of the tapes than anyone, and he knew how bad they were for Nixon. What if Nixon pardoned all the men charged in the Watergate cover-up case, as well as others who might be charged? That would obviate the need for disclosure of the tapes and save Nixon the embarrassment, or worse, from their disclosure. This was another example of pardons that would not have surprised the seventeenth-century English parliamentarians who sought to limit the sovereign's pardon power. Buzhardt's proposed pardons had nothing to do with mercy or generosity to others; they would have existed solely to advance the self-interest of the president who granted them. (In keeping with this theme, Buzhardt thought that he himself might need a pardon because of his machinations to keep the tapes out of the prosecutors' hands.) Haig was interested enough in the idea to tell Buzhardt to make a list of the people to be pardoned, but the idea went no further, not least because it probably would not have accomplished its purpose. It's unlikely, to say the least, that such pardons from Nixon would have quelled the demands of prosecutors and legislators for the tapes.

Still, in a broader sense, the Supreme Court's decision in *United States v. Nixon* raised a question that historians have puzzled over for years. Why didn't Nixon just destroy the tapes? Butterfield disclosed the existence of the tapes in July 1973—and Haig immediately shut down the taping system—so why didn't Nixon short-circuit the disclosure fight by eliminating the material in question? As would become clear later, he regarded the tapes as his personal property. Why didn't that give him the right to do anything he wanted with them, including getting rid of them? In his memoir, Nixon gave two reasons for not destroying the tapes. First, he thought that at least some of the tapes would exonerate him from wrongdoing. But the second— and more persuasive—point was that "destruction of the tapes would create an indelible impression of guilt, and I simply did not believe that the revelation of anything I had actually done would be as bad as that impression."[12] Of course, it's impossible, at this late date, to prove with certainty what would have happened if Nixon had destroyed the tapes. Nixon may well have been right that destruction of the tapes would have hastened his political demise. But the Supreme Court made clear the costs to Nixon of allowing the tapes to survive.

By much the same reasoning, Nixon never seriously considered defying the Supreme Court's decision and refusing to turn over the tapes. By July 1974, it was too late for such a confrontation. Especially because the decision was unanimous and included the votes of two justices (Burger and Lewis Powell) whom Nixon himself had appointed, there would have been no political support for Nixon simply to ignore the Court's ruling. So, Nixon directed his lawyers to announce publicly that he would comply. (Sitting alone in San Clemente that night, he wrote in his diary, "My options have been reduced to only two: resign or be impeached.")[13] And there was worse to come. The June 23, 1972, tape—the smoking gun—was days away from public disclosure.

The Supreme Court's decision in *United States v. Nixon* was hailed at the time as a bracing ratification of the principle that no man was above the law. And it is true that the case forced Nixon to surrender the tapes. But the legacy of *United States v. Nixon* is more complicated. Until this case, the Supreme Court had never recognized the legal basis for a doctrine of "executive privilege." In *The Brethren*, Bob Woodward and Scott Armstrong provided a behind-the-scenes account of the Court's deliberations on the case. They found that some justices on the Court rejected the very idea of "executive privilege." Justice Byron White in particular thought that "the President should be treated like any citizen, no more, no less."[14] William Brennan and William Douglas felt similarly. But Burger, Powell, and Potter Stewart thought that the Court needed to recognize that presidential deliberations deserved some protection in the law. So, in the interest of preserving unanimity, the justices decided to unite behind the compromise that Burger struck in his opinion.

On behalf of the Court, Burger asserted that the Constitution did allow for an "executive privilege," which permitted the president to prevent disclosure of some internal communications within the White House. Burger cited "the valid need for protection of communications between high Government officials and those who advise and assist them in the performance of their manifold duties; the importance of this confidentiality is too plain to require further discussion. Human experience teaches that those who expect public dissemination of their remarks may well temper candor with a concern for appearances and for their own interests to the detriment of the decision making process." Further, Burger went on, "There is nothing novel about governmental confidentiality. The meetings of the Constitutional Convention in 1787 were conducted in complete privacy. . . . The President's need for complete candor and objectivity from advisers calls for great deference from the courts."

In the Nixon case, though, Burger said that the balance favored disclosure of the tapes. Allowing the privilege to withhold evidence that is demonstrably relevant in a criminal trial would cut deeply into the guarantee of due process of law and gravely impair the basic function of the courts. Here, he said, "the generalized interest in confidentiality . . . cannot prevail over the fundamental demands of due process of law in the fair administration of criminal justice." Far from rejecting outright Nixon's claim of privilege, the Court acknowledged the existence of that privilege and ruled only that in this case, the privilege must yield to the demands of the criminal justice system—but just barely.

In other words, the decision in *Nixon* amounted to an invitation for future presidents to resist disclosure of their internal deliberations and argue that the balance should be struck in favor of confidentiality. President Donald Trump pushed this strategy to its limit, when, after the Democrats took control of the House in the 2018 midterm elections, he refused to disclose virtually any information in response to demands for congressional oversight. He litigated each congressional subpoena, and between the inevitable delays of court processes and a conservative judiciary more sympathetic to the claims of the executive branch, Trump succeeded in preventing disclosure of almost everything that was sought. That, too, is a legacy of *United States v. Nixon*.

CHAPTER 10

Pardons and Self-Pardons

IN ONE WAY, FORD'S RESPONSE TO THE FINAL SPIRAL OF
Watergate resembled Nixon's; they both fled Washington. While
Nixon shuttled between foreign capitals and his vacation homes,
Ford kept up his frenetic pace of speeches on behalf of Republican
candidates around the country, which were often scheduled by Nixon's political team without any input from Ford's own staff. The vice
president's generic cheerleading on the road allowed him to avoid
both the closer scrutiny he would receive in Washington and the increasingly real prospect that he would soon take over as president.

Ford rarely let his guard down and when he did, he quickly pulled
back. After one long day in the spring of 1974, he was chatting with
Tom DeFrank, a young *Newsweek* reporter with whom Ford had a
friendly relationship. DeFrank could see that something was both-
ering Ford, especially when the vice president told the reporter to
put his notebook away. Ford asked DeFrank why he thought William
Safire had attacked him in a recent column in *The New York Times*.
"Well, Mr. Vice President, it's very simple," DeFrank recalled saying.
"They know Nixon is finished. They know he's a goner. They know
he can't survive, and they know sooner or later—probably sooner—
you're going to be President."

"I was not prepared for what happened then," DeFrank later recalled, "because without any delay at all, he blurted something out. And
he said, 'You're right. But when the pages of history are written, no one
will ever be able to say that Jerry Ford contributed to it.' If I'd had a pen

out, I would have dropped it because that was one of those holy smokes moments. Here was a Vice President of the United States telling me he knew it was over, and that he was going to be the next President of the United States at some point. He quickly recovered and recognized the enormity of what he had done, and he came around the table, and he said, 'You didn't hear that.' And I, without thinking said, 'But I did.'"

Suddenly, the mood between the two men shifted. "I was just scared to death, because I also knew that Gerald Ford was an imposing guy," DeFrank said. "He had about eight inches on me and he was towering over me. At this point, he grabbed my tie, and he held my tie and he said, 'Damn it, Tom, you're not leaving this office until we have some understanding.' Well, I knew what the understanding was; the understanding was he wanted me to admit to agree that I wouldn't use this. And I froze. . . . I was speechless, literally speechless, and he looked at me and he said, 'Write it when I'm dead. You can write it when I'm dead.'" (DeFrank honored Ford's demand and only disclosed the exchange, after Ford's death in 2006, in a book and in an interview with the historian Richard Norton Smith for an oral history project at Ford's presidential library and foundation.)[1]

––––––––––

Ford didn't want to acknowledge, even in private, that he would soon become president, but his oldest and best friend did. Unlike the vice president, Phil Buchen decided to take steps to prepare for a Ford administration—sort of.

Buchen and Ford were fraternity brothers at the University of Michigan, where they made an odd couple, at least in appearance. Ford was the strapping football hero, and Buchen, thanks to a childhood bout of polio, usually used a wheelchair. But they shared an interest in law and politics, and Ford had introduced his friend to the charms of Grand Rapids. While Buchen was enduring an unhappy summer job at a big New York law firm, Ford talked him into joining him instead in a new law partnership in Ford's hometown. They opened their doors shortly before Pearl Harbor in 1941. Ford promptly volunteered for the Navy—Buchen was exempt—and the pair reunited after Ford left the service in early 1946. Buchen was one of the few people in Grand Rapids who knew Ford was courting a beautiful young dancer named Betty Bloomer before her divorce from her first husband came through; Jerry and Betty married in 1948. That was also the year that Ford's political ambitions surfaced, and he won his race for Congress. Though no longer law partners, Ford and Buchen remained close friends in the decades to come.

One of the few formal assignments that Nixon gave Ford as vice president was to supervise the work of a committee studying technology privacy. (It was not an administration priority.) But Ford used that opportunity, in May 1974, to bring Buchen to Washington as the part-time director of the group. Buchen had never worked in D.C., but Ford found it comforting to have an old friend in close proximity.

Shortly after Buchen arrived, notwithstanding his lack of political experience, he recognized that the Nixon presidency appeared doomed. Whether through impeachment or resignation, Buchen thought that Nixon would soon be gone from the White House, and his old friend would be president of the United States. So, Buchen took it upon himself to set up an informal, and secret, transition committee. Buchen deputized Clay Whitehead, who ran the telecommunications policy office of the White House, to put together a planning document for a Ford presidency. To work with him, Whitehead recruited four young policy operatives, one of whom was Brian Lamb, who went on to found the C-SPAN television network. (Ford long maintained, including in his memoir, that he did not approve Buchen's project and had no idea that it was even underway. Some who knew Ford in this period think that he gave at least tacit approval to Buchen, but certainly Ford did nothing to assist Buchen and his colleagues in their labors. And Ford didn't see the product of their work until a day or so before he became president.)[2]

What, then, did the secret Buchen committee do? How did it tee up decisions for Ford to make if and when he became president? How useful was it in providing a guide to a possible transition?

The answers to these questions illustrate how little, not how much, Ford prepared for the presidency. Because the group had to operate in secret, they produced only the most banal and obvious advice. The report began with three "guiding principles":

Restoration of confidence and trust of the American people.

Assumption of control which is firm and efficient.

National feeling of unification and reconciliation enabled by the character and style of the new President.[3]

It was all valid as far as it went, but offered little specific guidance. Ford did follow the report's advice in two ways. It suggested that Kissinger not serve simultaneously as secretary of state and national security advisor. (Ford eventually replaced him as national security advisor with Brent Scowcroft.) And the report said the White House press secretary should be a journalist, not a public relations professional like Nixon's Ron Ziegler. (Ford named Jerald terHorst, a reporter for a Detroit newspaper, to the position.)

Two issues would dominate the first weeks of Ford's presidency—the fate of the White House tapes and other material related to Watergate, and the question of a pardon for Nixon. Buchen's paper didn't even mention them.

———

After Ford's meeting with Nixon in San Clemente, as events accelerated through the end of July, Ford continued to make his frenetic way around the country. On July 24, the Supreme Court ruled unanimously against Nixon. Two days later, Kissinger visited Nixon at La Casa Pacifica. "I was shocked," Kissinger recalled in his memoirs, "by the ravages just a week had wrought on Nixon's appearance. His coloring was pallid. Though he seemed composed, it clearly took every ounce of his energy to conduct a serious conversation. He sat on the sofa in his office looking over the Pacific, his gaze and thought focused on some distant prospect eclipsing the issues we were bringing before him."[4] The next day, Saturday, July 27, the House Judiciary Committee voted 27 to 11 to impeach the president for obstruction of justice. (Six Republicans joined all the Democrats in voting for the measure.) The passage of two more bipartisan articles of impeachment quickly followed. Ford, meanwhile, remained in a kind of parallel universe, on a three-day campaign swing through the Midwest on behalf of endangered Republicans. He returned to Washington on Wednesday, July 31, and promptly turned around and flew to Worcester, Massachusetts, to play in a golf tournament with his friend Tip O'Neill.[5]

Nixon finally returned from California to the White House on Monday, July 29, and the first thing he did was summon his lawyer Buzhardt, who had recovered enough from his heart attack to return to the office. Nixon wanted to talk about pardons.

Nixon hadn't discussed pardons much since he considered using them for the Watergate burglars in the early days after the break-in. But that notion faded once the legal process picked up steam; it would have been too politically damaging to short-circuit it with pardons, and Nixon apparently didn't consider the possibility again. Overall, Nixon's use of the pardon power was roughly similar to other twentieth-century presidents'. He granted a total of 863 pardons and 60 commutations, virtually all of them processed in routine fashion through the pardon attorney in the Justice Department. Nixon's one modestly controversial act of clemency took place two days before Christmas in 1971, when he commuted the sentence of Jimmy Hoffa, the Teamsters leader, five years into a thirteen-year sentence for jury tampering and mail fraud. As a condition for the act of mercy, Nixon directed that Hoffa resign as president of the Teamsters and refrain from union activity until 1980. In any event, Hoffa disappeared in 1975, presumably murdered, and his body has never been found.

With impeachment and removal a near-certainty, even before the smoking gun tape was revealed to prosecutors and the public, Nixon now had his own criminal exposure to worry about—which got him to thinking about a pardon. After the Supreme Court's opinion in the tapes case the previous week, Buzhardt had raised the possibility with Haig of mooting the whole controversy by having Nixon pardon himself and all the cover-up defendants and then resigning.[6]

Nixon didn't go for that idea at the time, but he did invite Buzhardt to the Oval Office and began a long and crucial meeting on July 29 that explains much of what happened over the following two months.[7] For the rest of his life, Nixon would maintain that he never sought out a pardon—that the decision was Ford's alone. That wasn't true. This meeting with Buzhardt showed that Nixon did want a pardon—desperately. Even in his diminished state—exhausted, enraged, physically diminished, as Kissinger saw, by the ravages of Watergate—Nixon still knew how to manipulate people and processes. By his own cynical standards, Nixon had made untold errors in handling Watergate, but he wasn't going to blow it when it came to preserving his own freedom.

Nixon began with Buzhardt by asking a question that has bedeviled lawyers and scholars for decades: could Nixon pardon himself?[8]

Since no president has ever pardoned himself, the legitimacy of a presidential self-pardon has never been addressed by any court, much less the Supreme Court. For that reason, Buzhardt could offer Nixon only an informed opinion, not a definite answer. Buzhardt's own research on the issue centered on the text of Article II, which states that the president "shall have Power to grant Reprieves and Pardons for Offences against the United States, except in Cases of Impeachment." Buzhardt's conclusion was straightforward. Since the text of the Constitution did not *prohibit* the president from pardoning himself, he had the right to do it. That's a plausible answer, but even then, others thought the issue was not so simple. At almost the same time that Buzhardt examined this question, the Department of Justice looked at it, too, in a secret memorandum prepared by Mary Lawton, who was the acting assistant attorney general in the Office of Legal Counsel. Her analysis was brief: the text of the Constitution "raises the question whether the President can pardon himself," she wrote. "Under the fundamental rule that no one may be a judge in his own case, it would seem that the question should be answered in the negative."[9]

That single sentence—unadorned by any further analysis—remains the only discussion of the self-pardon question by a senior official in the government. At a minimum, the question of self-pardon deserves more scrutiny than this one throwaway line. Self-pardon raises profound questions. What is the purpose of the pardon power? Whom does the power serve? And who gets to decide those answers?

In the debates over the Constitution in Philadelphia in 1787, the pardon power was discussed only briefly and the question of self-pardons not at all. But it is possible to intuit some Framers' views of the possibility. At the Constitutional Convention, Edmund Randolph argued that treason was such a serious crime that it should be excluded from a president's pardon power, especially because the president himself may be guilty. James Wilson responded, "If [the president] be himself party to the guilt he can be impeached and prosecuted." Wilson's response, which carried the day, suggests that self-pardon is not a possibility because if a president pardoned himself, he could not be "prosecuted." (Wilson's answer also suggests that the Supreme Court's 2024 decision in *Trump v. United States*, limiting the ability to prosecute ex-presidents, is inconsistent with this Framer's belief.)

Another argument against the legitimacy of self-pardons rests on the structure of the Constitution. Several provisions of the Constitution guard against self-dealing. For example, the vice president is designated the president of the Senate, but the Constitution directs that the chief justice, not the vice president, presides over impeachment trials of the president. This is because the vice president would have too much of an interest in the president's removal and thus his or her own succession as president. The text of the Impeachment Clause of the Constitution also suggests an argument against self-pardons. Article I, Section 3, which describes the impeachment process, states that "the Party convicted shall nevertheless be liable and subject to Indictment, Trial, Judgment and Punishment, according to law." Since the Constitution is clear that the pardon power does not cover impeachments, this clause may mean that a president who was impeached by the House and convicted by the Senate could still be criminally prosecuted for the underlying conduct, even if that president tried to pardon himself.

There is also a larger point against self-pardons. While it is true that the president's pardon power was based on the king's, the Constitution makes abundantly clear that the president's authority, in other areas, is far more limited than the king's. The idea of an unlimited and unreviewable power is in tension with the overall Madisonian concept of checks and balances. To cite just one difference between royal authority and that of the executive branch, the king serves for life, and the president must be elected by the voters and then serves only a limited term of four years at a time. To cite another, a president can veto a law passed by Congress but Congress can override that veto. It may follow, then, that the pardon power is similarly limited, especially when it comes to self-dealing. And in certain circumstances, the courts have already found some limitations on the pardon power. A president can't pardon for a crime that has not yet been committed, nor can a president's pardon expunge the record of an underlying conviction.[10]

Still, the question about self-pardons remains open. Despite the powerful legal and historical arguments against such pardons, the textual argument in favor of them remains strong, especially when, as now, textual arguments are ascendant at the Supreme Court. It's a straightforward point: if the text of the Constitution does not prohibit self-pardons, they are not prohibited. As Justice Antonin Scalia, the father of textualism, said, "The text is the law, and it is the text that must be observed."[11] One interested party endorsed this view. On June 4, 2018, President Donald Trump tweeted, "As has been stated by numerous legal scholars, I have the absolute right to PARDON myself, but why would I do that when I have done nothing wrong?"

In his conversation with Buzhardt in the Oval Office on July 29, Nixon grasped the legal uncertainty regarding a self-pardon, and he also knew how bad it would look if he tried to issue one to himself. So, in that first conference on the subject in the Oval Office, Nixon told Buzhardt that he didn't want to pardon himself at that time. But that was just the beginning of Nixon's scheming. He was doing his usual free associating, which Nixon's staffers often found maddening, but he clearly had a scenario in mind.

So, Nixon asked: if he resigned, could Ford pardon him?

Yes, Buzhardt said.

Okay, Nixon went on, could Ford agree in advance that he would pardon Nixon if he resigned?

Here, both men recognized that they were entering sensitive territory. Nixon knew that Ford was no crook. He wasn't going to make a corrupt deal, or even a questionable one, to make himself president. For starters, Nixon had long recognized that Ford didn't hunger to be president, which was one reason he chose Ford as his vice president in the first place. For these reasons, Nixon knew that Ford would recoil at the idea of an explicit deal, especially if Nixon approached him directly and proposed a presidency-for-pardon trade.

But that didn't end the issue—far from it. Nixon still wanted a way to guarantee that he would get a pardon even if he didn't hear such a promise directly from Ford. Maybe the best idea would be to find a trusted intermediary who could feel Ford out on the issue and plant the idea of a pardon. Nixon needed someone he could trust but also with enough heft and credibility to make that kind of proposal. Only one person fit the bill: Al Haig.

But Nixon wanted to be able to deny that he had ever instructed his chief of staff to make a deal with Ford. The president needed, as it were, a cutout for his cutout. That's where Buzhardt came in. Because Buzhardt represented Nixon as a lawyer, Nixon thought their conversations would be protected by privilege. (Since Buzhardt actually worked for the government, not for Nixon personally, the privilege didn't exactly work that way, but Nixon thought it did.) Buzhardt could go to Haig and persuade him to approach Ford with the suggestion that he agree to pardon Nixon. This plan had another advantage. Haig, as a nonlawyer, wouldn't know the law of pardons or the mechanics of how they worked. Buzhardt could explain the law in a way that Haig could pass along to Ford.

So, as a result of this conversation on July 29, Buzhardt had his assignment from Nixon: he would prompt Haig to talk to Ford about pardoning Nixon. Buzhardt went back to his office and scribbled out a set of notes about pardons. It included a short summary of the law and various options for how Ford, as president, could deliver a pardon to his predecessor. After explaining the process to Haig, Buzhardt would just hand the paper over to Haig for use in his conversation with Ford.

That set the stage for the extraordinary events of August 1, 1974.

CHAPTER 11

The Sixth Option

FINALLY, EVERYONE WAS BACK AT THE WHITE HOUSE.
Nixon had returned from San Clemente, Ford from the campaign
trail. Events were building toward a climax. The House Judiciary
Committee had approved articles of impeachment. The smoking gun
tape was about to be released. The events of Thursday, August 1, 1974,
a series of hushed conversations in the West Wing and Old Executive
Office Building, set the course for all that followed—Nixon's resignation a week later and Ford's pardon of him in a little more than a
month.

After Nixon and Ford, the key figure was Alexander Haig. As
Nixon's chief of staff during this period, when the president was
withdrawn and preoccupied with his survival, Haig took on a nearly
superhuman workload. Ever since he and Kissinger unilaterally increased the alert level for American nuclear forces the previous
October, Haig saw that there were essentially no constraints on his
authority, and he acted accordingly. He didn't have a specific ideological agenda—he was not a policy person—but he thrived on the
exercise of power. He pushed decisions through the system. Like the
general he had been before he came to the White House, he was an
action officer. He accomplished tasks.

Nixon generally began his workday with Haig around 9 a.m., but
on August 1, the president summoned his chief of staff an hour earlier.
His tone was matter-of-fact, and he had a simple message to impart.

"Al, it's over," Nixon said. "We've done our best. We haven't got the votes. I can't govern. Impeachment would drag on for six months. For the sake of the country, this process must be ended." Nixon said he would take his family to Camp David for the weekend and then resign in a speech to the nation on the following Monday, August 5. Haig didn't try to talk him out of it, though he thought the precise date might be a bit hasty. Haig had been briefed on the content of the June 23, 1972, tape, and he agreed that it was indeed a smoking gun. He regarded Nixon's position as hopeless. In this early morning conversation, Nixon had one instruction for Haig: "Al, you've got to tell Ford to get ready. Tell him I want absolute secrecy. Tell him what's coming. Explain the reasoning. But don't tell him when."[1]

Just as notable as what Nixon said in this conversation was what he didn't say. Nixon said nothing to Haig about a pardon. That, Nixon knew, was the job of Buzhardt, the White House counsel. Nixon recognized how much Haig relied on Buzhardt, and Nixon knew that Haig would check with Buzhardt before entering into such a consequential conversation with Ford. The lawyer would lay out the process for a pardon to Haig, and he, in turn, would tell Ford. And that, on the morning of August 1, was what happened next. Haig went to Buzhardt to understand the mechanics of resignation and pardon before he talked to Ford.

Buzhardt was ready for him. Based on his conversation with Nixon on July 29, the lawyer was going to tell Haig what to say to Ford. Buzhardt even wrote it out for Haig. Buzhardt presented Haig with a list of possibilities, scribbled out in his own hand on a legal pad. As Buzhardt laid it out, Haig should present six possible scenarios for Ford to consider:

1. Nixon could temporarily step aside under the provisions of the 25th Amendment to defend himself in an impeachment trial in front of the Senate. Ford would then be Acting President until the trial was resolved, one way or the other.
2. Nixon could delay resigning, hoping that the tide would somehow turn in his favor.

3. Nixon could try to persuade the House to vote for censure, rather than impeachment.
4. Nixon could pardon himself, then resign.
5. Nixon could pardon some or all of the Watergate defendants, then pardon himself, then resign.
6. Nixon could resign and then Ford could pardon him.[2]

Buzhardt was engaging in the classic bureaucratic maneuver of appearing to present options while steering his boss in a predetermined direction. This was Buzhardt's way of complying with Nixon's instruction to push Ford toward a pardon. Option 1 was bizarrely complex and clearly a nonstarter. Options 2 and 3 were out of the question because both Houses of Congress were now hopeless causes for Nixon, and his situation would deteriorate further when the smoking gun tape was released. Options 4 and 5 were out, because Nixon told Buzhardt that he would not pardon himself. Only Option 6 made sense—which was Buzhardt's, and Nixon's, goal all along: Ford pardons Nixon. As if there were any doubt about Buzhardt's (and Nixon's) real agenda, the lawyer also handed Haig a draft of a document that Ford, as president, could use to issue a formal pardon to Nixon. Haig thanked Buzhardt for the briefing and took the draft pardon and the list of six options with him. Then Haig called Ford and said he had to meet with him urgently—and privately.

Ford canceled what had been on his schedule and invited Haig to join him in his office in the OEOB. There Haig received an unwelcome surprise: the presence of Robert Hartmann, Ford's chief of staff and speechwriter. By this point, Haig and Hartmann had established a rich loathing for one another. Haig thought Hartmann was a drunken degenerate; Hartmann thought Haig was a power-mad bully. Both thought the other was a leaker of bad stories about their internal rivals. In light of Hartmann's presence, Haig dialed back what he was going to say. Rather than pass along Nixon's message of his plan to resign—and Buzhardt's list of options—Haig decided to keep it simpler. Haig said he had learned the contents of the smoking gun tape of June 23. It would be very damaging to Nixon. "Mr. Vice President," Haig said, "I think you should prepare yourself for changes in your life. I can't predict what will happen, or when, but I think you should hold yourself in readiness."[3] Puzzled by Haig's urgency to deliver such a vague message, Ford cut the encounter short and went to the Capitol for meetings with his former colleagues.

But Haig was not to be dissuaded. While Ford was at the Capitol, Haig tracked him down again and asked for another meeting—this time one-on-one. Ford agreed to see him in his office in the OEOB at 3:30 p.m. As it happened, Ford was scheduled to meet at that time with Rogers Morton, Nixon's secretary of the interior and an old friend of Ford's. Haig's visit preempted that meeting, but Haig, ever-calculating, told Ford's assistant to keep Morton's name on the schedule, so Haig's visit would not draw attention from Ford's staff, especially Hartmann.

This second meeting between Ford and Haig on August 1 was the most scrutinized and controversial of Ford's vice presidency. Only the two men were present, so only they knew precisely what was said. But Ford and Haig described the meeting several times—in their books and in interviews—and they both discussed the meeting contemporaneously with others. At this late date, it's not possible to discern all the subtleties of the exchange, but the broad outlines appear clear.

In this second meeting, Haig spoke more bluntly than he did earlier in the day, when Hartmann was present.[4]

"Mr. Vice President," Haig said, "the President has made up his mind to resign." The smoking gun tape of June 23—which Ford had still not heard—was highly incriminating and would be impossible for Nixon to survive. In the morning meeting, Haig said resignation was a possibility; now he acknowledged that it was a certainty. Ford was going to be president—sooner rather than later. Haig asked if Ford was prepared for the job. Ford said if it came to that, he would be ready.

Then Haig moved to the real purpose of this private meeting with Ford. He said he had spoken to "White House lawyers" about the logistics surrounding the endgame, and it turned out there were several different scenarios. Haig took the two papers that Buzhardt had prepared—the list of six options and the draft pardon—and handed them to the vice president. They went over it together. Haig said he wasn't a lawyer. He didn't know the details of how these things worked. But he was just passing the paper along to Ford so he would understand what the lawyers regarded as the possibilities.

Ford noticed that three of the options involved pardons, and he began asking Haig questions about the pardon power. As a member of Congress and vice president, Ford had little experience with pardons. He didn't really know how they worked. Could Ford, as president, pardon someone—Nixon—who had not yet been convicted? Haig said he understood that the answer was yes. What if the person hadn't even been charged yet? Could someone who was not yet facing charges be pardoned? Haig said he didn't know. The real reasons for the pardon, Haig thought, were to let the country move on from Watergate and as a simple act of mercy to a man who had suffered a catastrophic reversal of fortune. It would be in the "national interest" for Ford to grant Nixon a pardon, Haig said.

Both Ford and Haig agreed that Ford made no commitment at the meeting, which lasted nearly an hour. Ford was starting to recognize the consequences of his policy of avoiding information about the progress of Watergate and of failing to plan, or even envision, his own transition to the presidency. What Haig told him was news to him, and in the rush of events, Ford lacked the opportunity to understand his options in any depth. (Toward the end of Ford's life, in a conversation with the journalist Bob Woodward, Ford said that Haig was even more direct in their conversation on August 1, 1974. Ford told Woodward that Haig offered a straight-up trade: the presidency for a pardon. But Ford told Woodward that he turned the deal down.)[5]

When the meeting with Haig was over, Ford summoned Hartmann to join him.[6] Ford was in a pensive mood, his head swimming with what he had just heard. He was starting to understand that he would soon be president and compelled to make decisions which he had heretofore avoided even considering. Ford swore Hartmann to secrecy about what he was going to tell him. Ford recounted that Haig said the June 23 tape was worse than anyone expected. Ford didn't exactly tell his aide that Nixon would soon be resigning as a result, but that was the clear implication of his words. Ford then read from the Buzhardt documents that Haig had left him, including the draft pardon. One possibility, Ford told Hartmann, was that Nixon would resign and Ford would pardon him.

"What did you tell him?" Hartmann asked.

"I didn't tell him anything," Ford replied. "I told him I needed time to think about it." Ford wondered what Hartmann thought of the idea of pardoning Nixon? Ford himself said he planned to talk to Betty about the idea, but he wanted Hartmann's opinion, too.

Here, Hartmann's temper surfaced. "I think you should have taken Haig by the scruff of the neck and the seat of the pants and thrown him the hell out of your office," Hartmann said. "And then you should have called an immediate press conference and told the world why." In Hartmann's view, Haig had proposed a deal for Ford: the presidency in return for a pardon for Nixon. That was inappropriate, in Hartmann's view, and Ford risked political embarrassment if news of the possible deal ever surfaced.

Ford didn't really acknowledge Hartmann's outburst—he was used to his aide's fury—and excused himself from the meeting. He had to go to the Naval Observatory to meet Betty to look at the house that was being renovated as an official residence for the vice president. On his way out the door, Ford ran into Jack Marsh, the former congressman who was now his national security advisor. "Ford looked thunderstruck," Marsh recalled. "I had never seen him that way—like someone had told him his house had burned down. It was the enormity of the developing situation." The new home for the VP was close to completion, and the Fords were planning on moving in in a few weeks. Distracted during the discussion of décor and china patterns, Ford muttered to his wife that he thought it was extremely unlikely that they would ever live there.

After the visit to the house, Ford returned to the office to shower for a dinner at the home of the *Washington Star*'s gossip columnist, Betty Beale. There, he avoided making news, then returned home to Alexandria with Betty, where, over bourbon-and-water, he discussed the events of the day.[7] Based on his conversations with Haig, it looked like they would be moving to the White House, sooner rather than later. "My God," Betty said. "This is going to change our whole life." And then they prayed together for guidance.[8]

As they continued talking, Ford showed his wife the two documents that Haig had handed him, the list of six options and the draft pardon. Ford presented the documents to Betty as a matter of curiosity, but Betty recognized the political peril that they represented. By giving him those documents, Betty said, it looked like Haig was proposing a deal—the presidency for a pardon. "You can't do that, Jerry," she said. Ford stewed about this. Betty thought that Haig might believe that they had made a deal that afternoon.

To rule out that impression, Ford called Haig at 1:30 a.m. Just so we're clear, Ford told Haig, in our conversation there had been "no decision and no deal."[9]

Haig agreed and signed off quickly, but he was furious. He didn't like being called out as a schemer—even though he *was* a schemer.

Ford arrived early at the OEOB early the next morning, Friday, August 2, and asked to see St. Clair, the outside lawyer who was handling Nixon's defense against impeachment in Congress. He wanted to know if St. Clair shared Haig's dire assessment of Nixon's fate. St. Clair did. He said that once the June 23 tape was released, Nixon's chances were nonexistent in the House and nearly that bad in the Senate. But Ford also wanted to ask St. Clair about the options that "White House lawyers" had presented. What did St. Clair think about the possibility of Ford pardoning Nixon? St. Clair had good enough political instincts to dodge that question, saying that he had not prepared any advice for Nixon or Haig about pardons. (Ford apparently thought that St. Clair was one of the "White House lawyers" that Haig had consulted; Ford didn't realize that Haig had spoken only to Buzhardt about pardons.)

Even with the clear message from his wife, which mirrored the one from Hartmann, Ford remained almost oblivious to the problem that Haig's approach represented. So, on that Friday morning, Hartmann called in reinforcements in what he regarded as an effort to save Ford from himself. He asked Marsh, the national security advisor, to speak to Ford about Haig. Ford showed Marsh the handwritten documents, and Marsh immediately recognized Buzhardt's handwriting, because they had worked together at the Pentagon. (In these days before emails and texts, this was often the best way to identify the origin of documents.)

Marsh agreed with Hartmann, which carried additional weight with Ford because Marsh didn't have Hartmann's contentious history with Haig. "I realized right away that Haig jeopardized the Vice President the moment he spoke the word pardon," Marsh recalled. He told Ford, "You can't be involved in anything that might at some point sound like some kind of deal."

In that moment, Ford turned defensive. "Haig was not suggesting a deal," he told Marsh. "These options hadn't even originated with him . . . I said nothing to signal approval or disapproval of any of them."[10]

Hartmann and Marsh felt like they still needed to drive their message home, so they decided to deploy the most powerful weapon they could summon—Bryce Harlow. He belonged to the long-vanished species known as the Washington "wise man," who dipped in and out of government service and maintained an impeccable reputation for rectitude. Harlow had been advising Republican presidents since 1953. Ford revered him. When Harlow arrived in the OEOB on the afternoon of August 2 and heard the story of what went on the previous day, he proved to be even more suspicious of the Haig overture than Hartmann and Marsh were. (Hartmann took notes of Harlow's reaction.)[11]

"Well, Mr. Vice President," Harlow said, "the thing is that I cannot for a moment believe that all this was Al Haig's own idea or that the matters he discussed originated with 'the White House staff.'" Harlow said Haig's overture obviously originated with Nixon himself, and it was Nixon who wanted to test your reaction to the pardon question.

"But the President knows that he must be able to swear under oath that he never discussed this with you and that you must be able to swear that you never discussed it with him. Therefore, he sends Haig, and therefore, I would not advise you to try to clarify the matter with the President himself. That would only make matters worse, if that's possible." (Harlow was almost right about the sequence of events, but even he underestimated Nixon's deviousness. Nixon did not spell out his pardon plan to Haig; he did so to Buzhardt, knowing that the lawyer would pass the message to Haig, who would, in turn, put the proposition to Ford.)

Harlow had an idea about how Ford could try to untangle the mess. "The most urgent thing, Mr. Vice President," Harlow said, "is to tell Al Haig, straight out and unequivocally, that whatever discussions you and he had yesterday and last night were purely hypothetical and conversational, that you will in no manner, affirmatively or negatively, advise him or the President as to his future course, and nothing you may have said is to be represented to the President, or to anyone else, to the contrary." (In his book, Hartmann said that Harlow's "soliloquy" went on for much longer than he even quoted.)[12]

Taken aback by this scolding from a man he admired, Ford immediately set out to write out a statement, based on Harlow's instructions, which he would make on the phone to Haig. He asked Hartmann and Harlow to remain in the room so that he would have witnesses to what he told the chief of staff. At that point, Ford made his second call to Haig in two days to emphasize the message that there was no deal for a resignation or a pardon. When Ford and Haig connected, the vice president recalled that he read his script "slowly so that there could be no ambiguities." He told Haig, "I want you to understand that I have no intention of recommending what the President should do about resigning or not resigning and that nothing we talked about yesterday afternoon should be given any consideration in whatever decision the President may wish to make."

"You're right," Haig said, and that ended the conversation.[13] (Hartmann thought Ford was so rattled by the experience that he flushed the paper with his statement down the toilet.)[14]

————

What, then, is one to make of these events of August 1 and 2? The accounts of the participants—in their own books, in interviews with journalists, and in oral histories—are consistent in every important particular. The question is what it all meant.

To some, the interactions between Ford and Haig suggest that there was in fact a deal—a trade of the presidency for a pardon—notwithstanding the disavowals of both men.[15] That was not the case. There was no deal, no trade. Ford was unprepared for Haig's overture about pardons. If Ford had thought at all about a pardon for Nixon at that moment, he had not considered it fully, and he was never going to agree to a pardon on the basis of that initial meeting in his office. Plus, as Hartmann, Marsh, Harlow, and Betty Ford recognized, it would have been unseemly (or worse) if Ford had made such an agreement with Haig.

There is another reason why there was no "trade": Haig, on Nixon's behalf, at that point had nothing to trade. By the first week in August, Nixon's presidency was doomed; he was going to be forced out of office one way or another, through impeachment and removal, or through resignation. Even if he were so inclined, Ford didn't have to trade for the presidency. He was going to be president, and he didn't have to promise Haig and Nixon anything to take office. He made no such promise.

But even in the absence of a trade, Haig's overture to Ford on August 1 marked an important turning point in the story, one that reflects broader truths about pardons. First, Haig forced Ford to think about pardons, something he had willfully refused to do at that point. Ford and even more so his staff now recognized that they had to understand the pardon process, and they began to educate themselves accordingly. But even more importantly, Nixon and Haig showed the inherently political nature of presidential pardons. Unapologetically, even shamelessly, the two men campaigned for Ford to pardon Nixon. They later claimed that was not what they were doing, but that, too, was strategic—and untrue. Nixon was behind the scenes; Haig was out front as the action officer. But they were both working for the same goal—a pardon. And they were just getting started.

CHAPTER 12

Party in Interest

THEN NIXON CHANGED HIS MIND. HE WAS NOT GOING TO resign after all.

Nixon and Haig had spent the afternoon of Friday, August 2, planning the details for his resignation. They talked about what Nixon wanted to say in his farewell speech. (Raymond Price, Nixon's speechwriter, had started to draft it.) They discussed where Nixon would go after he left the White House (probably San Clemente), and they weighed how they might transition the presidency to Ford. It was a typically meandering conversation, and nothing was decided with certainty, but one thing was clear: Nixon was resigning.[1]

Then, in the early evening, Nixon's family gathered with him in the Lincoln Sitting Room. Bebe Rebozo was at the White House as well. Pat Nixon, daughters Julie and Tricia and their husbands David Eisenhower and Ed Cox huddled around Nixon in his favorite armchair. The president told his family about the June 23 tape—the smoking gun. Nixon said his advisers thought the disclosure of the tape would make his situation in Congress hopeless. The family wasn't sure and prevailed upon Nixon to call Haig and get a transcript of the tape, so they could make their own evaluation. As Tricia Cox recalled in her diary, "In about ten minutes Manolo brought us the papers bearing the bothersome words."[2] (Manolo Sanchez was Nixon's loyal and long-serving valet.)

The two daughters and their husbands excused themselves to study the transcript. After a few minutes, they returned with their

collective verdict. The smoking gun was not so bad. It could be ex-
plained. Nixon should not resign but fight on. Nixon recalled, "Pat,
who had let the others do most of the talking in our meeting, told me
that now, as always before, she was for fighting to the finish."[3]

Nixon was moved by the loyalty of his family, and they left him to
ponder his fate alone. "I decided that instead of resigning on Monday
night," Nixon wrote, "I would release the June 23 tape and see the reaction to it." After several more hours of rumination, as Friday night
turned into Saturday morning, Nixon called Haig and said he would
not resign. "Let them impeach me. We'll fight it out to the end," he
told his chief of staff.

––––––––

For all that Ford knew, based on his conversation with Haig, resignation was a done deal, and still, over the weekend, the vice president kept up his campaign duties. On Saturday, August 3, Ford tore
around three cities in Mississippi, talking up the local candidates
and avoiding the subject of impeachment. During a press conference,
though, he couldn't duck it. Ford acknowledged Nixon's precarious
status and said he "may be" impeached. He also repeated his defense
of Nixon: "My views are just as strong today as they were two days
ago. I believe the President is innocent of any impeachable offense,
and I haven't changed my mind." Asked about his meeting with Haig,
Ford dissembled: "It was not an extraordinary meeting, if that's what
you want me to say. It was an ordinary meeting of the kind we frequently have and had no extraordinary implications." Eager to escape
the questions, he said, "I am going on from here to New Orleans. I am
going to give a speech there this evening, and play, maybe, some golf
tomorrow." (He did.)

On Saturday afternoon, Nixon went to Camp David for a morose
weekend with his family. His family had persuaded him to put off
the decision until he saw the reaction to the smoking gun tape after
it was released on Monday. On Sunday, Nixon summoned Haig,
St. Clair, and a few more assistants to try to put together a statement
that would offer a more sympathetic gloss on the words that Nixon
and Haldeman spoke on June 23, 1972. Haig, St. Clair, and Pat Bu-

chanan brought along their wives, because they thought it would be their last chance to see Camp David.[4] (They also brought several secretaries, because none of the men knew how to type.) Diane Sawyer, aide to press secretary Ron Ziegler, stopped by Kissinger's office on Sunday before joining the group on the helicopter to Camp David. Kissinger asked her if she thought the effort to save Nixon was worthwhile, in light of the pending release of the smoking gun. "Beautiful, clever Diane was nonplussed," Kissinger later wrote. "She had not read the tape but she was beginning to think that there would never be a climax, simply an endless hemorrhaging. 'As likely as not,' she said, 'the tape will be drowned out by the political uproar.'"[5]

Nixon himself had listened to the smoking gun tape in May and then assured his lawyers and staff that there was nothing incriminating on it. So, St. Clair and the others had based their arguments to Congress on the assumption that there were no other shoes to drop. With the smoking gun tape now before them, Nixon's advocates were furious at him for deceiving them as well as dubious about his chances of survival.

At this point, in fact, some people around Nixon were as concerned for their own reputations as for the president's fate, which now seemed preordained. Nixon told St. Clair to write a preemptive defense for the smoking gun tape, but the statement he drafted turned into something very different. After a perfunctory statement that Nixon had not interfered with the FBI's investigation of Watergate, the statement concluded in this extraordinary way:

Among the conversations I listened to in May were two of those of June 23. Although I recognized that these presented potential problems, I did not inform my staff or my Counsel of it, or those arguing my case, nor did I amend my submission to the Judiciary Committee in order to include and reflect it. At the time, I did not realize the implications which these conversations now appear to have. As a result, those arguing my case, as well as those passing judgment on the case, did so with information that was incomplete and in some respects erroneous.

This was a serious act of omission for which I take full responsibility and which I deeply regret.

In simple terms, Nixon's lawyer was throwing his client under the bus. Far from minimizing the smoking gun, which was why Nixon summoned the group to Camp David, St. Clair and the others were exacerbating the crisis. The statement revealed that Nixon lied even to those whose sole mission was to try to help him. When Haig showed Nixon that part of the statement, he protested at first but then shrugged and said, "The hell with it. It doesn't really matter. They can put out whatever they want." As Haig observed, with some poignancy, Nixon had even lost the ability to control a statement that would be issued in his own name.[6]

On Monday morning, August 5, Ford gave a speech to the Disabled American Veterans meeting in New Orleans, where he was introduced, apparently by accident, as "Mr. President." He then got on Air Force Two, the unloved Corsair, and flew back to Washington. He returned to the OEOB in late afternoon, when Nixon released sixty-four tape transcripts, including the June 23 smoking gun, as well as the statement exonerating his lawyers.

The transcript showed that on June 23, 1972, six days after the Watergate break-in, Nixon and Haldeman agreed on a plan to demand that the CIA instruct the FBI to shut down the Watergate investigation on spurious national security grounds. (Haldeman and Ehrlichman did in fact make that attempt, but the CIA officials, to their credit, refused.) In other words, the transcript showed that Nixon had been in on the Watergate cover-up from almost the very beginning.

The reaction was as cataclysmic as expected. The Republicans on the Judiciary Committee who had voted against the impeachment articles announced that they had changed their minds and now favored impeachment. Nixon's support in the Senate appeared to evaporate as well. Impeachment and conviction were now a certainty. News reports called attention to the fact that a president who was impeached and convicted lost his government-funded pension and staff. (These were considerable, especially in 1974 dollars, and the amounts in-cluded $900,000 for a transition period, a lifetime $60,000 per year salary, $96,000 for staff per year, and Secret Service protection.) A president who resigned kept those benefits. Nixon clearly knew about the difference for him between being forced out of office and resign-ing. This was not a small thing for someone like Nixon, who owned two luxurious residences but had little cash of his own.

For Ford, the release of the smoking gun tape marked a belated but final turning point. On the afternoon of Monday, August 5, Ford recognized that he was going to be president and took his first inde-pendent action. No longer a team player for Nixon, he was his own man, and he began to take steps accordingly.

————

Still, Ford's declaration of independence was a modest one. Hart-mann drafted a statement, which came out just after Nixon released the smoking gun tape of June 23, 1972. Ford did not address the con-tents of the tape, but he acknowledged that his own perspective had changed: "I have come to the conclusion that the public interest is no longer served by repetition of my previously expressed belief that based on all of the available evidence known to me and to the Amer-ican people, the President is not guilty of an impeachable offense. . . . I intend to respectfully decline to discuss impeachment matters in public or in response to questions until the facts are more fully avail-able." Despite the convoluted syntax of the statement, the meaning was clear enough: Ford was finished defending Nixon.

As with his pardon advocacy during the previous week, Haig was still acting as the point man for Nixon's well-being. In this moment, that meant pushing Nixon toward resignation rather than resistance. Haig stayed in close touch with Capitol Hill, and he knew that the House was overwhelmingly set for impeachment and the Senate was well beyond the required two-thirds in favor of conviction. Haig knew that continuing to fight this losing battle would accomplish nothing for Nixon except extended humiliation and the loss of his pension. And, to be sure, the country would be paralyzed for the weeks, if not months, it would take for the constitutional process to play out.

Haig's effort was of a piece with his encouragement to Ford to pardon his predecessor. Haig wanted a dignified exit for Nixon followed by a prosecution-free retirement.

Haig was monitoring Nixon's shifting moods and reporting back to Ford by phone. On that Monday night, shortly after the transcript was released, Nixon took his family on a cruise on the presidential yacht, *Sequoia*, in part so they wouldn't have to watch news coverage. There, Nixon told Haig that he wanted a cabinet meeting the following morning. But the president didn't commit to what he was going to say there. Haig's deputy called Ford at home and invited the vice president to the cabinet session on Tuesday morning, August 6.

The cabinet meeting itself bordered on the surreal. Ford and the cabinet assembled as ordered at 10 a.m., but the president didn't show until an hour later. Kissinger, an astute judge of power, noticed that while the group was waiting around, the cabinet members formed a respectful circle around the vice president, who was usually ignored in these sessions.[7] At last Nixon arrived and opened a leather portfolio to read his remarks. "I would like to discuss the most important issue confronting the nation—and confronting us internationally too: inflation." As the men (all men) around the table exchanged nervous looks, Nixon droned on about economic policy. Had the president completely lost touch with reality? All anyone wanted to know was whether he was going to resign. Did Nixon really think the cabinet needed to hear his thoughts on inflation? No one had the fortitude to interrupt.

With little warning or transition, Nixon turned to Watergate and a defense of his conduct. Alluding to the disclosures in the June 23 tape, he insisted that he did want to protect national security interests in the investigation of the break-in, but he also acknowledged that "certain political interests" were present as well. He denied that he had engaged in obstruction of justice or committed an impeachable offense. Nixon then rambled into a defense of his record on foreign policy, especially the opening of China and the conclusion of the American role in the Vietnam War. No one could tell where he was going.

At last, Nixon turned away from his prepared text and to the matter at hand—in a way. He said the United States was not a parliamentary system, where the head of government could be removed on the whim of a majority of legislators. "I will accept whatever verdict the Senate hands down," he said, "and I recognize the possibility that the outcome won't be favorable. A very important consideration here is my sworn promise to uphold the Constitution. And it provides the process. . . . I have made the decision. I ask for your support of this process." Nixon had expressed himself in a confusing way, but it did appear that he was saying he was going to fight his impeachment in a trial in the Senate.

In response, Ford later recounted, "the silence was deafening."[8] Not a single member of the cabinet spoke up in support of Nixon's apparent decision to fight on. Instead, Ford himself spoke up, a rare interjection in a setting where presidents were rarely interrupted.

"Mr. President, with your indulgence," Ford said, "I have something to say."

"Well, Jerry, go ahead," Nixon said.

"Everyone here recognizes the difficult position I'm in," he said. "No one regrets more than I do this whole tragic episode. I have deep personal sympathy for you, Mr. President, and your fine family. But I wish to emphasize that had I known what has been disclosed in reference to Watergate in the last twenty-four hours, I would not have made a number of the statements I made either as Minority Leader or as Vice President. I came to a decision yesterday and you may be aware that I informed the press that because of commitments to Congress and the public, I'll have no further comment on the issue because I'm a party in interest. I'm sure there will be an impeachment in the House. I can't predict the Senate outcome. I will make no comment concerning this. You have given us the finest foreign policy this country has ever had. A super job, and the people appreciate it. Let me assure you that I expect to continue to support the Administration's foreign policy and the fight against inflation."

According to Ford, Nixon seemed taken aback by his vice president's presumption, but Nixon said, "I think your position is exactly correct," though it wasn't clear which position—about inflation or impeachment—Nixon was approving.

Ford's comments essentially disowning Nixon opened the way for others to speak up. William Saxbe, a former Ohio senator who was serving as Nixon's fifth attorney general in the last two-and-a-half years, openly questioned Nixon's "ability to govern."

Nixon took offense: "Bill, I have the ability just as I have had for the last five and a half years." But the president found no support for that proposition. Even George H. W. Bush, who was present in his capacity as chairman of the Republican National Committee, questioned whether Nixon could restore public faith in his leadership. When it became clear that Nixon would not get the vote of confidence that he had sought from his own cabinet, he brought the meeting to a close. Kissinger followed him into the Oval Office and said resignation was his only option. Nixon seemed to agree, but Kissinger, like Haig, couldn't be sure that the decision would stick.

As it happened, the Fords had earlier invited Phil Buchen to dinner at their home in Alexandria on that Tuesday night, and the engagement went forward, despite everything that was happening around them. At first, the two men avoided the topic on their minds and instead chatted about old friends from Grand Rapids. Then, after a drink, Buchen let Ford know about the secret project he had hatched with Clay Whitehead back in May—the transition plan in case Ford became president. According to his own account, Ford acted offended that Buchen took it upon himself to plan a presidency that might never happen.[9] If it had leaked, Ford said, it would have looked like he was scheming to take over.

Still, suddenly daunted by the task in front of him, Ford began to consider the multitude of issues he would soon confront: appointments (including of a new vice president), policy priorities, his schedule, an inaugural address, to name a few. Whitehead and his young charges had made a start, but the vice president decided he needed some heavy hitters. Ford asked Betty to find the family address book, and he gave Buchen names to start calling for help. And thus, late on the night of August 6, Gerald Ford started to decide what he would do if he became president.

*Nixon bids farewell to the White House after his resignation
on August 9, 1974.* DAVID HUME KENNERLY/CENTER FOR
CREATIVE PHOTOGRAPHY/U OF ARIZONA

CHAPTER 13

The Sun Sets on Nixon

FOR STARTERS, FORD WANTED TO MOVE ON FROM THE subjects of the past—chiefly, Richard Nixon—and separate himself and his new administration from Watergate and everything associated with it. Ford would establish his own agenda and stick to it. Presidents often have this particular misguided notion about the course of events. When it comes to which issues that they must confront, and when, they think they have more power than they do. (Declaring "Infrastructure Week," as President Donald Trump repeatedly tried to do, didn't make it so.)

Still, Ford gave Buchen those marching orders—clean break, fresh start—as the lawyer worked through the night of August 6–7, assembling Ford's wise men (all men) to aid in his transition. The group included Bryce Harlow, Rogers Morton, Nixon's secretary of the interior, and Bill Scranton, the former governor of Pennsylvania, but they couldn't do much more than agree to help at that point. Even if they were already in Washington, events were moving too fast for the group to assemble, much less provide a coherent plan for a new presidency. Meanwhile, on the morning of Wednesday, August 7, Nixon was still equivocating about what he was going to do: resign or fight. Haig called Ford just after eight in the morning to say that Nixon had not made up his mind.

Ford was scheduled to leave on a twelve-day campaign swing through the West, but he decided to cancel it. Previously, Ford had been loath to change his schedule because of one Nixon crisis or another, for fear of drawing attention to himself. But the time for such pretense had clearly passed. On that Wednesday, he asked for briefings on foreign policy from Kissinger's White House deputy and on congressional relations from Nixon's chief lobbyist. And for what he assumed would probably be the last time, Ford went to the Capitol to get a 75-cent haircut from his favorite barber, Morrison Hansborough.[1]

In the Oval Office at that moment, the Republican establishment asserted itself. Hugh Scott, the Republican leader in the Senate, John Rhodes, who was Ford's successor as the top Republican in the House, and Barry Goldwater, the spiritual leader of the GOP as well as its 1964 presidential nominee, went to talk truth to Nixon. The three legislators had been counting votes. At that point, it was beyond dispute that impeachment was a certainty in the House. Nixon needed thirty-four votes in the Senate to remain in office. How many could Nixon get? "Maybe sixteen to eighteen" votes for acquittal, Goldwater said.

Nixon asked Scott if he agreed. "I'd say maybe fifteen," he said. "But it's grim and they're not very firm."

Then Goldwater, who always had a competitive relationship with Nixon and disdained the president's congenital dishonesty, twisted the knife: "Some are very worried about what's been going on and are undecided. I'm one of them."

It was an emotional session, and the three visitors understood Nixon's pain. They didn't seek a commitment from Nixon, and he didn't offer one. But he did, by negative implication, provide a clue of what was on his mind. "I'm not interested in pensions," he said. "I'm not interested in pardons or amnesty. I'm going to make this decision for the best interests of the country."[2] (Each sentence was a lie.) But following that meeting, Nixon ended his equivocations. He told Haig that he would resign in a speech from the Oval Office the following night, Thursday, August 8.

———

With the clock ticking down on Nixon's presidency, the minds of two principal Watergate figures turned to the possibility of pardons, even as the president was disclaiming interest in one for himself. Haldeman and Ehrlichman were banking on a phenomenon that would become more pronounced in later years. Presidents who were in their final days in office, when there was no chance of political account- ability, would give unpopular (and often unwise) pardons to people who didn't deserve them. These last-minute pardons reflected the opposite of political courage on the part of the presidents who prof- fered them. The pardons were often crass gifts, given out of pique or self-interest, in the vague (and often forlorn) hope that they would be ignored or forgotten in the crush of events in the change of admin- istrations. That, in any event, seems to have been Haldeman's hope when he spoke to Nixon on August 7.

The previous day, Haldeman had talked to Ron Ziegler, the press secretary whom he had brought into the administration years earlier. Haldeman said he wanted to talk to the president one more time be- fore Nixon made the final decision to resign. Ziegler made the call happen after the three legislators came to the Oval Office with their dire prognosis for Nixon. "Bob," Nixon told Haldeman, "I want you to know that I have decided I must resign."[3]

Haldeman expressed sorrow, but he quickly moved to his own agenda for the call. "There is one point I would like to raise, which I would never mention unless I was sure you were totally committed to the resignation. I firmly believe that before you leave office you should exercise your constitutional authority and grant pardons to all those who have been or may be charged with any crimes in con- nection with Watergate. I think it's imperative that you bring Wa- tergate to an end before you leave—for the sake of the country and especially for your successor."

Nixon seemed taken aback by the request and said he hadn't given the issue of pardons any thought (which was not true). From the first weeks after the Watergate break-in, he had thought about pardons for the burglars, and he had just talked to Buzhardt about the prospects of a pardon for himself. As for Haldeman's request, Nixon promised to consider the issue. Haldeman said he would forward a written re- quest, which spelled out his reasons in greater depth. After the call, racing the clock in the fading hours of Nixon's presidency, Halde- man worked with his lawyers to draw up a proposal, which included a political sweetener for the blanket Watergate pardons. As Haldeman recalled, "I also recommended a pardon to all Vietnam draft evaders on the grounds that these two acts would eliminate the two major traumas of the Nixon Presidency, and enable President Ford to start with a clean slate."[4] (At around the same time, Ehrlichman tried to make a similar pitch for a pardon for himself, but he couldn't get through to Nixon, so he reached out with his plea to Nixon's daughter Julie and to his secretary Rose Mary Woods.)[5]

Haldeman tried to get his talking points to Nixon, but couldn't reach him directly, so he connected instead with Haig—who was appalled. He saw Haldeman's request as a shakedown, a threat that if he wasn't pardoned, he would turn into a witness against Nixon. Worse yet, Haig knew that Howard Hunt had asked for a pardon in the early days of Watergate. Nixon's acquiescence in Hunt's demands represented a key part of the cover-up that had led Nixon to the point of resignation. To Haig, Haldeman's talk of healing and compassion, much less benefit to the new president, were so much camouflage for Haldeman's self-interest. In his brief call with Haldeman, Haig kept a civil tongue but offered no encouragement. And he never raised the issue with the president. There was, of course, some irony in Haig's outrage at what he saw as Haldeman's attempted shakedown; at this time, Haig was acting as Nixon's instrument in shaking down Ford for a pardon of Nixon.

But Nixon, through Buzhardt, did become aware of Haldeman's proposal, and the president later displayed an almost perverse sense of admiration for his former aide's moxie, even as he dismissed the idea on the merits. Buzhardt showed Nixon a letter from Haldeman's lawyer. As Nixon later wrote, "Haldeman, ever the efficient Chief of Staff, had included a specially typed page to insert in my resignation speech announcing the pardon and proclaiming a Vietnam amnesty."[6] Nixon pronounced Haldeman's idea "unthinkable," by which he meant a terrible proposal. Still, Haldeman's idea for a kind of double amnesty—for Watergate villains and draft evaders—reflected a common conceptual flaw about pardons. Haldeman acted as if presidential pardons were a sort of holistic whole, which the public evaluates as a single, unified legacy. (Nixon and Charles Colson made the same conceptual

To that end, on the afternoon of August 8, Haig arranged a cloak-and-dagger face-to-face meeting with the prosecutor.[7] Haig knew that a Jaworski visit to the White House would draw attention, so Haig asked the prosecutor to come to his home. Haig sent a staff car to pick up Jaworski, but he told the prosecutor to wait a half-block away from the Jefferson, so no one would see him get in. The car took Jaworski to the chief of staff's house in Wesley Heights, an afflu-ent enclave in Washington. Haig would travel from the White House in his own car "in the hope of giving the impression that I was on personal business."[8] It is a measure of the importance Haig attached to the meeting that he took two hours away from the White House on a momentous day—the day the president would announce his resignation—to see Jaworski.

In the meeting over coffee served by Haig's wife, Pat, the pair cir-cled each other warily. Haig had hired Jaworski as special prosecu-tor nine months earlier, and they had what the prosecutor called "a strange kinship." Over those months, they had argued about several issues, especially access to Nixon's tapes, but they were both mem-bers of the same establishment—interested in stability, rather than dramatic change, in government. It was unspoken, but Haig intended this meeting to advance that shared agenda.

Haig told Jaworski that Nixon would be resigning that night and that he would be taking his papers and the tapes with him to Cali-fornia, as was his right. The White House would begin shipping the papers on Friday, as soon as Nixon's resignation became effective. Jaworski had resolved in advance of the meeting to make no com-mitments, and he took in that information without agreeing with Nixon's belief that he had the right to the papers. Jaworski said only that his office would need continuing access to the papers, wherever the originals happened to be located. Haig agreed. Haig said further that Haldeman and Ehrlichman, who were both about to go on trial against Jaworski's prosecutors, had sought pardons, which Nixon would not be granting. If either side called Nixon as a witness in the cover-up trial, Haig said, Nixon would take the Fifth and refuse to testify.

Haig then turned to the main point of his agenda, which was, in

mistake a year earlier when they considered joint pardons f
tergate burglars and the Gainesville antiwar protesters.)

Pardons are individual acts for individual beneficiaries
pardon standing on its own merits; a good one doesn't ma
bad one in anyone's accounting. At least on this occasion
hours in office, Nixon recognized that he couldn't hide an
pardon (Watergate) behind a popular one (Vietnam). But
see, Nixon was wrong in a literal sense in calling Halde
"unthinkable" because it turned out that others did think
Watergate mercy to Vietnam amnesty.

———

On Thursday morning, August 8, Ford still didn't kno
when he would become president or if Nixon was going
his mind again. Ford started his workday across the stree
White House in Blair House, the official guest residence
presented the Congressional Medal of Honor to the fami
eral soldiers who had been killed in Vietnam. Near the (
somber duty, Haig called and said Nixon wanted to spe
The visit from the three Republican grandees had sealed l
cision to resign. Ford crossed Pennsylvania Avenue and
the Oval Office. There, in a straightforward, almost ma
conversation, Nixon said he would be resigning in a spe
nation that night. Ford would become president the foll
August 9, at noon.

With Nixon's decision now in place, Haig set off on a
sion. Haig felt he had, by midwifing the resignation, pr
country from the chaos of an impeachment trial (with
result) and preserved Nixon's pension and staff. But Haig
ished doing Nixon's bidding—and his advocacy wouldn'
Nixon's presidency either. There was still the chance that
gate special prosecutor would bring charges against Nixon
wanted to do everything he could to prevent that possibilit
vious week, he had started urging Ford to pardon Nixon
now began to work the other side of the equation as well—
Jaworski not to bring any charges against Nixon.

its own way, very Nixonian. Haig said Nixon was resigning of his own accord and sought no agreement from Jaworski in return. This was not a resignation in return for an agreement not to prosecute him. Nixon was leaving office solely for the good of the country. But as with Nixon's denials about seeking a pardon or protecting his pension, nonprosecution was precisely what Haig (and Nixon) wanted. Jaworski didn't have to agree to it at this point, and he did not. But as Haig probably assumed, if he did not actually know, Jaworski agreed with him—that he already thought a prosecution of the former president would not be in the public interest and would rather be a threat to the national stability that mattered so much to them both. In this important way, even though nothing was formally agreed to, Haig and Jaworski on the day of Nixon's resignation were allies.

———

There was no time to assemble the transition team that Buchen had started to recruit the previous evening, so Ford brought together his vice presidential staff to make plans for the transition, to the extent it was possible on such short notice. Ford made clear that he wanted Kissinger to stay on as secretary of state. Hartmann was already at work on an inaugural address. Buchen had recruited Jerald ter-Horst, the Washington bureau chief of *The Detroit News*, as press secretary. Ford had known terHorst since his first campaign for the House, in 1948. (These were the days when regional newspapers still had bureaus in Washington.) The vice president's first choice for the swearing-in location was the Capitol, like other presidents, and Ford, of course, had a special fondness for his professional home of several decades. But there was no time to set that up. Nixon himself suggested to Ford a simple swearing-in session in the Oval Office. But Ford's people insisted on the East Room of the White House, so that at least a couple hundred dignitaries, as well as Ford's family, could attend.

Then there was the question of who would administer the oath, a job traditionally assigned to the chief justice of the United States. It was quickly established that Warren Burger was at a conference in the Netherlands. But Jack Marsh tracked Burger down by phone and passed the receiver to Ford, who asked respectfully if the chief justice would agree to attend. "Oh, I *want* to be there," Burger said.[9] An Air Force aircraft was summoned to fetch Burger for the swearing-in. (Equally dramatic, if less consequential, a Secret Service helicopter picked up Jack Ford, the family's middle son, by a stream in Yellowstone Park, where he was working a summer job as a forest ranger, so he could make it to his father's inauguration.)[10]

Strangely enough, despite all the activity, Ford made it home to Alexandria only a little later than usual for dinner with Betty on Thursday, August 8. Together, they watched Nixon's fifteen-minute farewell address, which was, as Nixon said that night, the thirty-seventh time he had addressed the nation from the Oval Office. The remarks were long on recitations of his accomplishments, especially in foreign policy, and short on contrition. "I regret deeply any injuries that may have been done in the course of the events that led to this decision," he said. "I would say only that if some of my judgments were wrong—and some were wrong—they were made in what I believed at the time to be the best interest of the Nation." He acknowledged, with justification, that an early departure from office was contrary to his character as an indefatigable political warrior. "I have never been a quitter. To leave office before my term is completed is abhorrent to every instinct in my body. But as President, I must put the interests of America first," he said. "Therefore, I shall resign the Presidency effective at noon tomorrow. Vice President Ford will be sworn in as President at that hour in this office." (As if to prove that he never gives up, Nixon said that Ford would take the oath, as Nixon had suggested, "in this office"—the Oval Office. But Ford was going to use the East Room.)

After the speech, Ford met briefly with the reporters who had taken to assembling around the clock in front of his modest home in suburban Virginia. He said Nixon's resignation was "one of the greatest personal sacrifices for the country" and promised a continuation of his foreign policy, with Kissinger in charge. After a few hours of sleep, Ford enacted a ritual that would become emblematic of his modest style, which was a noted contrast with the imperial pretensions of the Nixon White House. Every day, including after he became president (but before he and Betty moved to the White House), Ford stepped out of the front door in his bathrobe and retrieved the newspapers that the fourteen-year-old papergirl had just delivered.

On the day that Ford would become president, he arrived at the White House complex early, but he went first to his vice presidential office in the OEOB, keeping his distance from Nixon during his final hours in office. Over breakfast in the Lincoln Sitting Room, Nixon observed the formal requirement for resignation. He signed a letter of a single sentence to the secretary of state: "I hereby resign the Office of President of the United States."

Then Nixon went to the East Room for one of the strangest events of his political career. (The Ford family was not present.) It was a speech to say goodbye to his cabinet and staff, but it was unlike any public remarks he had ever given. For one thing, Nixon wore his glasses, which he never did in public, and he also had no prepared text—and seemingly no plan—for what he was going to say. The speech offered an unobstructed view into his troubled soul. Rage, self-pity, pathos, unintentional candor—it was all there. Above all, there was Nixon's fierce determination that he would, as he had so many times before, rise from the wreckage. "You are here to say goodbye to us," he said, "and we don't have a good word for it in English—the best is *au revoir*. We will see you again."

Nixon rambled about his financial predicament. "I only wish that I were a wealthy man. At the present time, I have got to find a way to pay my taxes," he said, to a nervous chuckle from the audience. He celebrated his parents, whom he almost never discussed in public. "I remember my old man. I think that they would have called him sort of a little man, common man. He didn't consider himself that way," he said, and then turned to his mother: "Nobody will ever write a book, probably, about my mother. Well, I guess all of you would say this about your mother: my mother was a saint." He read a long excerpt from Theodore Roosevelt's diary, from just after his wife died: "When she had just become a mother, when her life seemed to be just begun and when the years seemed so bright before her, then by a strange and terrible fate death came to her. And when my heart's dearest died, the light went from my life forever."

But the lesson Nixon drew from this story was a characteristic one. "We think, as T.R. said, that the light had left his life forever," he said. "Not true. It is only a beginning, always. The young must know it; the old must know it. It must always sustain us, because the greatness comes not when things go always good for you, but the greatness comes and you are really tested"—as, of course, Nixon himself had just been tested; resilience and a comeback were always possible. And then, to conclude, Nixon offered the most revealing lesson, even if that was not the one he intended. "Always give your best, never get discouraged, never be petty," he said. "Always remember, others may hate you, but those who hate you don't win unless you hate them, and then you destroy yourself." In fact, Nixon's hatred of his political adversaries created the conditions for Watergate and led to this destruction of his presidency.

Moments later, Nixon and his wife, Pat, along with Jerry and Betty Ford walked together to the helicopter that would take the Nixons away from the White House for the last time. It's customary for the vice president always to walk a few steps behind the president, but on this occasion, the four of them walked in parallel to the helicopter, a sign of the changing of the guard in the White House and in the country. Just before Nixon boarded the helicopter, he turned back to the White House and raised his arms in his famous V-for-victory sign. Marine One lifted off for Andrews Air Force Base and the flight to San Clemente. When the aircraft took off, it was Air Force One, but at noon, when it was over Missouri, the radio call sign changed to SAM 27000, because the president of the United States was no longer on board.

Back inside the White House, the East Room was quickly reset, for one of the most extraordinary transformations, and events, in its history.

CHAPTER 14

Nightmare's End

THERE IS NO SUCH THING, OF COURSE, AS A PERFECT PO-
litical speech. But on August 9, 1974, in the East Room of the White
House, following his swearing-in by Chief Justice Burger, Gerald
Ford came close to giving one.

In just eight minutes, the new president acknowledged the unprecedented nature of his arrival in the presidency, established a new
course and direction, and offered grace to his fallen predecessor. And
Ford did it in the kind of plainspoken language that sounded right
coming from him. "I assume the Presidency under extraordinary
circumstances never before experienced by Americans. This is an
hour of history that troubles our minds and hurts our hearts," he
said. "Therefore, I feel it is my first duty to make an unprecedented
compact with my countrymen. Not an inaugural address, not a fire-
side chat, not a campaign speech—just a little straight talk among
friends. . . . I am acutely aware that you have not elected me as your
President by your ballots, and so I ask you to confirm me as your
President with your prayers."

Standing at a simple wooden lectern bearing the presidential seal,
with his wife and the chief justice seated in gold chairs behind him,
Ford rocked slightly as he spoke, his Midwestern twang noticeable in
the words with longer vowels. By clear implication, though certainly
not by name, he repudiated Nixon: "I believe that truth is the glue
that holds government together, not only our government but civi-
lization itself. That bond, though strained, is unbroken at home and

abroad. In all my public and private acts as your President, I expect to follow my instincts of openness and candor with full confidence that honesty is always the best policy in the end."

As if there were any doubt about what he meant, Ford added this passage of straightforward eloquence: "My fellow Americans, our long national nightmare is over. Our Constitution works; our great Republic is a government of laws and not of men. Here, the people rule." (Ford and Hartmann had quarreled over the use of the word "nightmare." Ford worried it was too unkind to Nixon, but decided ultimately to keep it in. It turned out to be the most famous thing Ford ever said.)

Recognizing the sting of those words, and reflecting his own fundamental generosity, Ford asked for kindness toward Nixon and his family. "In the beginning, I asked you to pray for me," he said. "Before closing, I ask again your prayers, for Richard Nixon and for his family. May our former President, who brought peace to millions, find it for himself. May God bless and comfort his wonderful wife and daughters, whose love and loyalty will forever be a shining legacy to all who bear the lonely burdens of the White House."

Ford closed with simple words that served as a reminder that he had held national office for well less than a year. He was still new and unfamiliar to most Americans. "I now solemnly reaffirm my promise I made to you last December 6: to uphold the Constitution, to do what is right as God gives me to see the right, and to do the very best I can for America," he said. "God helping me, I will not let you down."

———

At that point, two Gerald Ford presidencies began to unfold, one in public and the other in private. Ford's public reign was serene, almost joyful. The reaction to his inaugural address—his "straight talk among friends"—was rapturous, even across political boundaries. By intention and also by temperament, Ford posed a stylistic contrast to Nixon, and the people celebrated the change. Where Nixon was dark and secretive, Ford was open and accessible; where Nixon glowered, Ford glowed.

Shortly after his inauguration, Ford went to the White House

Press Room, to introduce terHorst as the new press secretary. Just days earlier, terHorst had been one of the reporters in that room, and his former colleagues welcomed him with applause. That was a departure from journalistic custom—"no cheering in the press box" is the cliché—but the transformation from the warfare of the Ziegler years merited an exception. On Capitol Hill, too, the mood had shifted. On the first Monday of his presidency, Ford addressed a joint session of Congress. There, he said, "I do not want a honeymoon with you. I want a good marriage." The standing ovation he received made it sound like he might get both. The sudden and welcome outbreak of peace gave millions of Americans the opportunity to opt out of Washington news for the time being. It was August, after all, time for vacations. It was more fun, even more pressing, to think about whether Evel Knievel would make it across the Snake River Canyon on September 8.

The presidency that was unfolding behind the scenes was very different from the one on display to the public. It wasn't that Ford's personality changed. He was genial in both public and private. But the Ford administration was born in rancor and governed, at least initially, in chaos. In light of Ford's decision to eschew any sort of preparations for the presidency until literally hours before he took office, it was perhaps not surprising that he and his staff were not ready to take over. But one initial decision in particular created problems. One widely believed theory about Watergate held that the scandal stemmed from Nixon's decision to give too much power to his chief of staff. According to this explanation, there was no check on Haldeman's despotic impulses, which led to rampant illegalities. Whether this view was accurate or not, Ford embraced it and decided to address the problem by abolishing the position of chief of staff in his White House. Instead, a group of about six officials would form "spokes of the wheel" and each have access to the president as equals.

Still, the key figure, as under Nixon, was Al Haig. When Nixon was in office, Haig had so much power that Jaworski referred to him as "our 37½ President."[1] In the first days after Ford took over, the new president had not yet sorted out all the titles for his advisers, but Haig was still the chief of staff—the head "spoke"—in fact if not in name. It wasn't clear how long he would stay on under Ford, but he was not one to surrender power without a push. On the very Friday afternoon that Ford took office, Haig convened a meeting for the new president with the top holdover staff members from the Nixon administration. Notably, for that session in the Roosevelt Room, there was no place set for Bob Hartmann or Jack Marsh from Ford's vice presidential staff—who had been designated as two of the new spokes of the wheel. Haig prepared the following memorandum and gave it to the new president for his use in the session:

The main purposes of this meeting are to:

(1) Reassure the staff of your respect, your need for their help, and your regard for President Nixon.

(2) Inform the staff of the role the Transition Team will play for the next few weeks and their relation to it.

We suggest this be a fairly short meeting covering the following general points:

1. The stress on the staff in these last few days and indeed the last year.

2. How important it is that they stayed in Mr. Nixon's service.

3. The special and heroic role of Al Haig.

4. Your personal need for the staff to remain intact and in place for a time to help you and the Transition Team.

5. The Team members will be in touch with them and General Haig will be actively involved in the Transition Team's efforts.

DO NOTS—At this time, do not commit yourself to dealing directly with anyone but Al Haig.

DO—Ask each staff member to be alert to problems and to make suggestions to Al Haig or to Transition Team members.[2]

Despite all the references in the memo to the "Transition Team," the "team" scarcely even existed at that point, as its members were still attempting to reach Washington and convene for the first time. (Donald Rumsfeld, a Transition Team member who was at the time U.S. ambassador to NATO, was en route to Washington from Brussels. He was met at the airport by his protégé and former assistant, Dick Cheney, and together they scrambled to the White House.) As a result, the immediate practical effect of the transition to Ford was that little changed: Haig was still in charge.

Even on Ford's first day, one of the main problems of the "spokes" model surfaced, and it concerned a president's most precious commodity: his time. No single person—not even Haig—was in charge of Ford's schedule, so he was immediately pulled in different directions. Kissinger, who was another spoke, arranged on that first day for Ford to meet with a group of diplomats from around the world, to assure them of the continuity in American foreign policy. The CIA also wanted to give Ford an intelligence briefing. TerHorst needed Ford to instruct him what to tell the press. Hartmann wanted Ford's input on his first address to Congress. And Ford himself wanted to settle on a nominee for vice president. (Once the nominee was confirmed, thanks to the Twenty-fifth Amendment, the United States would have an unelected vice president as well as an unelected president.) Also, before too long, Ford would have to decide whether he would run for a full term as president. There weren't enough hours in the day to deal with it all, and there was no one in charge to tee up the decisions for the president.

———

And then, still, there was Nixon. He may have resigned but his habits and expectations did not change with his departure from the job. On that final trip on Air Force One, he took about thirty-four family members and staffers with him, which was comparable to a sitting president's entourage. One reason the group was a little smaller was that Ziegler, in a final act of contempt for the press corps, had excluded the customary pool of reporters who usually traveled on Air Force One. When the aircraft arrived at Marine Corps Air Station El Toro, in Orange County, about five thousand supporters had gathered to welcome Nixon home to California. This was the reminder that Nixon needed that even though he had been repudiated in the capital, he retained a significant reservoir of support in the country at large. As so often happened in his career, Nixon was down, but not out.

In a brief speech, he elaborated on his theme of *au revoir*—he would be seeing them all again. After all, he was only sixty-one years old. "With all the time that I have which could be useful," he said, "I am going to continue to work for peace among all the world. I intend to continue to work for opportunity and understanding among the people of America."[3] With the cheers still echoing, Nixon and his family stepped on a Marine helicopter for the short ride to San Clemente and his Western White House.

There, as his first act, he placed a call to Al Haig and said, "You know those boxes up in EOB? Ship them out here. Send everything out here. I want all my records, all my papers and all my tapes."

———————

It is impossible to understand the events of the following month—including Ford's pardon of Nixon—without seeing the central role of the struggle over Nixon's papers and tapes. They are, in many respects, the same story. Ford wanted to put everything about Nixon behind him; by pressing the fight over his papers, Nixon made that impossible. To be sure, Nixon wanted his papers, but he also wanted the leverage over Ford that the papers gave him. He and his allies inside and outside the government employed that leverage to get what else Nixon wanted—a presidential pardon. Seen in this way, Nixon used his papers as a form of extortion—and it worked.

The struggle over the papers—and its connection to the pardon—involved three very famous people: Nixon, Ford, and Haig. It also featured someone whom history has largely forgotten: Benton Becker.

Born in 1938 and raised in and around Washington, D.C., Becker was a high school football player who never lost his beefy build or his aggressive attitude. He went to college and law school at the University of Maryland and then joined the Justice Department as a junior trial attorney in the early 1960s, when Robert F. Kennedy was the attorney general. Becker admired the Kennedys, but he was more sympathetic to Republicans than most of the others in his family. At Justice, Becker was assigned to the team investigating New York congressman Adam Clayton Powell for taking kickbacks from his staff members. Because the evidence-gathering process raised issues of separation of powers, the House of Representatives created a small committee to deal with the prosecutors. One member was Jerry Ford, of Michigan, and though they were technically on opposite sides, he and Becker hit it off. Even though Becker was a good deal younger than most other staffers, he called Ford "Jerry." Even after Ford became president, when the two men were alone, Becker called him "Jerry," not "Mr. President."

In 1970, at the instigation of the Nixon Justice Department, Ford conducted his ill-begotten campaign for the impeachment of Supreme Court Justice William Douglas. Ford had been supplied with dubious ammunition for his attack on Douglas—like his publication of an article in a racy magazine and some far-fetched claims of financial misdeeds—and the congressman's speech drew broad condemnation. Ford decided he needed help beyond his own staff and reached out to Becker, who had just opened his own law practice. Becker helped Ford extricate himself from this problem of his own making—the investigation of Douglas went nowhere—and Ford was grateful for the help. When Nixon nominated Ford to be vice president three years later, Ford again called on Becker to help him navigate his confirmation.

A frosty encounter in this period had lasting implications. As part of the confirmation process, the FBI did an exhaustive background investigation of Ford. One day, when Becker was huddled with Ford, Haig, who was then Nixon's chief of staff, called Ford, who put Becker on the line, too. Haig was calling Ford to give him a heads-up about some information the FBI had found, which would have been a violation of the rules that had been established for the confirmation. But before the conversation went much further, Becker jumped in. "General, General, General," he said. "Let me give you my name. My name is Benton Becker, and I'm representing [Ford] before the House and the Senate, and before we're finished before these committees, I guarantee you, he will be asked and re-asked the question, 'Did the White House feed you any information about the FBI reports?' 'Did the White House prepare him improperly?' When that question is asked, General, the answer is going to be a truthful answer, and the answer is no. We don't need or want you to do this anymore. He's in good hands, he will be confirmed well, and it will be fine." Becker recalled his statement was followed by "the deadliest silence on the other end of the line which continued for about eight to ten seconds, followed by, 'May I have your name one more time, please?'" Becker told him. Haig remembered.

———

In the chaotic hours before Ford took office, Becker again volunteered his services. It was a precarious moment in his own life. Becker was under criminal investigation. Becker's brother had introduced him to a real estate developer named Joel Kline, who became a client when Becker went into private practice. It turned out that Kline was crooked, and he faced a Justice Department investigation for obstruction of justice and other crimes. After pleading guilty, Kline tried to reduce his sentence by turning on his lawyer and accusing Becker of tax fraud and perjury. By the time Becker volunteered to work for Vice President–designee Ford, Becker had been told that the Justice Department had cleared him of most, but not all, of the charges. (He was eventually cleared of all of them.) But throughout this critical period of 1973 and 1974, Becker was in the bizarre position of both representing Ford on the most critical and confidential matters and fending off a federal investigation of his own behavior.

Becker was just thirty-six years old and had no government job, but he had something more important: the new president's trust. At that point, the West Wing and OEOB were filled with hundreds of executive branch employees. All but about a dozen of them had been hired by Nixon or his subordinates. With Becker, who was just a volunteer, Ford was happy to have one person whose loyalty was to Ford alone.

The new president had not looked into the issue of Nixon's papers and tapes and, in any event, he believed he had more important issues to address. As soon as Becker reported for duty, Ford told Becker to deal with the situation. Just figure out what was going on, don't let anything come or go, until we figure out what we are going to do.

To this day, it's not clear how many of Nixon's papers disappeared in the days immediately before and after he resigned. In this period, the lead role was taken by William Gulley, an irascible character who had long served as the head of the White House Military Affairs Office. During service to four presidents, Gulley had become a master at using government resources to serve his patrons. He found a way for the government to fund an air-conditioned movie theater at the LBJ Ranch and flew in stone crabs at $500 per pound for a farewell dinner at Camp David for Haldeman and Ehrlichman.[4] A close ally of Nixon and Haig, Gulley later boasted that he "started shipping stuff out to San Clemente as fast as it fell into my hands."[5] Burn bags, which were used to destroy sensitive documents, were also apparently in heavy use during these tense days.

It was Becker's job to stop the exodus of papers from the White House. On Saturday, August 10, shortly after Ford gave him that assignment, Becker walked from the West Wing to his temporary office in the OEOB, when he came upon a startling sight on West Executive Avenue.

"There was a truck being loaded by enlisted men under the command of a colonel," Becker recalled. "The enlisted men were placing the OEOB boxes of Nixon's records and tapes on that truck. I said, 'Colonel, are these the boxes from the fourth floor of the EOB containing the Nixon administration records and tapes.' He said, 'Yes, sir. They are.' I said, 'Well, what are you doing?' He said, 'We're taking them to Andrews Air Force Base. We're shipping them out today.' I said, 'Someone gave you that instruction?' He said, 'Yes, General Haig gave me that instruction.' I said, 'Are you aware that President Ford has issued instruction that these boxes shall not leave the White House?' He said, 'Sir, I take my orders from General Haig.' I said, 'Very well.'

"So, I recognized two Secret Service agents at the gate at the White House," Becker continued, "and I went over to them. Without giving them a reason, I said, 'Do you see that truck?' I said, 'I'm going in to see the President of the United States, I'm going to talk to him about that truck. That truck cannot, under any circumstances, leave these White House grounds. And I'm leaving it up to you to see to it that that truck does not leave here.' I said, 'I don't care if you have to shoot the tires out, that truck does not leave here.' He said, 'Yes, sir. You may be assured of that.'

"I turned around and went back into the White House, went upstairs to the Oval Office. The President was alone and I walked in. I was allowed to walk in immediately. 'I'm sorry to interrupt you, but . . .' and I told him what I just observed and my conversation with the colonel. And before I was finished—I mean, he had a telephone in his hand and his face was as red as a beet—'Get Haig in here.' Haig came in. President Ford said to me, 'Tell Al what you just told me.' The calmest, coolest Al Haig you ever saw, feigning surprise, said, 'Yeah, the damn colonels, they just don't know anything. They're so stupid. I'll take care of that colonel.' Haig quickly, immediately, put all the blame on the colonel. Haig said, 'Of course, I never ordered that.' But as sure as I'm alive, those records would have left the White House." (Haig was almost certainly lying to Ford, because Haig had just told Jaworski that Nixon's records were heading to San Clemente as soon as Ford took office.)

————————

On Ford's first day in office, terHorst gave his first press briefing as press secretary. After a few announcements, he took questions.

"Can you check for us, as to if President Ford's position is still as he stated on the Hill, that he is not in favor of immunity?" This was a reference to Ford's statement during his vice presidential confirmation hearings that "the public will not stand for" a pardon of President Nixon.

"I can assure you of that," terHorst answered.

"He is not in favor of immunity?"

That's right, terHorst said.

It was Ford's first day in office and whether the new president liked it or not, the issues of a pardon and the papers were not going away.

CHAPTER 15

Ford Settles In

FOR AS LONG AS NIXON WAS PRESIDENT, LEON JAWORSKI
was off the hook. Roger Dixon's memo of September 24, 1973, to then–
Attorney General Richardson was in effect: Justice Department policy
forbade the indictment of sitting presidents. But with Nixon's resignation, the door was now open, and Jaworski's prosecutors were raring
to make a case against the now former president. Jaworski wasn't.

The Watergate prosecutors no longer called themselves "Archie's
Orphans." By bringing the cover-up case against Nixon's closest aides
and then fighting and winning the tapes case before the Supreme
Court, Jaworski had won the respect of his staff. But he was never
one of them. As far as his staff could tell, Jaworski remained in his
funk following his argument in the Supreme Court. He missed his
home, family, and private income in Houston. When Jaworski was in
Washington, he still spent more time sulking at the Jefferson Hotel
than working in the office. He never came out and said it, but it was
clear to his staff that Jaworski felt he had completed his assignment.
He had brought the case that needed to be brought—the cover-up
case against Mitchell, Haldeman, Ehrlichman, and the others—and
the constitutional process for removing a president had proceeded
through the appropriate channels. Jaworski thought his work was
done.

After his meeting at Haig's home on August 8, Jaworski invited
three of his top aides to get a debrief from him at his suite at the Jefferson. (Notably, Jaworski chose not to return to the office and face

his full staff.) Jaworski summarized what happened. Nixon would resign that night. Jaworski made no commitments. Hearing this, James Vorenberg, a Harvard Law School professor who was on leave to serve as a senior assistant, said, "Come on, Leon!"[1] Vorenberg's point was clear. *Haig took all that time out of his day just to give you a heads-up? You don't want to prosecute Nixon, and he doesn't want you to prosecute Nixon. And you didn't agree on that?*

Unamused, Jaworski swore it was true, and the special prosecutor issued a statement on the night of Nixon's resignation speech: "There has been no agreement or understanding of any sort between the President and his representatives and the Special Prosecutor relating in any way to the President's resignation." So, the issue of whether to prosecute Nixon was at least technically open. Jaworski decided to hear out his subordinates. He told his staff he was ready to resign and return to Texas, but before he left he wanted to flesh out the debate on whether to ask the grand jury to indict Nixon.

Recalling this period, Jaworski later wrote, "Almost all of the lawyers expressed themselves in one form or another, and, without exception, they favored the return of an indictment."[2] George Frampton, one of the prosecutors, spoke for many when he pushed back on what he regarded as the best arguments against an indictment. First, Nixon had "suffered enough" and the country needed to get on to other subjects; second, Nixon did not initiate the cover-up but "rather fell into or was led into assisting the principal actors"; and third, Nixon "could not receive a fair trial." As for the first, Frampton said, Nixon had retired with a pension and staff. A multimillion-dollar book deal awaited him. Compared to the ordinary criminal defendant, his suffering was modest at best. Second, Nixon was the indispensable figure, as well as the main beneficiary, of the cover-up. And finally, the pretrial publicity surrounding the Watergate cover-up trial of Nixon's top aides was nearly as great as one involving Nixon would be, and that case was proceeding to trial without undue complications. The same would be true for a Nixon trial.

Jaworski acknowledged the power of his staff's arguments, but still he hesitated. To his staff of northeastern Ivy Leaguers, Jaworski could seem stolid and opaque, but they had come to see that his style had its virtues. As his press officer later wrote, "Partly from his southern manner and partly from his horse-trading instincts, Leon Jaworski is very good at being agreeable without agreeing to anything."[3] And Jaworski knew that sometimes it was better for someone to take a decision out of your hands than to make one yourself. The basic truth was that Jaworski didn't want to prosecute the now former president. Before Nixon resigned, the Justice Department policy served that purpose. Now that Nixon was gone from the White House, a pardon of Nixon by Ford would accomplish the same thing.

———————

In any new administration, there is a land grab for prime office space in the West Wing, near the Oval Office. But that didn't really happen in August 1974, because there were so few vacancies. Bob Hartmann snagged Rose Mary Woods's office—small but strategically adjacent to the president—and terHorst took Ziegler's press secretary space. But even though Haig no longer had the title, he remained in the customary suite for the chief of staff, and his immediate assistants also stayed in place. So did Henry Kissinger, who remained as national security advisor as well as secretary of state. In keeping with his sure public relations touch in those early days, Ford did make one change in the West Wing. He installed a portrait of Harry Truman, a celebrated Democrat, in the Cabinet Room, alongside Ford's favorite Republicans, like Dwight Eisenhower.

Ford's day-to-day challenges were daunting. After taking office on Friday, August 9, he chose to give a speech to a joint session of Congress on the following Monday. Other than Kissinger, Ford knew only one member of Nixon's cabinet, Rogers Morton, the secretary of the interior, and as president, Ford had to decide how many of them to keep on. Likewise, having decided on a "spokes of the wheel" approach, he had to decide how that would work and who would fill each role. At the same time, he deputized Jack Marsh to canvass political allies for their views on who should be vice president. World events didn't wait either. In Ford's first week, a long-gestating conflict in Cyprus between Greek and Turkish forces turned violent. On Friday, August 16, Ford hosted a previously scheduled State Dinner for King Hussein of Jordan. The following Monday, August 19, the American ambassador to Cyprus, Rodger Davies, was killed by a sniper outside the U.S. embassy.

Ford learned of the ambassador's death on his first trip as president, to give a speech to the Veterans of Foreign Wars in Chicago. It appeared to be a routine speech before a friendly audience, not least because Ford himself, a Navy veteran of the Pacific theater in World War II, was a VFW member. (It was also a good day for the president to be out of town, because this was the day the moving vans arrived at the White House from Alexandria so the Ford family could spend their first night in the White House.) But Ford planned something more consequential than the customary call for a strong defense and paean to veterans' service. Ford took seriously the notion of healing that he had raised in his inaugural remarks, and that included the wounds of the Vietnam War. There were about 100,000 draft evaders from the Vietnam era, many outside the United States, and their legal status remained unsettled. Ford wanted to give them a route to rejoin American society. After ordering secret consultations with the Veterans Administration and the Justice Department, Ford came up with a plan for "earned" amnesty. (The plan involved two years of good works in return for a clean record.) Ford knew the idea would be controversial before a conservative group like the VFW. As a result, Ford and his staff decided to omit the section on amnesty from advance copies of the speech. They didn't want to generate protests even before he arrived in Chicago.

In that section of the speech, Ford said he had ordered his administration to come up with a plan for the 100,000. "All, in a sense, are casualties, still abroad and absent without leave from the real America," he said. "I want them to come home if they want to work their way back. . . . In my judgment, these young Americans should have a second chance to contribute their fair share to the rebuilding of peace among ourselves and with all nations. So I am throwing the weight of my Presidency onto the scales of justice on the side of leniency. I foresee their earned reentry—earned reentry—into a new atmosphere of hope, hard work and mutual trust." As Ford knew would happen, the VFW audience grumbled at this section of the speech. That was fine with Ford. As he later wrote, "A liberal audience—Americans for Democratic Action, for example—would be pleased by the change of approach." But announcing it to a more conservative group was, as Ford intended, "a sign of strength on my part."[4]

Outside the hall, Ford's amnesty plan drew broad support. (The details proved to be complex, and only about 21,000 people attempted to take advantage of it.) The amnesty plan was widely seen as proof of Ford's seriousness about moving on from the rancor of the Nixon years. But the press missed a more specific message Ford was sending. The new president wasn't just reaching out to his political adversaries; he was interested in forgiveness as a general proposition, and that included a pardon to Nixon. When he was nominated to be vice president, Ford had, in his congressional testimony, rejected the idea of a pardon, but once in the Oval Office, he began to see the issue differently. In Ford's mind, even if few recognized it at the time, the Vietnam amnesty was a precursor for, and a justification of, a pardon for Richard Nixon.

———

Ford had wanted to name a vice president in his first week in office, but he couldn't quite close the deal in time. Bryce Harlow was in charge of the search, and he narrowed the list of candidates from sixteen to five. Harlow even devised a points system which ranked each of the contenders in categories like national stature, executive experience, and political appeal.[5] George Bush, the former Texas congressman and current chair of the Republican National Committee, led with 42 points, but he was closely followed by Rogers Morton, John Rhodes, and Tennessee senator Bill Brock. The fifth-place finisher was Nelson Rockefeller, who had just stepped down as New York's longtime governor. Harlow acknowledged that Rockefeller was opposed by the conservative wing of the party, and there was a risk that his famous name and long political history, including three runs for president, would overshadow Ford. But Ford thought that picking a strong VP demonstrated that he wasn't easily intimidated. Further, Ford didn't want to be thought of as a lame duck, so he was thinking of running on his own. As Harlow put it in a memo to Ford, "As for 1976, a Ford-

Rockefeller ticket should be an extremely formidable combination against any opponents the Democrats could offer. Therefore, the best choice is Rockefeller." (Harlow had noted one downside to Rockefeller, which was, at age sixty-six, he might be perceived as too old. In later years, especially in the next century, the upper age range for potential presidents expanded dramatically.)

Rockefeller temporized about the offer over the weekend—as he later put it, he never wanted to be vice president of anything—but he decided to accept. Rockefeller flew to Washington on his own Gulfstream jet, which was a far superior aircraft to the creaky one Ford endured as vice president. Ford announced the selection on August 20.

———

But Nixon—the person as well as the issues he represented—would not go away. TerHorst saw this better than anyone because reporters asked more questions about Nixon than any other subject. Though terHorst was an experienced reporter, he was new as a spokesman, much less for the president of the United States, and he made some cardinal errors. Trying to be responsive to his former colleagues, and reluctant to stonewall like Ziegler did, terHorst answered questions even when he wasn't sure of the facts. Since terHorst wasn't part of Ford's inner circle, he didn't know everything that was going on.

Answering questions from reporters on his first day, terHorst had settled the pardon issue: Ford was not going to grant one to Nixon. But then the questions began on the custody of Nixon's White House documents and tapes. That was a lot more complicated, and terHorst scrambled—both to find out what was actually happening with the material and what to tell reporters. TerHorst didn't know about Benton Becker's confrontation with the packed truck on West Exec and the resulting showdown with Haig in front of the president. Nor did terHorst know about another, similar event that took place on August 19. Buzhardt, who was still the top lawyer in the White House, told Jerry Jones, the holdover staff secretary and a longtime Haig aide, to box up all the White House tapes and place them in a waiting Air Force truck for transport to Nixon at San Clemente. Jones spent hours in the un-air-conditioned storage space in the OEOB cataloging and packing the tapes. At the last minute, though, Buzhardt tracked him down and told him to leave the tapes where they were.

While Jones was packing, Buzhardt was having a conversation with Phil Buchen, Ford's longtime friend and first law partner, who had not yet received a formal title in the new administration. Buchen himself didn't know what to do with the tapes, but he didn't want any irrevocable decisions made—like one to ship them to Nixon's custody, where he could do anything he wanted with them, including destroy them. In the end, Buchen convinced Buzhardt to tell Jones to stand down.

"Jerry," Buzhardt told him, "we just can't do this. If we let these tapes out of here, all hell is going to break loose. You and I may go to jail."[6]

But if the lawyers were confused about the legal status of the tapes, terHorst was even more baffled—and he had to answer questions from reporters. Here was a simple one: who owned the tapes? "I can't give you much on that," terHorst said. "As I mentioned, the tapes are in the protective custody of the Secret Service, but they have been ruled to be the personal property of President Nixon."

Ruled? By whom? TerHorst said it was a "formal" but unwritten decision by Buzhardt and St. Clair, Nixon's private defense lawyer, who was leaving the White House. TerHorst told the reporters that the tapes belonged to Nixon based on "historical precedent," going back to George Washington. The judgment of the White House lawyers was a "collective one." Every day there were more questions on the subject, and terHorst received minimal guidance from Buzhardt about what to say.

Later, terHorst was asked by a reporter if the president took part in the decision that the tapes belonged to Nixon.

"No, he did not," terHorst said. "This was made independently of President Ford."

"Does he concur in it?"

"Yes, he does."

But then other reporters followed up. There were continuing investigations, including the imminent cover-up trial, and the tapes were relevant evidence. How did Ford know that the investigators didn't need access to the tapes?

"I presume that was a judgment made by the respective legal counsels, both those who served President Nixon and those who served in the Special Prosecutor's office," terHorst said. It's a basic rule of public relations that a spokesman should not "presume" any facts, especially when, as here, terHorst was completely wrong.

"Are you saying," a reporter went on, "there was an agreement among the different staff, the Special Prosecutor, the Justice Department and the White House legal staff?"

"I assume there would be," terHorst said, "because I'm sure neither would just take unilateral action." ("Assume" is as perilous a word for spokesmen as "presume.") TerHorst's words were convoluted, but they were enough to prompt headlines that the special prosecutor had agreed that Nixon owned the tapes and could take them to California. Jaworski promptly issued a statement that he had been "informed" of Buzhardt's conclusion about the ownership of the tapes, but not "consulted."

It was chaos. Ford, who didn't want to be dealing with these issues at all, saw that his legal and communications staff were not collaborating successfully. He decided he wanted his own people in charge. He told terHorst to announce that Buzhardt as well as St. Clair would be leaving the White House. Phil Buchen would be the new White House counsel. This was a bitter blow for Buzhardt, who had risen from his sickbed to go back to work, only to be publicly fired by the White House press secretary.

Haig was even angrier. He believed that the office of White House Counsel was under his purview—part of his "spoke"—and he yelled at terHorst for announcing Buzhardt's departure without clearing it with him first. He called terHorst "the little executioner. Do you feel good? Executing a sick man?"[7]

Like many successful bureaucrats, Haig had a gift for managing up—that is, for pleasing his superiors. It was no surprise, then, that while Haig tangled with lower-level aides like Hartmann, Becker, and terHorst, he made himself invaluable to Ford, at least at first. And especially compared to those closest to Ford, Haig did have way more understanding of how the government, especially the executive branch, functioned on a day-to-day basis. But Ford failed to recognize where Haig's true loyalty lay. Haig owed his prominence and power to one man—Nixon—who promoted Haig to four-star general and then catapulted him to a position of extraordinary prominence. Haig was going to pay his patron back, even if it meant accepting a demotion to a mere spoke on a wheel, at least for a while. Haig was losing his title and his allies like Buzhardt, but the general was going to hang in at the White House long enough to get the former president what he really wanted. Haig vented to Jerry Jones. "I have lost the battle," Haig said. "But I will stay long enough to get Nixon the pardon."[8]

President Ford and his press secretary Jerald terHorst following his first White House press conference, on August 28, 1974. DAVID HUME KENNERLY/CENTER FOR CREATIVE PHOTOGRAPHY/U OF ARIZONA

CHAPTER 16

The Collapsing Floor

THE PROBLEM OF NIXON'S PAPERS WAS THREATENING TO bring down the White House—literally. Once Becker and Buchen put a stop to the immediate threat of removal of the documents and tapes to San Clemente, they directed that the papers all be held together in one place. It was an enormous amount of material. The controversy largely centered on the 950 reels of tape, but the papers from the Nixon presidency took up vastly more space, because, in this predigital era, there were about 42 million pages in a thousand boxes. They were moved to a locked space—a kind of extra-large closet—on the fourth floor of the OEOB. The closet didn't have a room number, though it ultimately came to be called Zone 128.[1] The volume of material created a serious problem. The Secret Service reported that the floor might collapse under all the weight.

Ford wanted a resolution. He saw the way that terHorst was being peppered with questions every day about the Nixon tapes and papers. The new president felt that he couldn't move forward with his agenda as long as these Nixon issues were plaguing him. Ford didn't want to deal with these issues at all, but he felt that he at least needed to know the law on the subject. He told Buchen to ask William Saxbe, the holdover attorney general, to resolve the issue. The matter was of such seriousness that rather than just pick up the phone and call in the question to the attorney general, Buchen drafted a letter to Saxbe for Ford's signature. "By this letter I am requesting your legal opinion concerning papers and other historical materials retained by the White House during the administration of former President Richard M. Nixon and now in the possession of the United States or its officials," Ford wrote. "I would like your advice concerning ownership of these materials and the obligations of the government with respect to subpoenas or court orders issued against the government or its officials pertaining to them." Saxbe gave the assignment to a lawyer on his staff named Antonin Scalia.

Scalia, who was thirty-eight at the time, had already led a peripatetic legal career. A graduate of Harvard Law School, he had started at a law firm in Cleveland, which he left just before he would have made partner, to begin teaching at the University of Virginia Law School. He developed an expertise in the infant field of cable television regulation and administrative law generally. He was a political conservative—a relative novelty in the legal academy—and he came to the attention of the Nixon administration. In 1971, Scalia was hired as the general counsel in the Office of Telecommunications Policy, and a year later he became the chairman of the Administrative Conference of the United States, a little known agency that is supposed to make the federal government function more efficiently. The Justice Department was a uniquely unstable agency in the Nixon years, with a rotating cast of attorneys general, but Scalia in early 1974 managed to be nominated to be the assistant attorney general for the Office of Legal Counsel. This was a prestigious post—William Rehnquist was a recent predecessor—where the occupant was expected to provide the last word on any in-house legal controversies within the executive branch.

Scalia had not yet come forward with the judicial philosophy that would make him famous. The concept of "originalism," which holds that the words of the Constitution should be interpreted according to their public meaning at the time of ratification, was not yet in wide circulation in 1974. But to be a conservative in that era still had ideological content, including a belief in a strong presidency. Nixon and his allies, including Scalia, believed that the presidency had been weakened by the activism of the other branches of government, and they resolved to steer power back to the president. This, in broad terms, reflected Scalia's worldview when Saxbe sent the president's question to him for a prompt answer.

Scalia replied with the literary grace that he would later display as a Supreme Court justice. His memo began, "Beginning with George Washington, every President of the United States has regarded all the papers and historical materials which accumulated in the White House during his administration, of a private or official nature, as his own property." In what would become typical Scalia fashion, he gave an erudite history of the issue, following the fates of presidential papers over the years. (The need for Scalia's analysis was so pressing that it appears that he sent drafts of his paper over to the White House before he delivered a finished product.) Scalia also said that if Nixon's tapes and papers were subpoenaed by other branches of government, Ford's White House should comply, while also giving Nixon's representatives access to the material. But Scalia's bottom line was clear: "To conclude that such materials are not the property of former President Nixon would be to reverse the almost unvaried understanding of all three branches of Government since the beginning of the Republic."

Scalia's artful prose hid some of the complexity of the issue. It was an "understanding" that the papers belonged to the president. The material was "regarded" as his property. This language obscured the fact that there was no law that said a president owned his presidential papers; nor was there any court decision, much less one by the Supreme Court, that held that the papers belonged to the president. It was a custom, or tradition, for a president to take his papers with him, but that was all it was. In this way, the legal opinion was an ideological document, one that reflected a tradition of presidential authority which Scalia wanted to preserve.

Saxbe cut-and-pasted Scalia's memo into his own message to the president, and the attorney general headed to the White House for a meeting on the subject. But before he did, someone in the Justice Department leaked Saxbe's memo to the press. This infuriated Ford's people at the White House, especially the prickly Bob Hartmann, because he thought Saxbe was trying to jam Ford by creating a public understanding that Nixon's papers belonged to him.

The meeting in the Oval Office became a showdown between Saxbe and Haig on one side and Hartmann and Becker on the other. Saxbe summarized the history that Scalia had outlined. Ulysses Grant held an auction of his papers. LBJ took every scrap with him to Texas. Nixon enjoyed the same rights. His papers belonged to him, and they should be shipped to him in San Clemente immediately. According to Saxbe, if Ford didn't send the papers posthaste, Nixon would sue for them and win. Haig agreed. Becker fought back, arguing that the precedents didn't apply. There had never been a full-scale taping system in place before, and the other presidents' materials were not the subject of ongoing criminal investigations.

The atmosphere in the room was fraught. Hartmann, who already had a rich loathing for Haig and was always alert to any slight, felt that Saxbe, a former senator, was condescending to Ford, who had been a mere congressman. "They thought Gerald Ford wasn't really very smart," Hartmann said, "and so he needed them to protect him from his own mistakes . . . hell, these little shits, they talked down to him and around him."[2] Becker, who had never been more than a mid-level federal prosecutor and was still a mere volunteer in the White House, was happy to challenge the attorney general on the merits. He recalled saying, "If you send those records, papers and tapes, to Richard Nixon, there will be a hell of a bonfire in San Clemente— and whatever happens in the remaining two and a half years [the remainder of Ford's presidency], is unimportant. Historians will write about the Ford presidency and this is what they will say, 'Jerry Ford committed the final act of the Watergate cover-up when he sent those records and papers and tapes to Nixon in California.'"

Ford disliked contention among his staffers, and he maintained a grumpy silence as the debate played out in front of him. "You could see red from the neck up, literally see the color change," Becker recalled. "I really angered him with that statement, and I meant to anger him. I wanted to shake him—you can't do that! Saxbe jumped in and said something like, 'I'm the Attorney General. You should listen to my advice.'"

In the end, Ford came down squarely on Becker's side. "Those damn things are not leaving here," he said. "They belong to the American people. They are going to stay here. They are not leaving."

It was, in many ways, a courageous decision on Ford's part, to reject the advice of his attorney general and stiff his predecessor on a matter that was obviously important to Nixon. Still, Ford's decision to hang on to the papers and tapes didn't really settle anything either. It meant that the records would remain in the White House complex, and terHorst and others would face continuing questions about what would happen to them. Becker was right. It would have been scandalous if Ford had allowed the papers and tapes to be shipped to Nixon, to do with them as he pleased. So, politically and even morally, Ford made the right decision. But that choice also meant that the issue would continue to plague Ford as the new president attempted to define his time in office. And by ruling against Nixon on control of the papers, Ford also felt, at least in part, that he owed Nixon one. So, in this way, Nixon won by losing. He didn't get his papers, but he did keep his issues in front of his successor, forcing Ford to keep looking for a way to put Nixon behind him.

It seemed at times that Nixon was haunting Ford. At one point in these early days, Hartmann received a tip that the Oval Office was still bugged.[3] This seemed improbable, but Hartmann told Becker, who looked into it. Becker found that there were still two microphones in the president's desk and two more embedded in the brass fixtures on the Oval Office wall. They were not currently connected to a tape recorder, but it wouldn't have been too difficult to crank up the old system.

Hartmann and Becker told Ford, who was apoplectic. "Dammit!" Hartmann recalled Ford saying, "They told me definitely there weren't any—that they had all been removed long ago." Haig had confirmed to him that no microphones were left. That night the four microphones were removed and presented to Becker, who found himself with a remarkable souvenir of his White House service. Ford was left to wonder what else was going on in his White House without his knowledge.

———

For the moment, though, these problems were inside baseball. For most people, the controversy over Nixon's papers was background noise. Instead, people heard endearing news about the new family that moved into the White House. For instance, Jerry and Betty Ford slept in the same bed, which represented a contrast to the Nixons and helped mark the First Couple as normal people. Polls showed Ford's favorability rating at around 70 percent, which was stratospheric for any president and more than double Nixon's last numbers. Inflation was still a problem, but no one could expect a new president to do anything about it in a couple of weeks.

On August 28, Ford passed another milestone as president by holding his first press conference. (In this era when newspapers were still dominant, the term "press conference" was still used, as opposed to the later formulation, "news conference.") Ford's opening remark illustrated something about the president and his era. "I have a very important and very serious announcement," he said. There was some confusion about the date of this first press conference because Betty Ford had originally announced her first press conference for this same day. "We worked this out between us in a calm and orderly way," Ford went on, deadpan. "She will postpone her press conference until next week, and until then, I will be making my own breakfast, my own lunch, and my own dinner." The joke was so lame that, even in 1974, it received only a polite chuckle. Then he called on Helen Thomas, of United Press International, for the first question.

"Mr. President," she said, "do you agree with the Bar Association that the law applies equally to all men, or do you agree with Governor Rockefeller that former President Nixon should have immunity from prosecution, and specifically, would you use your pardon authority, if necessary?" (Before he was nominated for vice president, Rockefeller had said he favored a pardon for Nixon.)

"Let me say at the outset that I made a statement in this room in the few moments after the swearing-in—that on that occasion I said . . . that I had hoped that our former President, who brought peace to millions, would find it for himself.

"Now, the expression made by Governor Rockefeller, I think, co-incides with the general view and the point of view of the American people. I subscribe to that point of view. But let me add, in the last ten days or two weeks, I have asked for prayers for guidance on this very important point. In this situation, I am the final authority. There have been no charges made, there has been no action by the courts, there has been no action by any jury and, until any legal process has been undertaken, I think it is unwise and untimely for me to make any commitment."

This answer, in which Ford paused awkwardly between sentences, seemed contradictory. Ford agreed with Rockefeller that there should be a pardon—but it was premature for Ford to commit to one. Reporters noticed and followed up. Was he in favor of a pardon?

"Of course, I make the final decision. And until it gets to me, I make no commitment one way or another. But I do have the right as President of the United States to make that decision."

Was he ruling it out?

"I am not ruling it out. It is an option and a proper option for any President."

But how was it fair for Special Prosecutor Jaworski to proceed against Nixon's aides when Nixon himself might get a pardon?

"I think the Special Prosecutor, Mr. Jaworski, has an obligation to take whatever action he sees fit in conformity with his oath of office, and that should include any and all individuals."

From there the questions veered off into other subjects—inflation, veterans' benefits, the federal budget, peace in the Middle East. Only about a third of the questions concerned Nixon. In answer to one more question about a pardon, he said, "I am not going to make any comment during the process of whatever charges are made." In reports on the press conference, most newspapers agreed with *The New York Times*, which interpreted the president as saying "until any legal process was undertaken, it would be untimely to commit on protection from prosecution or a pardon."

Overall, the press conference was a gentle affair, with respectful questions and straightforward answers. But as soon as Ford left the lectern in the East Room, he was furious. As he experienced the press conference, it was all about Nixon, and Ford hated it. He was not going to allow his presidency to be swallowed up by Watergate, as his predecessor's had been. It was time, he believed, to lance the boil.

CHAPTER 17

A Leak-Free Decision

ON THE MORNING OF AUGUST 28, JUST BEFORE FORD'S
press conference, the president received a memo from Leonard Garment, a lawyer in Nixon's counsel's office who remained on the White
House staff. Garment had been a law partner of Nixon's during his
exile years in New York, and he came to Washington with him. In a
Republican White House, Garment was an eccentric figure, a liberal
Democrat (and an accomplished jazz saxophonist) with a passion for
such issues as Native American rights. But he had been loyal to Nixon
throughout Watergate, and Garment stayed on during Ford's early
days as president.

The memo urged Ford to pardon Nixon—immediately. (Garment
even recruited Raymond Price, the holdover Nixon speechwriter, to
draft a proclamation announcing the pardon.) "My belief is that unless the President himself takes action by announcing a pardon today,
he will very likely lose control of the situation," Garment wrote. "The
national mood of conciliation will diminish; pressures for prosecution from different sources will accumulate; the political costs of intervention will become, or in any event seem, prohibitive. . . . There
will be a national sigh of relief. . . . The country trusts President Ford
and will follow him on this matter at this time."[1] Garment gave copies
of the memo to Haig, a longtime White House ally, and Buchen, and
Haig told Garment that he thought a pardon was going to happen.

It didn't happen on that day, but the momentum for a pardon,
at least inside the White House, was building. Henry Kissinger,

whom Ford respected more than anyone else in his White House, urged Ford to pardon Nixon. He told Ford that an indictment and trial would have "grave physical and psychological repercussions" on Nixon and hurt American credibility abroad.[2] The press conference on August 28 seemed to seal Ford's decision. "At the conclusion of the press conference, I walked back to the Oval Office and asked my advisers how long they thought this would go on," Ford later wrote in his memoir. "Was I going to be asked about Nixon's fate every time I met with the press?" He acknowledged that his answers at the press conference had been contradictory—that he said he was in favor of an immediate pardon and in favor of waiting until Jaworski obtained an indictment. "All this forced me to address the issue squarely for the first time," Ford went on. "I had to get the monkey off my back."[3]

Ford's extreme reaction to the press conference was curious but revealing. The session with reporters was hardly an all-out assault on the new president with questions about Nixon. True, there were more questions about Nixon than any other individual topic, but there were many more questions about other topics than about Nixon. News coverage of the press conference focused more on Ford's answers on those other subjects, like inflation, than about Nixon. A more experienced national politician would have recognized that the D.C. press corps has a short attention span. If Ford had just stuck to a single answer—like he was going to wait for a Nixon indictment before deciding about a pardon—he would have closed off the subject for the foreseeable future. But as a congressman and even as a vice president, Ford was used to picking and choosing the subjects on which he chose to speak out. He just didn't want to talk about Nixon, and he looked—he flailed—for a way to stop. A White House full of Nixon loyalists, like Haig, Price, and Garment, told the new president that the best and only way to put Nixon behind him was a pardon, and Ford was only too willing to believe them. He heard no contradictory voices, not because they didn't exist but because he didn't seek them out.

Ford stewed about the press conference for a day, and on the morning of Friday, August 30, just before Labor Day weekend, he left the White House early in the morning to speak at a commencement ceremony at Ohio State University, in Columbus. (Since Ohio State was the great rival of Ford's University of Michigan, speaking there was another gesture of healing and reconciliation. Still, Ford opened his remarks with a football joke that he wrote in at the last minute: "Thank you very much, and in keeping with my fight against inflation, I'm going to ask the Michigan team to keep the score down.") When Ford returned to the White House at midday, he summoned his closest aides, Hartmann, Buchen, and Marsh, as well as the ubiquitous Haig, to the Oval Office. He took the unusual step (for Ford) of swearing them all to secrecy for what they were about to discuss. "I want no leaks," he said.

Ford wanted to talk about a pardon for Nixon. He said he had been thinking about his answers at the press conference, and after he read the transcript, he realized he had not been clear.[4] He said he was disappointed in himself as a lawyer because he had answered without really understanding the law on presidential pardons, and he wanted to be brought up to speed. Buchen told him that he would get him the answers he wanted.

Then, as Hartmann recounted, there was a long pause as Ford leaned behind him and filled his pipe. In the silence of the Oval Office, the only sound was the ticking of an antique clock. Ford said he was "very much inclined" to grant Nixon a pardon from "further prosecution" as soon as he was sure he had the legal authority to do so. In other words, the president wasn't asking for advice; he was asking for affirmation, legal and otherwise.

When it was clear that the subject of the meeting was a pardon for Nixon, Haig offered to leave the room. He didn't say why—and he didn't explain why in interviews or in his memoir—but it seems clear that everyone in the room knew that he had already expressed his opinion on the subject. He was an ardent supporter of a pardon. Ford told him to stay where he was.

Then Ford spelled out his reasons. It wasn't just that he wanted to avoid the degrading spectacle of a former president being dragged into a prisoner's dock in a criminal court. It would take at least months before that happened. He thought that given the Supreme Court's rulings on pretrial publicity, the case would probably have to be delayed for a very long time. His concern was that each legal maneuver in the case would dominate the news. Ford would not be able to penetrate the noise. The president didn't put it this way, but his concern was as much about himself as about Nixon.

In light of the probable length of a Nixon prosecution, Ford thought there were only two possible outcomes. First, an acquittal, or second, a conviction and thus a demand from the public for mercy for Nixon. (These were not the only possible outcomes of a Nixon prosecution, but no one in the room challenged him.) But Ford thought in both circumstances, Nixon was never going to face a prison sentence.

"If eventually, why not now?" he said. If there was either going to be an acquittal or a pardon down the road, why not get it over with now and get on with the business of the nation?

Haig, Buchen, Marsh, and Hartmann reacted with silence. Hartmann, who had worked for Ford the longest, recognized when his boss wasn't interested in a debate. Buchen, who knew him the longest, spoke up first.

"I can't argue with what you feel is right," he said. "But is this the right time?"

"Will there *ever* be a right time?" Ford said.

Hartmann mentioned the fast-approaching midterm elections, where Republicans were already looking at a dismal showing, thanks to the hangover of Nixon scandals (and the shaky economy). "If you are thinking of doing this for political reasons," Hartmann said, "you ought to put it off until after the November elections."

"For the past five years, far too many decisions have been made in this room based on politics," Ford said. "This has nothing to do with politics. If I decide to give a pardon, it will be because it's the right thing to do."

Just then, Ford had to take a phone call. All four men left the room, and Haig didn't return. When the other three did, Ford asked Hartmann's opinion. "I think, Mr. President," he said with a smile, "the fit is really going to hit the shan." This was an inside joke of sorts. Susan Ford, the presidential daughter, had a frequently incontinent kitten named Shan.

Hartmann followed with a gentle protest. Ford said at the press conference that he would wait for a prosecution to decide on a pardon. An immediate pardon would be a shock. "The professional Nixon haters in the press and in the Congress will go right up the wall," Hartmann said. "You are going to have a firestorm of angry protest that will make the Saturday Night Massacre seem mild."

That might be true, Ford responded, but it would flare up and die down. "If I wait six months or a year, there will still be a 'firestorm' from the Nixon haters, as you call them. They wouldn't like it if I waited until he was on his deathbed. But most Americans will understand."

Marsh, the former congressman, was the last to give his opinion. He agreed with Hartmann that there would be an adverse reaction. But he said members of Congress, as a rule, didn't like it when politicians were prosecuted. They would believe that being forced from office was punishment enough for Nixon.

The discussion, such as it was, petered out from there. As is often the case, something very important was *not* said. Haig knew better than anyone that Jaworski did not want to bring a case against Nixon, and Jaworski was the final arbiter for that decision. In all likelihood, there was never going to be a criminal prosecution of Nixon, so a pardon was probably unnecessary. But Haig chose not to bring this crucial fact to Ford's attention, because it would have steered Ford away from Haig's, and Nixon's, preferred outcome—a pardon.

As the meeting wrapped up, Buchen said the best way to preserve the secrecy of the legal research about pardons was to assign it to Benton Becker, the volunteer (and criminal suspect) who had been helping out on issues relating to the Nixon tapes and papers. Ford agreed.

———

According to the minute-by-minute diary of the president's activities maintained by the Secret Service, this meeting took less than thirty minutes. It appears to have been the only conversation Ford had with

his advisers about the merits of a pardon, and it was more of an announcement than a conversation. As he said several times in his press
conference, the pardon decision was his alone to make.

But the implications of that decision for Ford's presidency would
involve a far larger group of people, and it was incumbent on him
to find out what they thought. "Leaks" have a pejorative reputation,
and so, to a lesser extent, do "trial balloons." But Ford would have
been better served if he had someone on his staff put the word out
that a pardon for Nixon was under serious and immediate consideration. Presidents from time immemorial have run their decisions
by members of Congress, especially of their own party, to test their
reactions or at least to prepare them for what's coming. As with any
political decision, the probable reaction may not have been disposi-
tive for Ford, but the information would have been immensely valuable. Instead, Ford confined the discussion to a tiny handful of aides
who were all sworn to secrecy and who, unlike many in Washington,
decided to keep their word.

The brief conversation on August 30 also revealed a failure of
strategic thinking on Ford's part. He talked with his aides about a
pardon for the former president, but they failed even to discuss the
still outstanding issue of Nixon's papers and tapes. Nixon wanted a
pardon, notwithstanding his occasional statements to the contrary.
He also wanted his presidential records, which Ford now controlled.
Above all, Ford wanted all Nixon issues behind him. The papers and
tapes gave Ford leverage to solve both problems at once. Ford could
have put out word through Haig that he would pardon Nixon but
only if the former president agreed to surrender his papers. Ford
never did. Instead, he moved ahead on plans for a pardon and let the
papers issue linger—with unfortunate consequences in the tumultu-
ous week ahead.

As for the legal issues surrounding pardons, Ford had at his disposal the entire resources of the executive branch, including the
Office of the White House Counsel and the Department of Justice,
which include some of the finest and most experienced lawyers in the
country. He was contemplating an enormously consequential issue—
whether to pardon his predecessor. He could have initiated instead a

process, which would have included deep research on the history and practice of pardons.

Instead, at about 9:30 p.m., on that Friday night, Benton Becker reported to the White House residence to receive his orders. Ford had questions that he wanted Becker to research.

(a) Could a President issue a pardon to someone who hadn't yet been charged with a crime?

(b) Could a President issue a pardon to an individual without citing the specific federal statutes for which the individual had been pardoned? (That is, could there be an across-the-board pardon for every federal crime?)

(c) Would a presidential pardon granted to an individual be binding upon the states, and thereby serve to bar state criminal prosecution? (This was relevant because Nixon was potentially involved in initiating the burglary of the office of Daniel Ellsberg's psychiatrist in Los Angeles. Burglary is a state, not federal, crime.)[5]

For Becker's Labor Day weekend assignment, secrecy was paramount. As Becker recalled, Ford told him, "I don't want you to work on this here. I don't want anybody seeing this. Go someplace."

Over the course of the weekend, Becker took his mission to the library of his law firm, where he was on leave, the library of the Supreme Court, and the law library at American University. "I'd keep books out and I'd mark the page," he recalled. "If it was on page 412, there was a case I was looking at, I would mark it 537 and have a separate code to myself in case some curious little law clerk was curious about what Becker is looking at." The answers to Ford's questions, if not all their implications, were straightforward. First, a president could issue a pardon before any charges were filed. Second, a president could issue an across-the-board pardon covering all federal crimes. Third, a presidential pardon could not create immunity for state criminal offenses. (This turned out to be of no consequence because Nixon was never investigated by California prosecutors in connection with the Ellsberg matter.)

Becker took his research a step further, and he found what he regarded as the holy grail—a heretofore obscure Supreme Court case from 1915. Becker became so intrigued with this case that he went to the Supreme Court library (in secret, of course) and tracked down the briefs that had been filed by the parties. More to the point, thanks to an introduction from Becker, Gerald Ford also became obsessed with *Burdick v. United States.*

––––––––––

The case emerged from the rough-and-tumble world of the New York harbor around the turn of the last century. George Burdick was a crusading journalist at the *New York Tribune*, who wrote a series of stories exposing corruption, including bribery and smuggling, at the Customs Service. The United States attorney in Manhattan wanted to follow up with prosecutions of the malefactors, so he subpoenaed Burdick to testify before the grand jury and identify his sources. Burdick was not a target of prosecutors; in fact, they lauded him for his disclosures. But Burdick refused to testify, citing both a reporter's privilege to protect his sources and his Fifth Amendment privilege against self-incrimination. (The reporter's privilege quickly fell out of the case, because, then as now, there is no reporter's privilege in federal court.)

The New York prosecutors faced the dilemma of how to overcome Burdick's Fifth Amendment rights. They came up with a novel solution. They obtained a pardon of Burdick from President Woodrow Wilson, absolving him of any federal crime he may have committed from birth until the day the pardon was issued. Because Burdick now faced no possibility of prosecution, the prosecutors argued that the journalist no longer had a privilege against self-incrimination. But Burdick still refused to testify in the grand jury. After being held in contempt and jailed, Burdick appealed to the Supreme Court.

The justices awarded Burdick a unanimous victory, dismissing the contempt finding against him and ordering him released from jail. Justice Joseph McKenna held that the granting of a pardon alone does not make it effective; the pardon must be *accepted* by the recipient, and Burdick did not accept Wilson's pardon. Because Burdick did not accept the pardon, it had no legal effect. As McKenna put it, "Granting, then, that the pardon was legally issued and was sufficient for immunity, it was Burdick's right to refuse it." The opinion then went on to explain why someone like Burdick might refuse a pardon. In what Becker (and later Ford) regarded as the key passage, McKenna stated, a pardon "carries an imputation of guilt; acceptance a confession of it."

On Saturday morning, Ford held a meeting at the White House with top officials at the Defense and Justice Departments about his plan for earned amnesty for Vietnam War resisters. He didn't discuss with them his linkage of that action to his planned pardon for Nixon, but his insistence on the meeting—over Labor Day weekend no less—underscored the intensity of his interest in the subject. From there, Ford went to play golf at the all-male Burning Tree golf course, and then he and his family made their first trip to Camp David for the rest of the weekend.

It was Tuesday, September 3, before Becker had the opportunity to present the results of his research to Ford. They spent most of their time talking about the *Burdick* case. They focused on the issue of "acceptance" of a pardon. At one level, they thought that could work in Ford's favor. They were somewhat concerned about the issue Helen Thomas raised in the first question at the press conference: if Ford pardoned Nixon, did that put the former president above the law? Was it too sweet a deal to let Nixon walk away with no consequences? But *Burdick* said that Nixon would be confessing to wrongdoing if he accepted a pardon. That was no free ride.

Becker and Ford were also concerned about a different issue—one largely of their own invention. Would Nixon accept a pardon? Even when Nixon resigned as president, he had refused to admit wrongdoing in connection with the Watergate cover-up. In light of Nixon's defiance on that issue, coupled with the language in *Burdick* that acceptance of a pardon "carries an imputation of guilt," would Nixon accept a pardon? The real answer was: of course Nixon would accept a pardon. Ford knew since Haig's approach to him at the beginning of August that Nixon wanted a pardon. A pardon was a gift to Nixon. But thanks to Becker and Ford's reading of this obscure 1915 Supreme Court case, they convinced themselves that Ford would have to persuade Nixon to take a pardon. It was an extraordinary turn of events: Nixon was in exile, and Ford was in the White House, but when it came to the pardon, Ford thought he was the supplicant and Nixon the boss.

CHAPTER 18

Delivering the Pumpkin

EVERY MORNING PROMPTLY AT 7 A.M., RICHARD NIXON, private citizen, went to his office in San Clemente in suit and tie.

Casa Pacifica had been built in 1925 by Henry Hamilton Cotton, a local industrialist, in the style of a hacienda, which the California rich of that era preferred.[1] But by the standards of the 1970s, to say nothing of the later McMansion era, the place in San Clemente was modest in size. It was almost all on one level, with small rooms built in a square around a courtyard with a fountain. The only room on the upper level was a tiny office—just eight by ten feet—where Nixon could look out at the ocean. Still, like so much else in Nixon's presidency, the house brought with it a measure of scandal. The White House had sunk more than $6 million in taxpayer money to turn Casa Pacifica into the "Western White House." The expenditures included $156,000 for landscaping and a $1,800 flagpole as well as a cluster of small buildings for Nixon's staff on the adjacent Coast Guard base.

At least for the time being, the staff that accompanied Nixon on the final Air Force One journey remained with him. Ron Ziegler, the press secretary, served as gatekeeper, along with his young assistant, Diane Sawyer. The staff was expected to join Nixon every morning at 7:30, and the former president seemed to have a hard time recognizing that he was no longer in charge of the government. One morning in the first week, Nixon greeted his staff with the words, "I've called you here to discuss an important topic. And that is, what are we going to do about the economy in the coming year?"

Nixon's mind was on survival as well as relevance. From his first day in California, he was demanding that his papers, including the White House tapes, be turned over to him in California. In part, he wanted the material for the reason he started the taping system in the first place—to write his memoirs. Nixon long had a fixation on his place in history, and he wanted the chance to write a first draft himself. At least as importantly, writing a memoir represented his only real chance of making the money which his real-estate-rich cash-poor lifestyle required. Other than his friends Rebozo (the Miami banker) and Abplanalp (the spray nozzle inventor), the first outsider to visit Nixon was Irving "Swifty" Lazar, the celebrated literary agent of his day. Lazar told the former president that if he wrote candidly, including about Watergate, his memoir could command an advance of $2 million.

But access to Nixon's tapes and papers had more significance than just as research material. Nixon knew that previous presidents had taken their papers with them—no questions asked—and he wanted the same treatment from his successor. His sense of his own dignity and importance required it. Nixon knew that the White House and West Wing were still full of his loyalists, and he didn't hesitate to take advantage. He remained in regular touch with Haig—usually demanding that more papers be sent to him—but his most important ally was Bill Gulley, the head of the White House military office. (Ziegler, his most devout courtier, was also in touch with Haig, and he was also insisting, at top volume, that Nixon receive his papers.)

Unknown to the public, Gulley was a powerful figure in the White House back to the Johnson administration. He controlled access to the vast resources of the armed forces, including troops and planes, that could be put at a president's disposal. In the name of "security" or "communications," he built additions to presidential homes that vastly increased their value. He shuttled presidents' family members around the world on private planes. Through the dispensation of such perks, he won great loyalty from the presidents he served and repaid that support as well. More than almost any staffer, he knew the real desires of each president, and he knew what Nixon wanted—his stuff, all of it.

From the moment that Nixon resigned, Gulley took charge of the project of sending him his belongings—and as many of the papers as he could get away with delivering. As he recalled later, "I started shipping stuff to San Clemente as fast as it came into my hands, things that weren't yet under lock and key."[2] Working feverishly in the first weeks after Nixon's resignation, Gulley sent possessions like clothing and furniture belonging to the former First Family, but he also tried to spirit away as many papers as possible—as much as 400,000 pounds of material to San Clemente. To this day, it's not clear what exactly Gulley was able to send to Nixon until Ford rejected Saxbe's advice (and accepted Becker's) and shut down the transfer of papers.

Gulley made several trips back and forth between the White House and San Clemente, and he saw that Nixon in exile was physically transformed—hollow-eyed and exhausted. Nixon was also furious about his treatment by the new regime. As Gulley recalled of one trip in mid-August, Nixon greeted him by saying, "What are those bastards going to do to me?"[3]

"They're after your ass," Gulley answered, then referred to Ford's longstanding aides. "Marsh and Hartmann are referring to you as a crook."

"I'm not going to deal with those fucking bastards," Nixon responded. "I'm entitled to anything that any other former President is entitled to. Goddam, you know what I did for Johnson, and you know what I did for Ike and Truman, and goddam, I expect to be treated the same way. When I travel, I expect military aircraft; I expect the same support I provided. I expect communications and medical personnel, everything they had. And goddam it, you tell Ford I expect it."

There is a revealing contrast in the way Ford and Nixon thought of the papers and tapes stored in the OEOB. Ford evaluated the arguments about custody and decided, on the merits, that they should remain with the U.S. government. Nixon had a more strategic approach. He wanted the papers for his own use—to write his memoirs and to be treated like other presidents—but also for leverage over the new administration. Even before the questions at the press conference on August 28 irritated Ford so much, Nixon knew that Ford would be willing to pay a price to get the issue of the papers off his plate. Nixon was nothing if not a skilled negotiator; he understood, to cite one famous example, that a shared antipathy for the Soviet Union could bring the United States and China to a seemingly unlikely rapprochement. Nixon didn't have to say what the papers could get him, but the people around him knew: a pardon.

But for that, he would need a lawyer.

————

Herbert J. Miller Jr., known as Jack, was an anomaly: a Kennedy Republican. In 1961, Attorney General Robert F. Kennedy had named Miller as the assistant attorney general in charge of the Criminal Division, which enjoyed a storied run under his leadership. (One successful prosecution was that of Teamsters leader Jimmy Hoffa; it was the prison sentence for this case that Nixon commuted in 1971.) Nixon always possessed a mixture of jealousy and admiration for the glamour and success of the Kennedys, and hiring Miller was a way of purchasing some Kennedy magic. (Miller was a pallbearer at RFK's funeral in 1968; the next year, he represented Ted Kennedy in the aftermath of the Chappaquiddick incident, where Kennedy left the scene of a fatal accident after driving his car off a bridge on Martha's Vineyard.) At the same time, Miller was a loyal Republican, who even made an unsuccessful run for lieutenant governor of Maryland in 1970. The combination appealed to Nixon.

After leaving the government, Miller had started a firm, Miller, Cassidy, Larroca & Lewin, with a group of hot young litigators, mostly Democrats, which created a measure of awkwardness. Immediately after Nixon resigned, Nathan Lewin, one of Miller's partners, wrote an article in *The New Republic* arguing that Jaworski should prosecute Nixon for his role in the Watergate cover-up. But that turned out to matter less to Nixon than Miller's record of having negotiated a sweet deal for Richard Kleindienst with Jaworski's office. Kleindienst, who was one of Nixon's rotating series of attorneys general, gave false testimony to Congress about the Nixon administration's dealings with the ITT conglomerate. Instead of being charged with perjury, a felony, Kleindienst was allowed to plead guilty to a misdemeanor and sentenced to a $100 fine and no jail time. Miller also represented Richard Moore, a former White House lawyer and minor Watergate figure, and Moore was the one who suggested to Nixon that he retain Miller. Ziegler then reached out to Miller on Saturday, August 24, and Miller agreed to sign on.

Miller had a higher priority even than meeting his client for the first time. Thanks to media attention like his partner's article in *The New Republic*, Miller was worried that Jaworski was going to obtain an indictment of Nixon at any moment. That was an irrevocable step, which Miller wanted to prevent if at all possible. So, over that first weekend, Miller visited Jaworski at the Jefferson Hotel and implored him not to indict Nixon right away.

Jaworski was receptive—surprisingly so, Miller thought. Miller was learning what Jaworski's subordinates (and Haig) had found out over the past year: Jaworski didn't want to indict Nixon. The prosecutor told Miller that he thought an indictment of a former president would make the United States look like a "banana republic." This was not a country where the new regime tried to imprison the old. Worse yet, a trial of Nixon would have to be delayed many months, if not longer, to deal with the poisonous anti-Nixon environment within the jury pool of Washington, D.C. So, according to Jaworski, the specter of a criminal trial of a former president would linger in the country seemingly for an eternity.

Miller set two young associates to work on the representation, which was a tightly held secret for the time being. Bill Jeffress and Thomas Rowe were sworn to secrecy and told to start learning the story of the White House documents and tapes—and who did, and should, own them. In addition, they were told to start preparing a memo to Jaworski arguing that he should not prosecute Nixon. Above all, though, the two young lawyers discovered Miller's top priority for the firm's representation of Nixon: obtaining a presidential pardon for the former president. This was such a big secret, even within the firm, that they spoke of it in code. The pardon was "the pumpkin," and the job was to get President Ford to deliver the pumpkin.

Confident now that Nixon would not be facing imminent charges, Miller made his first visit to San Clemente. Like Gulley, Miller found

Nixon to be physically diminished and emotionally overwrought. He felt wronged by everyone—the press, the public, his onetime allies in Congress, and his successor in the White House. Miller made clear to Nixon that the best outcome for him was a presidential pardon. That would take the possibility of criminal prosecution off the table for the rest of his life and allow him to start rebuilding his reputation and his finances. At first, Nixon was resistant—or at least he said he was resistant. Accepting a pardon suggested that he knew he had done something wrong, and that was not something that he wanted to acknowledge. This brief resistance may have been a show for the benefit of his new lawyer; even before he resigned, Nixon had made clear to Haig and Buzhardt that he wanted a pardon. And it didn't take much convincing from Miller for Nixon to sign on to the pardon strategy. The lawyer's job back in Washington was to make a pardon happen. (At the time, thanks to his conversations with Becker, Ford was convinced, and had convinced himself, that he would have to persuade Nixon to accept a pardon.)

As Miller and Nixon parted ways, there was a moment of awkwardness. Even in exile, Nixon liked to present visitors with a tie clip bearing his presidential seal. When he gave one to Miller, though, he saw that the lawyer was already wearing a clip—a gift from John F. Kennedy commemorating *PT-109*, which represented JFK's World War II heroism in the Pacific.

————

What followed, over the next two weeks, was a peculiar three-way negotiation between Jaworski, Ford's lawyers, and Nixon's lawyers that was, at its core, barely a negotiation at all. All three sides wanted the same thing—for Ford to pardon Nixon. The only question was how to get there in politically acceptable ways for all three parties.

Jaworski never really came out of his funk following the Supreme Court argument in *United States v. Nixon* in July. He spent more time back home at his ranch in Texas, and when he was in Washington, he lingered at the Jefferson Hotel more than at the office. He felt his work was done. The country had been spared a continuation of the Nixon presidency, and the Watergate cover-up case was heading to trial on October 1. Jaworski was looking for an exit strategy, and a pardon would make everyone happy—except his staff and, though this wasn't Jaworski's concern, the American people.

Some of Jaworski's concerns related to Nixon as a person. He understood the strain Nixon had been under, and Jaworski, in simple terms, didn't want to kill him. As a former eminence in the American Bar Association, Jaworski was long acquainted with James Eastland, the Mississippi segregationist who was the longtime chairman of the Senate Judiciary Committee. One day shortly after Nixon's resignation, Eastland summoned Jaworski to his Senate office so the senator could recount a recent conversation with the former president. "He was crying," Eastland told Jaworski. "He said, 'Jim, don't let Jaworski put me in that trial with Haldeman and Ehrlichman. I can't take any more.'" Eastland shook his head. "He's in bad shape, Leon."[4]

Still, the prosecutor had to figure out how to bring the Nixon matter to a conclusion. Jaworski was as puzzled as anyone by Ford's garbled answers at his press conference on August 28. What was Ford saying about a pardon for Nixon? Was he going to issue one right away? Was he going to wait until there was an indictment? Was he going to pardon Nixon at all? Jaworski had watched the press conference on television, but then he asked his staff to track down a transcript, to see if he could untangle Ford's real intentions. It didn't help. Jaworski still didn't understand what Ford planned to do.

Jaworski chose to use Ford's ambiguity as an opportunity. Though Jaworski himself did not want to indict Nixon, he still headed an office of restless young prosecutors who did. (The conflict was largely generational. The only other leading figure in the office who opposed a Nixon indictment was James Neal, the Tennessee lawyer whom Jaworski brought in to lead the prosecution team in the cover-up trial. Neal was the only lawyer in the office who was somewhat close in age to Jaworski.) Office firebrands, like Richard Ben-Veniste and George Frampton, saw the approaching cover-up trial as an opportunity to bring a case against Nixon. According to the plan at that time, the trial of Mitchell, Haldeman, Ehrlichman, and the others was scheduled to begin on October 1, and it would last about six weeks. After the close of testimony, the jury would be sequestered until it reached a decision. When the jury was sequestered, according to the office hawks, that would be the time to indict Nixon, because there would be no argument that the cover-up jury was influenced by the news. To this group, Nixon was at least as culpable as those who were going to trial, so it would be wrong, almost immoral, to prosecute Nixon's underlings but not the man himself.

Jaworski understood the appeal of this argument, though he disagreed with it; that's why he saw the decision on Nixon as "a monkey on my back," as he described it at the time. (Ford used the same metaphor for his Nixon problem.) But Jaworski, ever the poker player, wanted to know if he was even going to have to decide whether to indict Nixon. If Ford was going to pardon Nixon anyway, he thought there was no reason to indict him in the first place. So, Jaworski decided to use the ambiguity of Ford's statement at his press conference as an opportunity to take the monkey off his back and put it on the new president's. Jaworski acted in response to a memo from Philip Lacovara, his counsel, who wrote:

> Since President Ford is now publicly on record as having expressed a willingness to assume the responsibility for the exercise of the ultimate constitutional powers that are his, I believe he should be asked to face this issue *now* and make the operative judgment concerning the former President, rather than leaving this matter in the limbo of uncertainty that has been created.

In other words, Jaworski would ask Ford to decide *now* whether he was going to pardon Nixon and thus spare Jaworski the decision of whether to indict him. And Jaworski had a convenient way to do so, because Phil Buchen, Ford's new counsel, also happened to be living in the Jefferson Hotel.

CHAPTER 19

The Prosecution Caves

INSIDE THE OFFICES OF THE WATERGATE SPECIAL PROSE-
cutor, the days after Nixon's resignation were tense and fraught. Many
of the younger lawyers knew that there were negotiations going on
above their pay grade. They were suspicious that Jaworski was going
to betray their hard work by giving Nixon a pass. As George Frampton, one of the firebrands, put it in a memo to Jaworski at this time,
"I fear that history may yet judge this venture a failure should your
decision be to 'call it a day' and not indict former President Nixon."[1]
Jaworski wasn't talking to them much, so some of the staff took to
trying to monitor his comings and goings. One office rumor had
Jaworski filling his briefcase with confidential office documents to
share with Buchen. This story was scotched when Jaworski was seen
opening his briefcase—revealing only a bottle of bourbon.

Some lower-level prosecutors on Jaworski's team, who had basically been shut out of the decision of what to do about Nixon, chose
a comic take on the issue. Ben-Veniste bought a movie poster from
King Kong and mounted it in the office of the cover-up trial team.
There, the lawyers would joke about whose back the monkey was
on—Jaworski's, Ford's, or someone else's.

The joke was no joke. It reflected what was going on between
Jaworski and Buchen, in their conversations at the Jefferson Hotel
and elsewhere. Both men wanted Ford to pardon Nixon, but neither
wanted responsibility for the decision. Jaworski didn't want his fin-
gerprints on the pardon, and at the same time, Buchen wanted Ja-

worski's help in easing Ford's path. Each wanted the monkey on the other's back. Still, on the main point, the pair were aligned. The pardon was the way to go. And events were heading that way.

For this reason, Jaworski was in good spirits when he returned to Washington on Tuesday, September 3, after spending Labor Day weekend on his ranch in Texas. He was confident that the pardon would bring his tenure as special prosecutor to a close. Not one normally to share much about his home life, Jaworski told his staff how pleased he was that his champion quarter horse Magnolia Pay had just sired some new foals.[2]

In the fast-moving events of late August and early September, the pardon had subsumed the subject that preoccupied the Ford White House in the earlier part of August: what to do about Nixon's papers and tapes. But that issue still needed to be decided. What was going to happen to all the material that was taxing the floorboards of the Old Executive Office Building? Where would it go? And who, ultimately, owned it? Ford told Buchen to get the issue of papers settled with Nixon's lawyer, so all the issues with the former president could be wrapped up and concluded at the same time.

But the reordering of the issues—pardon first, papers second— shifted the power dynamics even more between Ford and Nixon. Ford, Buchen, and Becker were already worried that they had to convince Nixon to accept the pardon. If Ford was going to pardon Nixon anyway, that greatly strengthened Nixon's hand when it came to the papers. If Nixon knew he was going to get a pardon, his lawyer could take a hard line on the papers, which he did, at the next Jefferson Hotel summit.

––––––––––

Buchen didn't want reporters to see that he was meeting with Nixon's lawyer at the White House, so he invited Jack Miller to meet him at his suite at the Jefferson on September 3. Benton Becker, the volunteer at the center of all Nixon-related matters for Ford, came along, too. Buchen was a decent and honest man who had spent his professional life with a modest law practice in Grand Rapids. He had no experience in high-stakes political matters, which he demonstrated, to his detriment, at the beginning of his meeting with Miller.

Buchen volunteered that Ford was strongly considering pardoning Nixon. It wasn't a done deal, but Buchen thought Miller and Nixon should know.[3] This information gave Miller considerable leverage in the negotiations that followed, which Nixon's lawyer put to good use. Indeed, he told Buchen that he couldn't even be sure that Nixon would accept a pardon, with its imputation of guilt. But in the end, Miller said he could probably get Nixon to accept a pardon.

Buchen said, "Look, I think it's important that there be a statement of true contrition from the former President. The President [Ford] tells me that we can't dictate that statement, but in the interests of both your client and the President, I hope you could persuade your client to develop something that would tell the world, 'Yes, he did it, and he's accepting the pardon because he's guilty.'"[4]

Miller said he had his doubts about that possibility. Nixon was still distraught about the whole situation. He didn't want to talk about Watergate at all, much less admit wrongdoing. Well, Buchen replied, the statement is not a precondition for a pardon, but please do your best to get an admission from him.

Thus, the meeting began with Buchen—and implicitly Ford—as supplicants to Nixon. Buchen was asking Nixon to give up his claim to the papers and to admit culpability on Watergate. But regardless of how Nixon responded to those requests, Ford was going to pardon him anyway. That was an inept way for Buchen to "negotiate," but it was what Ford wanted.

Miller came to the meeting with a proposal that he called a compromise on the papers, and the three men came to agreement on the rough terms. The tapes and documents would be moved to a federal facility near San Clemente, and they would be jointly owned by Nixon and the federal government. The materials would be available for court subpoenas for between three and five years. Two keys would be necessary to open the storage facility—one in Nixon's possession, the other with the General Services Administration. After five years, Nixon could order that the tapes and the papers be destroyed. As the meeting ended, Miller said he thought he could get Nixon's agreement on the plan. The plan was an extraordinary capitulation on the part of the Ford White House. The material was to be located for Nixon's convenience, and the government could only examine them with a subpoena—and Nixon would eventually enjoy the right to destroy these irreplaceable historical records.

In fact, Buchen didn't have to make any concessions to Nixon on the papers, because they weren't Nixon's to give. As Scalia had determined, and Saxbe then told Ford, the longstanding tradition was for former presidents to retain custody of their papers. (Nixon knew this better than anyone and had been raging about it ever since he stepped down.) But that was just a tradition and not a law, and besides, the Nixon papers were different from those of his predecessors in many ways. For starters, the papers constituted important evidence in an ongoing criminal investigation, including of Nixon himself, who was seeking to spirit the papers away from the eyes of his pursuers. Moreover, early in Nixon's presidency, he had donated some of his papers to the National Archives and taken a $576,000 tax deduction, which had already been disallowed by the Internal Revenue Service. (Later in 1974, Edward Morgan, who prepared Nixon's tax return, pleaded guilty to conspiring to violate the tax laws by using backdated documents in connection with the donation.) Jaworski's office was investigating Nixon's role in the events surrounding the gift to the Archives and the tax deduction. Worse yet, on August 8, 1974, the last full day of Nixon's presidency, he had written to Arthur Sampson, the administrator of the General Services Administration, purporting to modify the terms of his donation. The letter preserved Nixon's access to the papers and added, "Prior to January 1, 1985, no person or persons shall have the right of Access to such Materials except the undersigned and those who may be designated in writing by the undersigned." Plus, Ehrlichman and other defendants in the fast-approaching Watergate cover-up trial were also seeking access to the papers to assist in their defense. The papers had also been subpoenaed in several civil lawsuits that had arisen out of the Watergate scandals. In spite of all these complex and confusing issues surrounding the papers, Nixon was claiming sole control of the papers he had already donated to the government as well as those on the fourth floor of the OEOB.

After Miller left, Jaworski came from his own suite at the Jefferson to visit Buchen's. Jaworski wanted an update about Ford's thinking about a pardon. Buchen said it was still on track, but he wanted Jaworski's assurance that he wouldn't object to a pardon. Jaworski kept to himself that he knew that his staff would object—vociferously—to a pardon, but he told Buchen that he himself had no objection. (Far from it.)

With the knowledge that he and Jaworski were basically aligned on the pardon, Buchen said he needed two things from the prosecutor to smooth the path. Buchen wanted a list of pending investigations of Nixon and an estimate of how long it would take to bring Nixon to trial in a prosecution for the Watergate cover-up.

Both of these issues—the number of investigations and the timeline for a Nixon trial—were crucial to Ford. Buchen knew that Ford didn't want to have to answer questions about Nixon for the rest of his term. (And as president, Ford was quickly leaning into the idea that he would run on his own in 1976.) So, it was in Buchen's interest for Jaworski to describe the Nixon case as stretching out for many months, if not years. To that end, too, Ford would want to know that there were many possible cases against Nixon, not just the cover-up prosecution of his former aides that was to begin shortly before Judge Sirica. To clinch the case for a defensible pardon, Buchen needed from Jaworski the possibility of lots of long-running cases against Nixon. Jaworski was happy to supply them both.

Jaworski returned to the prosecution office and commissioned Henry Ruth, his second in command, to write a memo listing the subject areas of all the outstanding investigations of Nixon. With the caution that none of these areas might lead to actual charges, Ruth produced a memo with ten subjects. They included:

- Tax deductions relating to the gift of papers to the National Archives.
- Transfer of the national security wiretap records from the FBI to the White House.
- Misuse of IRS through attempted initiation of audits of Nixon's "enemies."
- Other misuse of IRS information.
- Filing of a challenge to the *Washington Post*'s ownership of two Florida television stations.

- The handling of campaign contributions by Bebe Rebozo for Nixon's personal benefit.
- Ordering the wiretapping of telephone of John Sears, a White House aide.
- Bribery from the dairy industry over price supports.
- Ordering false testimony at confirmation hearing of Attorney General Richard Kleindienst.
- Obstruction of justice in connection with the break-in to the office of Daniel Ellsberg's psychiatrist.

To an outside observer, this long list of pending investigations might well represent a good argument *against* a pardon. Surely someone who was possibly implicated in so many crimes did not deserve a pardon. But in the strange calculus of Ford and Jaworski at that moment, the long list made a pardon more likely, because Ford believed the continuation of all these investigations would pose a distraction for the country and interfere with his own agenda. Likewise, Jaworski knew that more investigations meant more pressure from his staff to indict Nixon. A pardon solved both Ford's and Jaworski's problems.

Jaworski responded to Buchen's second request in a letter. "You have inquired as to my opinion regarding the length of the delay that would follow, in the event of the indictment of former President Richard M. Nixon, before a trial could reasonably be had by a fair and impartial jury as guaranteed by the Constitution," he wrote.[5] Answering that question, Jaworski told Buchen that a trial of an ex-president would be "unprecedented" and that the delay in seating a fair jury would be "a period of nine months to a year, and perhaps longer." On the morning of Wednesday, September 4, Jaworski had Ruth's memo and his own letter hand-delivered to Buchen at the White House.

The two communications were exactly what Buchen (and Ford) needed: proof that, given the range of subject areas, the continuing investigations of Nixon would be nearly endless and that an actual trial of Nixon would likely stretch into 1976. The implicit message of both was that a pardon of Nixon would spare the country, not just the former president, a long ordeal.

———

Meanwhile, Jack Miller, Nixon's lawyer, and his associates were producing their own brief arguing to Jaworski that he shouldn't indict the former president. Miller's argument matched up well with what Jaworski had already said and what Buchen wanted to hear. "The purpose of this memorandum is solely to demonstrate that one—and probably the most crucial—legal prerequisite to indicting and prosecuting Mr. Nixon does not exist: the ability of this government to assure him a fair trial."[6] The seventeen-page memo relied heavily on the Supreme Court's decision in 1966 to overturn the conviction of Sam Sheppard, a Cleveland osteopath who was tried for murdering his wife in a highly publicized case. "The Sheppard murder was sensational news and the media reacted accordingly. In the course they destroyed the state's ability to afford Sheppard a fair trial," Miller wrote. "The sensation of Watergate is a hundredfold that of the Sheppard murder." Miller concluded, "In short, no delay in trial, no change of venue, and no screening of prospective jurors could assure that the passions aroused by Watergate, the impeachment proceedings, and the President's resignation would dissipate to the point where Mr. Nixon could receive the fair trial to which he is entitled."

From the perspective of a half-century after Nixon's resignation, the most striking thing about the arguments by Nixon, Jaworski, and Ford, as well as their representatives, is what they *didn't* say. Some of the finest lawyers in the country came up with every argument they could think of for why Richard Nixon should not be prosecuted after he left office. And it seems not even to have occurred to any of them that the Constitution gave Nixon, as an ex-president, any kind of immunity from prosecution. But that is what the Supreme Court held in July 2024 in the case of former President Donald Trump.

If that Supreme Court ruling had been in effect in 1974, Richard Nixon would not have needed a pardon. His conduct in supervising the Watergate cover-up would likely not only have been off-limits for prosecution. It would have been unlawful even for federal prosecutors to investigate it in the first place.

Philip Buchen (with cane), Alexander Haig, and Benton Becker
discuss the pardon with Ford in the Oval Office on September 5, 1974.
DAVID HUME KENNERLY/CENTER FOR CREATIVE PHOTOGRAPHY/
U OF ARIZONA

CHAPTER 20

From Nixon to Trump

THE INVESTIGATION OF RICHARD NIXON HAD CLEAR PAR-
allels and major contrasts to the prosecution of Donald Trump, which
began in 2023. There were similarities between the underlying conduct of both presidents; however, the response of the legal system,
especially the Supreme Court, was very different.

Both Nixon and Trump were subjects of investigations of possible
criminal conduct committed while they were in office. (Both also
considered pardoning key witnesses against them as a way of containing the scandals.) Both were beneficiaries of the Justice Department policy against indictments of sitting presidents. But their status
changed after each left the presidency, Nixon on August 9, 1974, and
Trump on January 20, 2021. At that point, each man was fair game
for prosecutors, or so it appeared. That was why Nixon hired Jack
Miller and why Miller worked so hard to forestall an indictment of
Nixon and secure a pardon for him.

Trump, on the other hand, was indicted for his conduct in office
during his first term. On August 1, 2023, in federal district court in
Washington, Trump was charged in connection with his efforts, as
president, to overturn the results of the 2020 election.[1] The indictment
alleged that after losing to Joe Biden, Trump conspired to change the
true outcome by spreading false claims of election fraud to obstruct
the collecting, counting, and certifying of the election results. At the
heart of the case was the claim that Trump and his co-conspirators
organized fraudulent slates of electoral votes which were to be substi-

tuted for the legitimate slates when Congress met to certify the results on January 6, 2021. The case had clear echoes of Watergate. Trump used his authority and persuasive powers as president to pressure Congress to do what the law forbade—declare him the winner of an election that he lost. Nixon also used his power and influence to do what the law forbade—prevent a legitimate investigation of the Watergate break-in. In a broader sense, though, viewed through the prism of democratic values, Trump's alleged conduct was worse than Nixon's. Nixon obstructed justice to preserve the support of voters who probably would have voted for him anyway; Trump broke the law to win an election where the voters had already rejected him.

Trump's lawyers argued what the Nixon lawyers did not: that the Constitution provided Trump with immunity from being prosecuted for crimes committed while he was president. On December 1, 2023, District Judge Tanya Chutkan rejected that claim and set a trial date for March 4, 2024. After Trump appealed her ruling to the Court of Appeals for the D.C. Circuit, Jack Smith, the Justice Department prosecutor, asked the Supreme Court to do what the justices did in *United States v. Nixon*—skip the review by the Court of Appeals and hear the case directly, so that Trump's trial could proceed in a timely manner. Unlike in *Nixon*, the Supreme Court declined to expedite the Trump case. The appeals court affirmed Judge Chutkan's ruling against Trump, and then the Supreme Court agreed to review that decision in the normal, unexpedited way; several months passed before the justices delivered their opinion on July 1, 2024, the last day of the term. In this way, Trump won even before the justices reached the merits of his case. By delaying the resolution of the case for months, the Supreme Court made sure that Trump would not face trial until after the November 2024 election, if ever.

Trump won on the merits as well, as the Supreme Court voted 6 to 3 to overturn the judgment of the Court of Appeals. In his opinion for the Court, Chief Justice John Roberts gave Trump a degree of deference that was inconceivable for Nixon. In *United States v. Nixon*, Chief Justice Warren Burger for a unanimous court ordered Nixon to produce certain White House tapes in response to a trial subpoena because "when the ground for asserting privilege as to subpoenaed materials sought for use in a criminal trial is based only on the generalized interest in confidentiality, it cannot prevail over the fundamental demands of due process of law in the fair administration of criminal justice." Roberts's opinion in *Trump v. United States* struck a very different balance. In broad terms, Roberts held that a former president enjoys immunity for "official" actions in office and can only be prosecuted for "unofficial" conduct. No such distinction occurred to anyone in 1974. In those days, everyone assumed that former presidents were not above the law—period. Even in the argument of the Trump case in 2024, the contrast to the Nixon case was obvious. Justice Ketanji Brown Jackson asked Trump's lawyer, "So what was up with the pardon for President Nixon? I mean, if everybody thought that presidents couldn't be prosecuted, then what was that about?" (There wasn't an answer.) In any event, the legal issues in the federal Trump prosecutions became moot when Smith dismissed the cases after Trump won the 2024 election.

In theory, the Supreme Court's opinion in *Trump v. United States* allowed for the possibility of some prosecutions of former presidents, but under the standards laid down by Roberts, it was clear that Nixon could not have been prosecuted for the Watergate cover-up. As we've seen, the strongest evidence that Nixon obstructed justice in the Watergate investigation was the so-called smoking gun tape of June 23, 1972. In that conversation, Nixon approved a plan for Haldeman, his chief of staff, to instruct the CIA to tell the FBI to curtail its investigation of the Watergate break-in on spurious national security grounds. Under *Trump v. United States*, Nixon's statement would not amount to obstruction of justice because it related to the president's "official" duties—that is, supervising the FBI and CIA. "Investigative and prosecutorial decision-making is 'the special province of the Executive Branch,'" Roberts wrote, "and the Constitution vests the entirety of the executive power in the President." Accordingly, "the President cannot be prosecuted for conduct within his exclusive constitutional authority."

Under Roberts's reasoning, the tape of the smoking gun conversation was off-limits even as evidence, as well as a crime itself, because Nixon and Haldeman were discussing official conduct. "What the prosecutor may not do, however," Roberts wrote, "is admit tes-

timony or private records of the President or his advisers probing
the official act itself. Allowing that sort of evidence would invite the
jury to inspect the President's motivations for his official actions and
to second-guess their propriety." This rule would have put most of
the White House tapes off-limits to the Watergate prosecutors, because their whole purpose in examining the tapes was to use them
"to inspect the President's motivations for his official actions and to
second-guess their propriety."

Roberts's opinion turned the lessons of Watergate on their head.
He defined "official" actions so broadly, and "unofficial" ones so nar-
rowly, that it was difficult to imagine that any prosecution of a former president for crimes in office could ever be successfully brought to
trial. More striking still, Roberts's "official" vs. "unofficial" distinction
cut exactly the wrong way. A president's unofficial actions pose modest risks for the nation and world. But because all presidents possess
extraordinary official powers, they are at their most dangerous when
they use them for criminal ends. As Justice Sonia Sotomayor observed
in her dissenting opinion, the majority appeared to offer immunity to
a president who "orders the Navy's Seal Team 6 to assassinate a political rival." In 1974, what made the smoking gun tape so incriminating
against Nixon was that he was abusing his official authority over the
CIA and FBI. Only a president can tell the nation's intelligence and law
enforcement agencies what to do, so only he could use them, as Nixon
did, for corrupt ends. And at that time, everyone understood that
Nixon might face criminal charges for doing so—and that was why, if
he was going to avoid that fate, he needed a pardon from his successor.

When Ford returned from Camp David after Labor Day weekend,
the decision to pardon Nixon looked settled. Becker had sold him
on the importance of the *Burdick* case. As Becker described it, *Burdick* meant that anyone who accepted a pardon acknowledged guilt.
Ford thought that interpretation would limit negative political fallout
from the pardon. In other words, Becker and Ford agreed that the
right way to see a pardon for Nixon was not just as a gift to the former president, but rather a trade of mercy for a confession of guilt. By

this point Ford was not interested in hearing debate on the subject—not that he ever heard a true contrary voice—but rather the subject turned to the mechanics of the pardon process. How should the pardon be delivered, and when?

Through all these discussions of the pardon and papers, Ford and his team had not yet heard directly from one person: Richard Nixon himself. At that point, just after Labor Day, Jack Miller had had only the briefest of conversations with Nixon. In his meetings with Buchen and Becker on September 3, Miller had made representations about the kind of deal that he thought Nixon would accept. But the lawyer couldn't be sure. Miller believed that they needed to get Nixon's approval in person. He asked Buchen if he wanted to go with him to San Clemente to meet with Nixon. Hobbled by the effects of polio, Buchen didn't travel well and begged off a quick trip across the country. Buchen said he (and Ford) would authorize Benton Becker to represent the president with Nixon. Becker said he'd be willing to make the trip to San Clemente, if Ford authorized it.

On the morning of Thursday, September 5, Ford again called together the members of his staff with whom he had discussed the plans for the pardon and the disposition of Nixon's papers and tapes. Buchen, Becker, and Haig gathered in the Oval Office, and they learned that Ford's plan to issue a pardon was no longer tentative or contingent. The president was restless, eager to get the Nixon problem off his plate.

"I want to make the announcement right away," Ford said, "How about tomorrow morning?"—that is, on Friday, September 6.

Buchen demurred, saying that his staff couldn't even produce the appropriate paperwork in time for a pardon the next morning. Besides, there were still a lot of loose ends, especially about the tapes and documents and Nixon's statement of contrition. Ford thought that the deal which Buchen and Miller had discussed at the Jefferson was too generous to Nixon. Ford didn't want Nixon to have enduring control over the papers and tapes. He repeated his view that the papers and tapes belonged to the American people. In that regard, though, and with some amusement, Ford mentioned a problem with possible future public access to the tapes: Henry Kissinger.

"Gentlemen, let me tell you," Ford said. "The other day Henry was in here, and we were talking about the tapes, and Henry told me that there were many times when he would meet with Nixon in the Oval Office, and the news of the day would be distressing to him. And he would issue a bizarre or wild instruction to Henry. Henry recalled, for example, an Algerian hijacking, and Nixon saying something like, 'Cut off all aid to Algeria and every country that touches it, and damn it, I want to send ships and boats in there. Do you hear me, Henry? I'm serious.' And Henry would respond, 'Yes, Mr. President.'" Kissinger would then ignore Nixon's outburst. But Ford told the group, "The 'Yes, Mr. President' would be on the tapes, and Kissinger was potentially embarrassed about that."

Considering Kissinger's concerns, Ford thought he would agree to greater limits on public disclosure of the tapes, but the president waved off any objections on the papers. He wanted the papers out of Nixon's hands, the pardon delivered, and the whole subject concluded. "I don't want any more horsing around," Ford said.[2]

Ford approved Becker as his emissary and reluctantly agreed to wait to issue the pardon until Becker and Miller had met with Nixon in San Clemente. But Ford wanted Becker to go straight from the White House to a flight to California on that Thursday. The president wanted the pardon done. "I will not wait one day later than Sunday to announce the pardon," Ford told his aides.

At the same time, Ford said that he was not going to agree to Nixon's terms on the papers. "I will never, ever give up those records. They belong to the American people. Be very firm out there." This was a baffling, contradictory instruction to Becker. Because Ford told Becker that he was definitely going to grant the pardon in seventy-two hours or less, he gave Becker no leverage to negotiate a "firm" deal on the papers or on Nixon's acknowledgment of wrongdoing.

As the meeting was breaking up, Ford put his arm around Becker and said, "I want you to be my eyes and ears." He wanted to know how Nixon looked, how his mental and physical health were holding up. "Tell me what you see," Ford said.

Haig, ever resourceful at mobilizing the government, scrambled a military jet from the president's fleet and told Becker it would be waiting for him at Andrews Air Force Base. Becker went home to grab a bag, but he didn't even tell his wife where he was going. Miller met him at the plane.

The aircraft was a twelve-seater, but Becker and Miller were the only passengers. As soon as the two men were settled in, the plane headed down the runway and into the sky, which had just turned dark on Thursday night.

Once the plane leveled off, the pilot emerged from the cockpit. "Mr. Becker, we are airborne," he said. "You are the commander of this flight."

Becker later recalled that he looked at the pilot "like he was crazy." Then Becker asked: "Has anyone even told you where we are going?"

CHAPTER 21

Showdown at Casa Pacifica

BECKER RECOGNIZED THE ODDITY OF HIS SITUATION. HE
was thirty-six years old, a former mid-level federal prosecutor who
was trying to establish his first private law practice. He was currently under investigation for criminal tax fraud for allegedly taking
kickbacks from one of his first clients. Becker was also flying across
the country on a secret assignment from the president of the United
States to negotiate with the previous president of the United States.
He was traveling on a military jet—as its "commander," no less.

Becker and Miller, Nixon's lawyer, worked on the plane. Becker
showed him the draft pardon that Buchen had prepared. There was
also a draft of an agreement on the papers and tapes, based on what
had been discussed at the Jefferson on the previous Tuesday. Becker
had also brought with him a copy of his treasured 1915 *Burdick* case
from the Supreme Court. (He left a copy of the full text of the case
with Ford in the Oval Office as well.) Though Ford wanted the issues
wrapped up quickly, Becker and Miller recognized that there was a
considerable agenda to cover with Nixon. There was the pardon; the
issues with the papers and tapes; and Nixon's statement of contrition
to go along with the pardon.

The plane landed a little after 11 p.m. local time at Marine Corps
Air Station El Toro, near Irvine, California. A waiting government
limousine took the two lawyers to Nixon's compound, about a half-
hour away. At around midnight, or 3 a.m. for the Washingtonians,
the pair was greeted by Ron Ziegler, Nixon's press secretary and cur-

rent gatekeeper, who, incongruously, was dressed as if he had just come from the beach. Miller spoke to Ziegler before the flight, and they agreed that this first meeting would simply be to set the schedule for conversations on Friday. But when Ziegler escorted the pair into his office in one of the outbuildings that the government had built for the Western White House, he took a different tack.

"Mr. Becker," Ziegler began, puffing on the first of a chain of cigarettes, "let's get one thing straight immediately. President Nixon is not issuing any statement whatsoever regarding Watergate, whether Jerry Ford pardons him or not." Taken aback, Becker noticed that Ziegler's demeanor, down to his hand gestures, seemed modeled on Nixon's. Becker noticed, too, that Ziegler used the honorific "President" for Nixon, while referring to his successor by his first name.

"Mr. Ziegler, you have the advantage on me," Becker replied. "I have never been to San Clemente before, and I have never before flown alone on a government aircraft, so I'm a bit confused. I don't know how to reach the pilot who flew me out here or the driver who dropped me off here. Can I use your phone so that I can reach those gentlemen, because I'm going home?"

Miller took the lead in shutting down the macho posturing and shifted the conversation to the next day's schedule. Ziegler said it would be fine to talk about the pardon at that point as well as the timing of the "return" of Nixon's presidential material. Becker said that was a nonstarter. There would be no "return" of the papers to Nixon. Becker said the documents and tapes were subject to subpoenas from various investigative bodies. Becker didn't have the legal right to turn them over to Nixon, even if he (and Ford) were so inclined, which they weren't. (Ziegler seemed unaware of the complexities of the documents issues.) Becker said that if Ziegler wanted to draft a statement to go along with the pardon, Becker would be happy to look at it. By 2 a.m. they had reached agreement on the schedule and agenda, if nothing else. They would talk again in the morning at nine, and the first subject would be the papers and tapes.

Becker and Miller were trundled off to the San Clemente Inn, whose lobby was still a shrine to the Nixon family. The two men decompressed with a couple of beers, and then Becker asked for a

5:30 a.m. wake-up call on Friday morning, so he could report back to Buchen at 8:30 a.m. Washington time.

––––––––––

For Becker, the morning brought two surprises. First, in their phone call, Buchen told Becker that Ford wanted to announce the pardon the following day, Saturday, September 7. Becker begged Buchen to put it off at least one more day. Ziegler had agreed to nothing. They hadn't even met with Nixon yet. The issues relating to the papers and Nixon's statement of contrition were entirely unsettled. Buchen reluctantly agreed, but said Ford would not wait longer than Sunday. In deference to the shortened schedule, Buchen said Becker could basically give up the fight on Nixon's statement of contrition. It would be good to get some kind of statement from the former president, but the pardon was going to happen anyway. The phone call from the hotel to the White House cost $11.40 (about $80 in 2024 dollars), and Becker was never reimbursed for the call or his room at the Inn.

The second surprise came at breakfast with Miller. David Kraslow, a reporter with Cox newspapers, approached the table where Miller and Becker were eating and asked why they were there. (Miller suspected that the desk clerk had tipped the reporter.)[1] The pair didn't reveal anything, but they figured that the confidentiality of their visit, which was so important to Ford, was going to be short-lived. It added to their urgency to get something, or anything, done before their cover was blown.

When the pair rejoined Ziegler at Casa Pacifica, there was another surprise of sorts, though it was something that Becker had expected all along. Ziegler noted that he was in moment-to-moment touch with Haig, who was still ensconced at the White House, nominally a member of Ford's staff. But Becker believed that Haig was scheming with Ziegler (and Nixon), telling them about Ford's demands, thus undercutting Becker's position in the negotiation.

When Becker and Miller joined Ziegler on Friday morning, they began discussing the agreement on the papers and tapes. They came up with a convoluted compromise, which was based on the one Miller put forward at the Jefferson. The agreement stated that the papers and tapes belonged to Nixon and that they would be deposited "temporarily" in a facility near San Clemente. But Nixon agreed that he would eventually "donate" the papers to the government. In the meantime, access would be controlled with two keys, one belonging to Nixon and one with the General Services Administration.

The process at Casa Pacifica was arduous, as Ziegler would excuse himself every few moments to check with Nixon, saying, "Let's see how he feels about this." On each occasion, Becker would do the same with Buchen by phone.

Further, according to their agreement, the White House tapes would be treated differently from the papers. The tapes would be designated as Nixon's property, but they would be "on deposit" with the government for five years. Prosecutors would have access to the tapes during that period. After five years, Nixon would have complete control of the tapes and could destroy them. In any event, the agreement called for the tapes to be destroyed at the time of Nixon's death or on September 1, 1984, whichever came first. By noon local time, there was an agreement on the papers and tapes, and they moved on to the pardon and Nixon's statement.[2] In the meantime, Kraslow reached out to Jerry terHorst, Ford's press secretary, and asked why Becker and Miller were in San Clemente. TerHorst checked with Buchen, who said they were meeting to discuss the fate of Nixon's papers, but Buchen said nothing to the press secretary about a pardon. So ter-Horst told Kraslow that the meeting only involved Nixon's papers, not a pardon. Over the next day or so, terHorst told the same thing— that there was no discussion of a pardon in San Clemente—to other reporters as well.

But that wasn't true. There was a lot of pardon talk in San Clemente. In later years, in books and interviews, Nixon claimed that he was reluctant to accept a pardon because he knew it came with an implicit acknowledgment of guilt—and, he insisted, he wasn't guilty of anything.[3] And Miller later recounted that when he urged Nixon to take a pardon, Nixon expressed some reluctance. There is reason to believe, however, that Nixon's supposed ambivalence about a pardon, especially after he received one, was a performance. When Nixon was still president and facing the real prospect of indictment, he made

clear to Buzhardt that he wanted a pardon. For all his professed uncertainty, he accepted the pardon once it was offered to him. When
Nixon had the pardon in hand and it extinguished the possibility
of criminal charges against him, he could safely boast that he never
wanted one in the first place because he did nothing wrong.

By Friday afternoon in San Clemente, Ziegler had relaxed somewhat. He noticed that Becker had used paper clips to hold together
the French cuffs on his shirt because he had forgotten cuff links. "You
must have a hard time making a living in Washington if you can't
afford cuff links," Nixon's press secretary said. Ziegler then removed
the cuff links he was wearing, which were embossed with Nixon's
presidential seal, and gave them to Becker. Ziegler also volunteered
that he had worked with a speechwriter and produced a statement by
Nixon to go with the pardon. He didn't let the two men see the draft,
but he read it out loud to Becker and Miller.

As Becker remembered, "The statement spoke of the pressures
of the office of the presidency and the necessity for reliance upon
the judgment and honesty of staff and the President's preoccupation
with the nation's international posture. It concluded by acknowledg-
ing that Nixon should have placed less reliance, and delegated less
authority, to staff members."

"What do you think?" Ziegler asked.

The pressure of time was getting to Becker. The afternoon was
slipping away, and it was already going to be nearly impossible to get
back to Washington on Friday night. If Becker was going to talk to
Ford on Saturday morning—with the pardon to come on Sunday—he
would have to leave San Clemente soon. Becker told Ziegler the truth.
The pardon was going to happen regardless of what Nixon said in a
statement. But Becker added that he thought no statement was better
than the one Ziegler suggested. He reminded Ziegler that the House
Judiciary Committee, in bipartisan fashion, approved impeachment
resolutions that pointed to specific misconduct by Nixon. At this late
date, it was pointless, even insulting, to suggest that the problem in
Watergate was just Nixon's failure to supervise his staff. Relaxing a
little, and punchy with exhaustion, Becker said the statement was a
"Ziegler-ism," just a protestation of innocence.

Ziegler went back to Nixon and the speechwriters. Tunafish sandwiches were delivered to Becker and Miller. The process continued through four drafts. By the end, Ziegler was asking Becker to provide his own editing contributions, which he declined to do. Preoccupied as always with the *Burdick* case, Becker insisted only that the statement include the word that Nixon "accepted" the pardon, because that, in Becker's view, would count as his acknowledgment of guilt. Ziegler made sure the former president used the word. In the other key passage of the final version of the statement, Nixon said, "one thing I can see clearly now is that I was wrong in not acting more decisively and more forthrightly in dealing with Watergate, particularly when it reached the state of judicial proceedings." In Becker's mind, Nixon's acceptance of the pardon, plus his acknowledgment that he had not acted "forthrightly," amounted to a confession to obstruction of justice.

It was now about 3 p.m. on Friday, and Becker really did have to get going. But there was still a piece of unfinished business at Casa Pacifica. Becker had to seal the deal with Nixon himself.

———

Back in Washington, Ford's honeymoon was still in full swing. On the day that Becker left for California, terHorst invited a photographer to document how the new president toasted his own English muffins for breakfast. On Friday, Ford met with his old friend Don Rumsfeld, the former congressman who at that moment was still ambassador to NATO. The "spokes of the wheel" organization for Ford's White House was already failing, as the president's advisers competed for his attention. Ford was arranging for Rumsfeld to take over as chief of staff. Later in the day, along with the first lady, Ford met with the leaders of major women's organizations, which was the kind of outreach that Nixon rarely did. On Friday night, Ford flew to Philadelphia for a celebration of the two-hundredth anniversary of the First Continental Congress. It would be the first of many events where Ford would mark the nation's Bicentennial during the rest of his term.

Ford was aware that Becker was in San Clemente and that negotiations were ongoing, but the president was serene at that point with his decision to grant the pardon. He had decided that was going to happen on Sunday, September 8, regardless of what Becker was able to achieve in California. He assigned Hartmann to draft the speech that would accompany the pardon. All through Friday, Becker was reporting by phone to Buchen, and on one of his last calls in the late afternoon, he learned that Buchen was in the Oval Office with Ford.

By that point, Becker, Miller, and Ziegler had reached agreement on the wording of the statement about the papers and tapes. Becker and Ziegler had concluded their talks about Nixon's statement to accompany the pardon. But Becker knew—and Ford knew—that Becker had not completed his assignment. He had not yet met with Nixon in person. Ford wanted Becker to size him up.

Through most of the day, as Becker now reported to Ford, Ziegler had refused to let Becker meet Nixon. The former president remained an Oz-like figure to whom Ziegler was making frequent pilgrimages.

Ford told Becker to keep pushing. The current president needed to know how the former president looked. Becker insisted again. Ziegler relented. Becker would be allowed to see Nixon in the flesh.

CHAPTER 22

The Last Cuff Links

"MR. PRESIDENT," RON ZIEGLER SAID, "THIS IS BENTON Becker."

Becker was shocked. The man in the suit in front of him did not look like Richard Nixon. He looked like Richard Nixon's father. The former president was just sixty-one years old, but Becker thought he looked eighty-five. His head seemed huge, disproportionate to his body, and the famous jowls hung low from his face. His face had deep wrinkles, and his hair was disheveled. His fingernails were yellowed, not because Nixon was a smoker—which he wasn't—but as a symptom of general decline. Nixon rose uneasily to the side of his desk and offered a weak handshake to his visitor and then sat back down with a thud.

The office in the compound's outbuilding was tiny and nearly bare of decoration. There was an American flag behind the desk, but almost nothing on the walls and shelves. It seemed like Nixon had just moved in. When the two men faced each other, there was a painful silence, until Nixon broke it.

"So, Mr. Becker, did you serve as a lawyer in my Administration?"

"No, sir."

"You're from Washington?"

"Yes, sir."

"How do you think the Redskins will do this year?"

Becker thought of something to say and tried to turn the conversation toward the purpose of his visit, but it wasn't easy. Nixon had trouble focusing. He didn't want to discuss anything of substance.

Sometimes his attention flagged. Miller and Ziegler, who were in the room at the beginning of the conversation, stepped out. It was just Nixon and Becker.

Becker placed the agreement about the papers and tapes on the desk between them and sought to go through it section by section. "I think you can be very proud of what we've done today for you and for the nation about your papers," Becker said. "President Ford certainly doesn't want to stop you from writing your memoirs. You will always be able to get copies to work with." With lawyerly precision, Becker was sure to say that Nixon could always look at "copies," not originals. Still, Becker believed Nixon wasn't really following what he was saying. He was so tired and weak. He barely responded as Becker went through the terms of the agreement.

After about thirty minutes on the papers, Becker changed the subject. "I'm sure Mr. Miller and Mr. Ziegler have told you that President Ford is considering a pardon, and I know they've shown you this document which, if the pardon is granted, will take this form," Becker said, producing Buchen's draft of the pardon itself. "And I've seen the statement that you plan to issue if the pardon is granted. I think that's a fine statement," Becker went on.

"There are certain things you should know about pardons that I should satisfy myself that you do know. Of course, you should know President Ford's view of pardons," Becker said. He went on to explain that he had done a lot of legal research on pardons, and he and President Ford had satisfied themselves that a pardon could be granted before any charges were filed, and that's what the president was going to do. Becker turned to the *Burdick* case. "The thing with pardons is that you can accept it or reject it. It's different from a commutation. When you were President and you commuted someone's sentence, they had to leave prison. They had no choice. But there's a choice with pardons. The leading case on the subject was when Wilson was President," Becker said.

It was almost like Becker was talking to himself. As Becker went through the implications of the *Burdick* case, Nixon was hearing but not really listening. But this part of the conversation was very important to Becker, because he wanted Nixon to understand the consequences of accepting the pardon. "You see," Becker said, "our view of the law is that acceptance of a pardon is an acknowledgement of guilt." Nixon nodded, but Becker couldn't be sure that he really understood the concept. But it was important to Becker (and presumably to Ford) that Nixon at least heard the words about *Burdick*. (To reinforce the importance of the *Burdick* case, Becker left a copy of it with Miller.)

The meeting wrapped up after forty-five minutes, and Becker packed up his briefcase and prepared to get into a car that Ziegler had summoned. He had almost gotten inside and left the compound when Ziegler came running up to him. "Mr. Becker! Mr. Becker!" Ziegler called after him, "The President wants to see you again." Becker had a brief kick of despair. "Oh, shit," he thought. "Everything's off." Nixon was going back on the deal. The trip was a waste of time. But the lawyer trudged back to Nixon's office.

Nixon was standing behind his office chair. "You've been a fine young man," Nixon said. "You've been so fair and thoughtful. You've been a gentleman. We've had enough bullies." Becker thought Nixon was on the verge of tears.

"I want to give you something," Nixon continued. "Look around this office. I don't have anything anymore. They took it all away from me. Everything I've had is gone. I tried to get you a Presidential tie pin and cuff links with my name on it, but I don't even have those anymore."

Becker said a gift wasn't necessary.

"There's nothing left from my presidency," Nixon said. Then he continued, "I asked Pat to get these—from my personal jewelry box."

Nixon handed Becker two little boxes—a tie pin and cuff links. "There aren't any more of these in the world," Nixon said. "You got the last ones." (The cuff links were identical to the ones Ziegler had given Becker earlier in the day.)

Becker thanked Nixon and headed with Miller to the military jet. Becker arrived home around 5 a.m. on Saturday morning, September 7.

Becker made it to the White House around 7 a.m., so he could speak to Ford before the president's golf game at Burning Tree. "I am not a doctor," Becker said, "but I have serious questions in my mind about whether President Nixon is going to be alive at the time of the election."

Ford said that the 1976 election was pretty far away.

"I don't mean '76," Becker said. "I mean '74."

In his memoir, Ford later wrote that the conversation with Becker had sealed his decision to pardon Nixon the next day, but his reasoning had contradictions. Ford said the seemingly dire state of Nixon's health was irrelevant to his decision to proceed. "I wanted it understood that my fundamental decision to grant a pardon had nothing to do with any sympathy I might feel for Nixon personally or any concern I might have had for the state of his health."[1] Rather, he went on, "Although I respected the tenet that no man should be above the law, public policy demanded that I put Nixon—and Watergate—behind us as quickly as possible." But he also said that sympathy for Nixon did play a part: "Being forced to resign the Presidency and live with that humiliation for the rest of his life was a severe punishment in itself, the equivalent to serving a jail term." Nor would a pardon deprive the American people of meaningful new information about Watergate. Then, as later, Ford asserted that the pardon fundamentally wasn't for the benefit of Nixon, but rather the country as a whole: "All the bad feelings that people had about Watergate and the cover-up would have boiled over again and the healing process would have been destroyed."

It was a busy Saturday for the president. Golf at Burning Tree was the first round of a two-day tournament, which Ford played with Melvin Laird, an old friend and former congressional colleague who had been Nixon's secretary of defense. (Ford didn't mention to Laird his plans for the pardon.) After golf, Ford met with a delegation of astronauts and cosmonauts who were planning to participate in the first joint space mission between the United States and the Soviet Union. In this early stage of his presidency, Ford was still closely aligned with Kissinger's (and Nixon's) policy of détente with the Soviets, and Ford wanted to promote this kind of cooperation. (Once

Ronald Reagan challenged Ford from the right for the Republican nomination in 1976, Ford responded with a harder line against the other superpower.)

Ford was in such a jolly mood that he decided to bring his Soviet guests, the cosmonauts and Anatoly Dobrynin, the longtime ambassador of the USSR to the United States, to a community event with his former neighbors in Alexandria, Virginia. It was the police department's annual picnic, and Ford wanted to show the visitors a classic American celebration.[2] There were hot dogs and hard-shell crabs, and the president demonstrated how to use a hammer to get at the meat. "A very great American delicacy," Ford promised.

In a short speech to the 250 people gathered in the heat, Ford promised that he and Betty were not going to sell their house in town, even though they now lived across the Potomac. And he welcomed his own guests. "The broader we can make our relationship," Ford said, "the better it is for us in America and for our friends in the Soviet Union."

————

Notwithstanding Ford's good spirits, the mood back at the White House was tense. Becker had checked in with Ziegler to make sure everything was ready to go. He said Nixon wanted to make some changes in his statement accepting the pardon. Nixon wanted all the references to "I" changed to "The White House." In other words, the sentence that began "I was wrong in not acting more decisively and more forthrightly . . ." would instead begin "The White House was wrong . . ." Becker said those changes would blow up the whole deal—a position he confirmed with the president after his golf game. Ford thought Nixon's statement was weak as it was, and he certainly was not going to tolerate the former president trying to minimize his conduct further. Ziegler and Nixon backed down, and the statement remained as it was. But the exchange underscored the precariousness of the situation.

Late on Saturday afternoon, Ford gathered his pardon team—Becker, Hartmann, Marsh, Buchen, and Haig—to make sure things were in order, and this time he added a new member, Jerry terHorst, his press secretary. In part, the decision to include terHorst was a simple matter of logistics. Ford needed him to set up the television broadcast for the next day and to summon reporters to the White House on a summer Sunday. Also, in this pre-digital age, it took some time to finalize documents and prepare copies for the press.

Until that meeting, terHorst had no idea that a pardon was coming. Ford had intentionally kept terHorst in the dark about the plan. Later, Ford said that he did so to protect terHorst—so that he wouldn't have to keep that knowledge from reporters. In fact, it had the opposite effect. The exclusion of the press secretary from the deliberations about the pardon, from even knowing that those discussions were taking place, put terHorst in a worse position, not a better one. Ter-Horst continued to tell reporters that no pardon was in the works, which was false. Moreover, Buchen had actively lied to terHorst about the meeting in San Clemente by saying that it wasn't about a pardon, and terHorst had passed along that falsehood to reporters. Ford and terHorst had known each other for many years, but as subject and reporter, not as principal and staffer. TerHorst still thought of himself as a truth-teller, even in this different position, and he was horrified both that he had been deceived and he, in turn, had deceived others. Worse yet, terHorst thought what Ford was doing was wrong on the merits. He believed what Ford had said back in his confirmation hearings for vice president—that the country wouldn't stand for a pardon.

After returning home from the White House, terHorst was up all Saturday night. He was furious, out of both pique and principle. He was a career journalist, new to government, but he knew what it meant to be a press secretary. How, he asked himself, was he supposed to do his job if the president didn't trust him enough to tell him when he was considering a tough decision? And what about the pardon itself? How was he supposed to defend it when he thought it was wrong?

So terHorst did what came naturally to a newspaper man. He started writing: "Without doubt this is the most difficult decision I ever have had to make . . ." After expressing his gratitude for being hired as White House press secretary, he went on:

As your spokesman, I do not know how I could credibly defend that action in the absence of a like decision to grant absolute pardon to the young men who evaded Vietnam military service as a matter of conscience and the absence of pardons for former aides and associates of Mr. Nixon who have been charged with crimes—and imprisoned—stemming from the same Watergate situation.

These are also men whose reputations and families have been grievously injured. Try as I can, it is impossible to conclude that the former president is more deserving of mercy than persons of lesser station in life whose offenses have had far less effect on our national wellbeing.

Thus it is with a heavy heart that I hereby tender my resignation as Press Secretary to the President, effective today. My prayers nonetheless remain with you, sir.

CHAPTER 23

"We Have All Played a Part"

FORD WAS A CHURCHGOING EPISCOPALIAN, BUT HE wasn't especially spiritual. He didn't believe in signs and portents, and once he made a decision, he didn't agonize about it. But if Ford had had a different turn of mind, if he were the kind to pay attention to cosmic messages from the universe, he might have seen trouble ahead on Sunday, September 8, 1974. It was one month since Nixon resigned, a time for taking stock, for completing one chapter and starting another. Ford's second month as president would be very different from his first.

That first month could scarcely have gone better. It wasn't that Ford had a lot of accomplishments to point to in such a short time, but he himself was the accomplishment. He appeared to be everything that Richard Nixon was not; he was open and honest and . . . normal. He didn't lie or scheme. His own approval rating remained over 70 percent, and a poll that dropped on this very day showed Ford beating Ted Kennedy, seen as the most likely Democrat, by double-digits in a hypothetical 1976 presidential contest. The American people had come to know Gerald Ford—the person, even more than the politician—and he had made a very good first impression.

On that Sunday, Ford went to the 8 a.m. service at St. John's Episcopal, the "Church of the Presidents," on Lafayette Square, just steps away from the White House, where every president since James Madison had worshipped. When Ford returned to the Oval Office, he gathered his pardon team—Buchen, Hartmann, and Marsh, plus terHorst (in his final hours on the job)—and he went over his speech one more time. He made one final change in the text, which revealed the lack of clarity in Ford's own mind about what he was doing. One line in Hartmann's draft read: "it is common knowledge that serious allegations and accusations hang like a sword over our former President's head as he tries to reshape his life." Ford took a felt-tip pen and added the words ". . . over our former President's head *threatening his health* as he tries to reshape his life." But in private before the pardon and later in public, Ford said the pardon was for the benefit of the public, not of Nixon personally. Earlier, in planning the speech, Hartmann had discussed with Ford the issue of Nixon's health, and Ford had explicitly said he didn't want to use it as a justification for the pardon. And other than through Becker's impression of the former president, Ford knew nothing about Nixon's health. Now, Ford was throwing it in at the last minute. Hartmann made a small protest about the change but surrendered quickly, given the press of time.[1]

The clock was increasingly a factor. By the time the speech text was locked, it was about 9:40, and the speech was set for eleven. In the remaining time, Ford planned to make a series of courtesy calls to leading members of Congress. Ford was not reaching out to his former colleagues to ask for their advice or even to test their reaction. It was just a last-minute ritual for major presidential announcements. The calls were quick:

9:48 a.m. Senator Mike Mansfield, the majority leader.

9:51 a.m. Congressman Carl Albert, the Speaker of the House.

9:56 a.m. Senator Hugh Scott, the Republican leader in the Senate.

Without exception, the reaction was incredulity. *Really? Now? Why now?* There wasn't time for much conversation, but the gist of the reactions, from both Republicans and Democrats, was clear. Ford could have previewed these reactions, and perhaps even tried to change some minds, if he had reached out earlier to both political allies and adversaries. But he had chosen to confine his consultations about the pardon to his tiny inner circle, and these loyal aides had told him, for the most part, what he wanted to hear.

10:10 a.m. Congressman Tip O'Neill, the majority leader in the

House and Ford's close friend. O'Neill was baffled. "I'm telling you right now, this will cost you the election," he said. "I hope it's not part of any deal."

Ford said there was no deal.

"Then why the hell are you doing it?"

Ford said Nixon was "sick" and depressed.

"Look, I know you're not calling me for advice," O'Neill said, "but I think it's too soon."

10:14 a.m. Ford spoke to Attorney General William Saxbe.

10:22 a.m. Congressman John McFall.

At that point, Ford was hustled out of the Oval Office, into his private study, so technicians could bring in cameras and lights for the television address. It was too late to set up a live transmission, so the plan was to record the speech and broadcast it a few moments later.

10:27 a.m. Vice President–designate Nelson Rockefeller (who supported the pardon).

10:31 a.m. Senator Barry Goldwater, who was awakened by the call while on vacation in California. "What are you pardoning him of?" he asked Ford. "It doesn't make any sense." Ford said the public had a right to know that Nixon was "clear." Goldwater scoffed: "He may be clear in your eyes, but he's not clear in mine."[2]

At around 10:45 a.m., with just minutes to go before the speech, terHorst popped his head into the president's study, ripped open the envelope containing his resignation letter, and handed it to Ford, who read it quickly and got the gist. His press secretary was quitting in protest over the pardon. Considering the magnitude of this act, and the venomous timing of its delivery, Ford was gracious in response. He said he was sorry that terHorst felt that way. "I know there will be controversy over this, but it's the right thing to do, and that's why I decided to do it now," Ford said. "I hope you can see that."

"I'm sorry, Mr. President," terHorst said, and they shook hands.[3]

As word of terHorst's decision spread to the handful of people in the West Wing, a measure of panic set it. They knew that the resignation in protest of a top official would be nearly as big news as the pardon itself. And it would provide an echo of the principled resignation of Elliot Richardson as attorney general in the Saturday

Night Massacre, just ten months earlier. TerHorst's sudden departure would portray Ford-as-Nixon, just the opposite impression that had been cultivated in that first month.

John Marsh, the soft-spoken former congressman, who was now part of Ford's staff, practically begged terHorst to take back his resignation.

"Don't hurt the President this way—not today," Marsh said.

TerHorst said he would think it over. While Ford was delivering his speech, terHorst wrote a handwritten note to Ford declining to change his decision to resign, "despite Jack Marsh's intercession." As a purported gesture to Ford, terHorst said in his note that he would not release the text of his resignation letter. But that was actually worse for Ford, because it concentrated public attention on terHorst's decision to resign rather than his debatable reasons for doing so.[4]

In keeping with the shambolic process that morning, the technicians had trouble installing the equipment for the speech. It was not until 11:16 a.m. that Ford took his place in the Oval Office and began his address to the nation.

———

Ford sat at his presidential desk, in front of a window with the curtains pulled back, with the summer sun shining on the foliage beside the Rose Garden. The recording of Ford's speech was so rushed and haphazard that no videotape of his first sentence survives, but this is what he said: "I have come to a decision which I felt I should tell you and all of my fellow American citizens, as soon as I was certain in my own mind and in my own conscience that it is the right thing to do." Ford was trying to address an issue that his fellow politicians identified right away. Why was it necessary to pardon Nixon at this moment? Why now?

A moment later, Ford tried to explain: "To procrastinate, to agonize, and to wait for a more favorable turn of events that may never come or more compelling external pressures that may as well be wrong as right, is itself a decision of sorts and a weak and potentially dangerous course for a President to follow." This was the opposite of the course that leaders usually follow. It's often smarter to avoid precipitous decisions, especially in a situation like this one, that might have sorted itself out on its own.

That was especially true here. Jaworski had signaled to Haig and Buchen that he did not favor an indictment of Nixon. True, Jaworski's staff wanted to proceed against the ex-president, but the decision ultimately belonged to the special prosecutor himself. If Jaworski was never going to indict Nixon, the pardon would not have been necessary. In the closed circle of advisers Ford consulted, none seemed to consider the possibility that there might never be an indictment. By waiting and listening, Ford might have avoided the problems that the pardon brought him and still achieved the result he sought—no Watergate trial for Nixon.

Next, Ford turned to the sources of guidance he sought, primarily, it seemed, divine intervention. In three straight paragraphs, he described how God had guided his decision. "As we are a nation under God, so I am sworn to uphold our laws with the help of God," he said. "And I have sought such guidance and searched my own conscience with special diligence to determine the right thing for me to do with respect to my predecessor in this place, Richard Nixon, and his loyal wife and family."

Then: "Theirs is an American tragedy in which we all have played a part."

This was an outrageous thing to say. Watergate was tragic, but "all" Americans did not play a part in it. Very few did. And the investigations—prosecutorial, congressional, and journalistic—were designed to create a measure of accountability for those who created the scandal. It was as if Ford was saying collective guilt paved the way for collective forgiveness, but there was neither the former nor, it turned out, the latter.

Ford then recited the line about the threat to Nixon's health and his effort to reshape his life, "a great part of which was spent in the service of this country and by the mandate of his people." Arguably, the abuse of that mandate made Nixon's culpability greater, not lesser.

The next section of the speech was based on Jaworski's letter from earlier in the week about the need for the delay in any trial of Nixon. "Many months and perhaps more years will have to pass before Richard Nixon could obtain a fair trial," Ford said. "A former President of the United States, instead of enjoying equal treatment with any other citizen accused of violating the law, would be cruelly and excessively penalized either in preserving the presumption of his innocence or in obtaining a speedy determination of his guilt in order to repay a legal debt to society." This was muddled thinking. Ford was saying that the courts would protect Nixon's rights—and that would be cruel and excessive.

Ford turned to the core of his justification for the pardon. It was for the benefit of the American people, not Nixon himself: "I dare not depend upon my personal sympathy as a long-time friend of the former President, nor my professional judgment as a lawyer, and I do not." (But he had just said that he acted out of personal sympathy for Nixon's health.) Here was the real reason: "I cannot prolong the bad dreams that continue to reopen a chapter that is closed. My conscience tells me that only I, as President, have the constitutional power to firmly shut and seal this book." The reference to "bad dreams" was a nod to the already famous line from Ford's inaugural speech, where he proclaimed that "our long national nightmare is over." The pardon, in Ford's reckoning, was another attempt to end that nightmare. Again, this was a faulty prediction about the effect of his actions. The pardon didn't end the country's nightmare—it extended it and began Ford's own.

Finally, in contradiction of what he had just said about the nation's interest being paramount, he concluded that "Richard Nixon and his loved ones have suffered enough," and he read the text of the pardon document itself. The dense legal language underlined the magnitude of the gift that Ford had presented to his predecessor. He granted "a full, free, and absolute pardon unto Richard Nixon for all offenses against the United States which he, Richard Nixon, has committed or may have committed or taken part in during the period from July 20, 1969 through August 9, 1974." (He said "July" but the document said "January.") Then, with resolution rather than joy, Ford picked up his pen and signed the document without further comment.

————

As a simple matter of political performance, Ford's announcement of the pardon was a disaster. In his obsession with secrecy on the subject, Ford failed to recruit supporters and surrogates (and some did exist), who would have been willing to support the decision or, even better, to press Ford to issue the pardon in the first place. As a result, in the immediate aftermath of the speech, opponents of the pardon mobilized and spoke out with greater speed and passion than its supporters. The bizarre timing for an important presidential speech—on a Sunday morning—suggested that the president had something to hide. The speech itself was anemic, poorly argued and weakly delivered. (The contrast to Ford's graceful and generous inaugural a month earlier, which was also less than ten minutes in length, was striking.)

Later, Ford's failure of stagecraft in connection with the pardon would be portrayed as almost an act of courage, as proof that he was acting on the merits rather than for crass political reasons. For a man who had devoted much of his career to attempting to secure a Republican majority in the House of Representatives, springing the pardon on the country in this way could scarcely have damaged his party's candidates more in the midterm election season. This wasn't courage; this was incompetence. And it all quickly got worse.

Moments after Ford's speech, Phil Buchen went to the White House briefing room to answer questions from reporters. (TerHorst introduced Buchen, but declined to speak, and his resignation was made public later in the afternoon.) Buchen had little experience in dealing with the press, and his confused and confusing presentation compounded the problems with the pardon. Nixon's letter accepting the pardon was released at this time, and reporters (along with anyone else who read it) saw that he had made a grudging, nearly nonexistent, acknowledgment of wrongdoing; Nixon had said only that he should have been more "forthcoming." But Buchen told the press that Nixon's letter "constitutes a statement of contrition which I believe will hasten the time when he and his family may achieve peace of mind and spirit and will much sooner bring peace of mind and spirit to all of our citizens."

Immediately challenged by reporters about Nixon's statement, Buchen said, "Well, my interpretation is that it comes very close to saying that he did wrong."

Buchen also gave reporters a copy of Saxbe's letter affirming the tradition that a president's papers belonged to him. In his remarks, Buchen referred to Nixon as "the owner" of the papers and tapes. He acknowledged that the agreement on that subject was "very complicated." But Buchen was clear that after the five-year window Nixon had the right to order the tapes "destroyed." Nixon could also "destroy" documents that he didn't want to donate to the government.

What if historians protest about the destruction of the tapes?

"I am sure the historians will protest," Buchen said, "but I think historians cannot complain if evidence for history is not perpetuated which should not have been created in the first place." (This was absurd. Historians study existing evidence, regardless of its origin.)

On the issue that would consume public interest in the immediate aftermath of the pardon, and for many years afterward, Buchen was emphatic: "There were no secret agreements made."

As is often the case with public statements, what was most striking about Buchen's hour-long press conference was what he didn't say. Ford and Becker had been obsessed with the *Burdick* case in the Supreme Court, which said that the acceptance of pardon amounted to an acknowledgment of guilt. But though Buchen mentioned the *Burdick* case once in passing, he never said Nixon's acceptance of the pardon meant that he was, in effect, pleading guilty to a crime. Buchen said only that Nixon's statement that he had failed to act "forthrightly" amounted to an acceptance of responsibility. In all, Buchen's press conference reinforced every negative impression of Ford's speech. Unintentionally, Buchen made clear the truth about the pardon—that it was a free pass, a total gift, a complete exoneration, with nothing of importance demanded of Nixon in return. When it came to the pardon as well as his papers, Nixon had gotten everything and given nothing.

Not long after Buchen's press conference, Evel Knievel's bid to vault over the Snake River Canyon in Idaho fizzled.

By that point, Ford himself was back at Burning Tree for a six-hour round of golf with Mel Laird on the second day of the club tournament. They played poorly and finished well back in the pack.

President Ford as he prepares to testify before a congressional subcommittee on October 17, 1974. DAVID HUME KENNERLY/ CENTER FOR CREATIVE PHOTOGRAPHY/U OF ARIZONA

CHAPTER 24

The Legacy of the Pardon

THE PUBLIC RESPONSE TO THE PARDON WAS A THUNDER-
clap of outrage. Ford's popularity in the Gallup poll dropped 21 per-
centage points in a single week. Elite opinion turned on Ford with a
vengeance. Newspaper editorials, which were at the time leading in-
dicators of public sentiment, raged. *The New York Times* wrote, "This
blundering intervention is a body blow to the President's own credibility, and to the public's reviving confidence in the integrity of its
Government." *The Washington Post* said that Ford's action was "nothing less than a continuation of the cover-up," which was a view shared
by Ford's hometown *Grand Rapids Press*.[1] Calls to the White House
ran eight-to-one against the pardon. Democrats, who had generally
treated the new president with deference, returned to their Nixon-era
battle stations. Senator Ted Kennedy led the charge. The pardon, Kennedy said, was "the culmination of the Watergate cover-up." There
was a measure of hysteria in some reactions, as when the American
Civil Liberties Union asserted, "If Ford's principle had been the rule
in Nuremberg, the Nazi leaders would have been let off and only the
people who carried out their schemes would have been tried."

Still, even the more tempered reactions refuted Ford's main justification for the pardon. If Ford thought the pardon would "firmly
shut and seal this book" of Watergate, it did the opposite. And Ford,
suddenly, was a new villain in the story. Above all, the public felt betrayed, because Ford had promised to be, and briefly seemed to be, so
different from Nixon.

Ford expected some negative reaction to the pardon, but he was astonished, and horrified, by what happened. In a model of understatement, he wrote in his memoir, "what I had failed to anticipate was the vehemence of the hostile reaction to my decision."[2] Ford wrote that what made matters worse was that "even some members of my staff failed to understand my motives." Buchen, in another press statement, called the pardon "an act of mercy." (Ford, still going back and forth about whether Nixon's well-being was a factor, said mercy had nothing to do with it.) Jack Hushen, terHorst's acting successor as press secretary, said Ford might pardon the rest of the Watergate defendants. (He had no such intention.) In response, the Senate immediately passed a resolution denouncing any further pardons. As Ford might have realized, the staff members' confusion resulted not from their inattention but from Ford's garbled reasoning.

In a small way, too, the reaction to the pardon also offered a lesson in the limits of a legal education. As lawyers, Ford and Becker had fixated on a single line in the Supreme Court's *Burdick* case, from 1915, as a justification for the pardon: "acceptance of a pardon was an acknowledgment of guilt." (This was the part of the opinion that Ford carried in his wallet for the rest of his life.) But not only did Ford and his advisers fail to call the public's attention to this passage, it wouldn't have mattered if they did. The plain facts of the Nixon pardon made the *Burdick* case irrelevant. The pardon made criminal prosecution of Nixon impossible; the former president's own statement, about his failure to be "forthcoming," displayed no meaningful contrition. For good reason, a citation to an obscure Supreme Court case was not going to convince ordinary citizens to ignore the facts in front of them. Nixon would not be held accountable.

The outrage about the pardon was especially intense among Democrats in Congress, who had battled Nixon for years. Four days after the pardon, Bella Abzug, an outspoken liberal from New York, filed a formal demand for information from Ford about the pardon. It was referred to William Hungate, a more moderate Democrat from Missouri, who chaired the criminal justice subcommittee of the House Judiciary Committee. Notwithstanding his temperamental differences with Abzug, Hungate thought Abzug's questions de served answers. On September 17, Hungate put Abzug's questions to Ford in a letter. The most important one involved the possibility of a deal—that Nixon had left office in return for a promise from Ford of a pardon. As Hungate's letter put it:

> Did Alexander Haig refer to or discuss a pardon for Richard M. Nixon with Richard M. Nixon or representatives of Mr. Nixon at any time during the week of August 4, 1974 or at any subsequent time? If so, what promises were made or conditions set for a pardon, if any?

At first, Buchen and the others in the White House dismissed the letter and other requests to the president for explanation with short, dismissive replies. But Ford started to hear back from his allies that even Republicans wanted answers.

In response, Ford did something extraordinary, even unprecedented. He agreed to testify in public under oath before Hungate's subcommittee. As far as anyone could tell, no president in American history had ever agreed to offer such testimony before Congress. Presidents rarely want anyone, much less a hostile Congress dominated by the opposition party, to learn about their internal deliberations. The testimony was a risk, but it was a good-faith effort to recapture the mantle of openness and integrity that Ford possessed before he threw it away with the pardon. Ford believed he had nothing to hide, and he told his staff to prepare an opening statement for Hungate's subcommittee that laid out the backstory of the pardon in some detail.

This created a problem, especially when it came to Haig. The Ford party line had been that there had been no discussions of a pardon for Nixon until after Ford became president; specifically, there were no "secret agreements," as Buchen put it in his press conference. But after Ford told Buchen to prepare answers to Hungate's questions, Buchen had to address the conversations between Ford and Haig about a pardon during the first week in August, just before Nixon resigned.

This set off the final battle between Ford's loyalists and Haig, who remained in the physical office, if not the actual job, of chief of staff.

Ford was unsure what to do with Haig. The general, even in civilian clothes, was still the only person in the White House who knew how to make the levers of government run, and Ford valued Haig's energy and competence. But Haig had continued to clash with Hartmann, and Ford could never be sure if Haig's loyalty ran more to Nixon than to him. On September 4, Creighton Abrams, the chief of staff of the Army, died at the age of fifty-nine. Ford and Haig himself wanted Haig to replace him, but the job required Senate confirmation, and both men realized that the hearings would turn into a recapitulation of Watergate, which they wanted to avoid. Henry Kissinger came up with an artful solution. He suggested, and Ford agreed, to name Haig the military commander of NATO, with command of all U.S. forces in Europe. Crucially, the job did not require Senate confirmation, and Ford announced the job change for Haig on September 15.[3] (Ford also officially abandoned his "spokes of the wheel" structure for his senior staff and named Rumsfeld as his chief of staff.)

As Buchen, Hartmann, and Marsh began to prepare for Ford's testimony, which was scheduled for October 17, Haig was still present in Washington. Shortly before that date, Haig received a call from Fred Buzhardt, the Nixon White House lawyer who was still on staff for Ford. He said that the draft testimony for Ford said that Haig, in early August, had offered the presidency to Ford in exchange for a pardon for Nixon; Ford would then say that he turned down any such deal. The draft no longer exists, so it's not exactly clear what it said, but the suggestion infuriated Haig. After hearing from Buzhardt, Haig raced to the White House and demanded to see the president. In his self-dramatizing way, Haig vowed to hold an immediate press conference, denouncing "the Grand Rapids group" if the testimony was not changed.

In time, Haig was admitted to the Oval Office and, according to Haig's memoir, Ford asked him, "What do you want?"

"The truth," he replied. "That's all."[4] Ford diffused the conflict between Haig and the others, and the president's testimony ultimately did not assert that Haig directly proposed a pardon-for-presidency trade. (Still, according to Ford's statement to Bob Woodward many years later, Haig did make that offer in so many words.)

Ford's testimony, in the Rayburn House Office Building, was a remarkable event, a detailed accounting of the process leading to a major presidential decision delivered under oath by the president himself. Considering the fierce reaction to the pardon, there was a measure of desperation in this unprecedented gesture by Ford, to try to save his presidency from the self-inflicted wound of the pardon. To do so, he returned to the plainspoken style that had served him well in the past. "We meet here today to review the facts and circumstances that were the basis for my pardon of former President Nixon on September 8, 1974," he began. "I want very much to have those facts and circumstances known. The American people want to know them. And Members of the Congress want to know them."

As Ford felt compelled to do for the rest of his presidency, and indeed for the rest of his life, he sought to explain why he pardoned Nixon. "That purpose was to change our national focus. I wanted to do all I could to shift our attentions from the pursuit of a fallen President to the pursuit of the urgent needs of a rising nation," he said. "We would needlessly be diverted from meeting those challenges if we as a people were to remain sharply divided over whether to indict, bring to trial, and punish a former President, who already is condemned to suffer long and deeply in the shame and disgrace brought upon the office he held."

Then, Ford went through the chronology leading up to September 8, recounting the events that prompted the pardon. He described his two meetings with Haig on August 1, when the then chief of staff told him that the smoking gun tape was about to come out and that Nixon would probably soon resign. The second was the important one, when Haig had contrived to be alone with Ford. In that meeting, Haig played out various scenarios for the next few days. Buzhardt had outlined six possibilities, and Haig had recited them for Ford. The last two were:

(5) Nixon could pardon some or all of the Watergate defendants, then pardon himself, then resign.

(6) Nixon could resign and then Ford could pardon him.

Ford testified that he expressed no preference for any of these outcomes and asked only for time to think through the options. "In summary," Ford said, "I assure you that there never was at any time any agreement whatsoever concerning a pardon to Mr. Nixon if he were to resign and I were to become President." (In this way, Ford finessed the issue of Haig's proposal. Ford said there was never an agreement, but he avoided saying whether Haig proposed one.)

As for when he became president, Ford testified that he began thinking about a pardon after his August 28 press conference: "Shortly afterwards I became greatly concerned that if Mr. Nixon's prosecution and trial were prolonged, the passions generated over a long period of time would seriously disrupt the healing of our country from the wounds of the past." At that point, he asked his advisers for legal precedents on pardons and learned that he could pardon Nixon before charges against him were filed. He authorized Benton Becker's trip to San Clemente and issued the pardon after he returned, on September 8. Ford said he understood that the papers and tapes were Nixon's property. "Those tapes belong to Mr. Nixon according to the Attorney General, but they are being held for the benefit of the Special Prosecutor, and I think that is the proper place for them to be kept," he said.

The questioning from committee members was respectful but direct. Lawrence Hogan, a Republican of Maryland, gave Ford a chance to play his *Burdick* card. "Mr. President, don't you feel that the very acceptance of the pardon by the former President is tantamount to an admission of guilt on his part?"

"I do, sir," Ford said.

Hogan went on, "So, those who say again that they would have preferred that the President admit his culpability before a pardon being issued again are overlooking that fact?"

Ford replied, "The acceptance of a pardon, according to the legal authorities—and we have checked them out very carefully—does indicate that by the acceptance, the person who has accepted it does, in effect, admit guilt." Then, as now, Ford's attempt to turn Nixon's acceptance into an acknowledgment of guilt persuaded few listeners.

Elizabeth Holtzman, a young New York Democrat, asked a question that has considerable historical resonance a half-century later. "I wondered whether anybody had brought to your attention the fact the Constitution specifically states that even though somebody is impeached, that person shall nonetheless be liable to punishment according to law," she said.

"Mrs. Holtzman," Ford answered, addressing the unmarried congresswoman with the honorific for a married woman, at a time before Ms. was in wide use, "I was fully cognizant of the fact that the President on resignation was accountable for any criminal charges. But I would like to say that the reason I gave the pardon was not as to Mr. Nixon himself. I repeat, and I repeat with emphasis, the purpose of the pardon was to try and get the United States, the Congress, the President, and the American people focusing on the serious problems we have both at home and abroad. . . . That was the principal reason for my granting of the pardon."

Both Ford and Holtzman were correct in their understanding of the Constitution in 1974—that "the President on resignation was accountable for any criminal charges." As of 2025, thanks to *Trump v. United States*, that is no longer the case.

———

In his testimony before Congress, as in his many explanations of the pardon over the remaining three decades of his life, Ford always did the same thing: he told the truth. Ford said he had not made a deal with Nixon (or Haig) to trade the presidency for a pardon, because he had made no such deal. Ford didn't always explain his justification for the pardon with great precision, but the basic ideas were clear enough. He thought the pardon would allow the country to move on from Watergate to more important subjects. A lesser factor, but still a significant one, was Ford's sympathy for Nixon's disgrace and his concern for his predecessor's health.

But Ford's candor, which was admirable on its own terms and

certainly a contrast to Nixon's dishonesty, should not obscure a larger truth about the pardon: it was a terrible decision. The pardon ended the only remaining opportunity for the government to demand a full accounting for what was at the time the most serious presidential scandal in American history. It let the person most responsible for the Watergate cover-up, and the chief beneficiary of its many crimes, get away with it, while his subordinates paid heavy prices. The pardon allowed Nixon, in the remaining two decades of his life, to minimize or even dismiss his misconduct in office. It contributed to the cynical view that powerful people escape consequences for their actions.

As for Ford's justifications, they were never very persuasive and look even less credible with the passage of time. The nation's business was proceeding without interruption after Nixon left office, and that would have continued if he had been indicted. To be sure, a Nixon indictment and trial would have received a great deal of attention, but it would not have brought the nation to a halt. Ford could never point to any accomplishments that he was able to achieve because the pardon cleared the way; there were none. In fact, the pardon probably made the government less able to address the nation's problems because it revived the partisan rancor of the Nixon years. As a veteran of Congress himself, Ford should have been able to predict that outcome; but because he chose not to test in advance his inclination to pardon Nixon with anyone but his close advisers inside the White House, he deprived himself of critical intelligence. With the pardon, Ford succeeded only in adding his own name to the roll call of Watergate wrongdoers, which was a fate he could have avoided, if only for selfish reasons. As for Ford's concern for Nixon's well-being and his desire to avoid the spectacle of a former president thrown in prison, a pardon after indictment or trial would have been far more defensible than Ford's preemptive strike against accountability. Ford's reputation never recovered after September 8, 1974, and that was the fate he deserved.

CHAPTER 25

Ford's Burden

EVEN IN EXILE, NIXON REMAINED A BIG STORY. REPORT-
ers still camped out near Casa Pacifica, in San Clemente, and news
helicopters scrambled whenever he left the property. On Sunday
morning, September 8, shortly before Ford announced the pardon in
Washington, Nixon and Pat were on the move in a limousine for the
two-hour journey to Palm Springs.

Walter Annenberg, the billionaire publishing baron who had
been Nixon's ambassador to the Court of St. James's, had invited
the Nixons to spend some time at Sunnylands, his vast estate that
bloomed in the California desert. The property, at the intersection of
Bob Hope Drive and Frank Sinatra Drive, covered two hundred acres
and included a 25,000-square-foot main residence (with twenty-two
bedrooms), eleven artificial lakes, a variety of guesthouses and outbuildings, and a private nine-hole golf course. Annenberg and his
wife were not there, but they put the estate and its thirty employees at
the Nixons' disposal.

Nixon secluded himself indoors, hiding from the helicopters
as well as the triple-digit heat. He didn't want reporters to have a
glimpse of him on the day of the pardon, which was also when he
released his own grudging statement that went along with it—his acknowledgment that "I was wrong in not acting more decisively and
more forthrightly in dealing with Watergate, particularly when it
reached the state of judicial proceedings."

More drama followed. On the very night of Ford's announcement of the pardon, the pain in Nixon's leg, which had flared earlier in Egypt, returned.[1] Doctors discovered a recurrence of phlebitis, with its accompanying risk of fatal blood clots. The pain and swelling didn't go away, and Nixon's longtime doctor in California recommended hospitalization. Nixon resisted, but the problems worsened when, after a few days, he returned to San Clemente. At last, on September 23, he checked into a local hospital where it was determined that a blood clot had broken off and traveled to a lung. Nixon was in intensive care for five days, at times near death.

Nixon's medical situation did have one salutary effect for him. The Watergate cover-up trial of Mitchell, Haldeman, Ehrlichman, and the others began on October 1, and both Jaworski's prosecutors and some of the defendants sought to force Nixon to testify. Citing his health, Nixon's lawyers refused. Judge Sirica, having presided over the Watergate investigation from the very beginning, knew better than to take Nixon's word about his condition (or anything else, for that matter). The judge ordered an independent medical examination by three different doctors. They reported back that Nixon was indeed incapable of returning to Washington to testify. The trial went on without him.

Even in the midst of a medical crisis, Nixon's fierce will asserted itself. He was never going to run for office again, but he would spend the rest of his life in a battle to defend his reputation and record. Stung by widespread skepticism that he was as ill as his doctors said, Nixon sent his physician on a media tour to make the case. Dr. Walter Tkach, Nixon's White House physician and a major general in the Air Force, came out to California to see him, and then Nixon had the doctor give a series of interviews describing his perilous condition. "The pardon did him no damn good," Tkach told one reporter. "It will require a miracle for him to recover. I don't know if I can pull him through." Offended, too, by the criticism of the pardon, Nixon called Ford one night in late September and offered to revoke his acceptance of the pardon.[2] It was an empty gesture—because it was not clear if pardons could be unaccepted—and Ford demurred on the offer. Still, the call to Ford showed that Nixon, even from a hospital bed, never stopped scheming for another public comeback. He was finally discharged from the hospital on November 14.

———

Jaworski's staff did a quick round of legal research to determine whether Ford's pardon of Nixon could be challenged in court. The answer was clear. The pardon was final and absolute and not subject to any sort of judicial review. Nixon was definitively in the clear from any threat of federal prosecution for crimes committed in office. This was fine with Jaworski. Nixon had been forced from office following the constitutional process of impeachment, and the pardon guaranteed that the nation would not experience the spectacle of a former president in the dock. Jaworski had sought this result all along, and he now felt his work was done. Plus, the cover-up trial of Nixon top aides was underway. (All defendants except a minor figure named Kenneth Parkinson were eventually convicted.) On October 13, 1974, Jaworski announced his resignation as special prosecutor.

With the prospect of a criminal prosecution ruled out, the outrage over Nixon's free ride in his post-presidency took a different form. Democrats in Congress turned their attention to the agreement that Jack Miller, Nixon's lawyer, had struck with Benton Becker and the Ford administration over the White House tapes and papers. At its core, that agreement was based on the shared assumption that the material from Nixon's White House belonged to Nixon himself; that was the tradition that Saxbe and Scalia had outlined in their memo for Ford. According to the agreement between Miller and Becker, the special prosecutor would have access to the papers and tapes for a limited time, but then Nixon could do with them what he wanted, including destroy them.

Both parts of the agreement—Nixon's ownership of the material and the prospect of its destruction—appalled many Democrats and even some Republicans. (At least initially, Ford was also opposed to Nixon's control of the material.) So, on September 18, just ten days after the pardon, Senator Gaylord Nelson, a Wisconsin Democrat, introduced a bill to guarantee that the papers and tapes would not be returned to Nixon's custody, at least until a final agreement could be negotiated. In a sign of how much the pardon curdled public opinion about Nixon, the bill passed the House and Senate with large majorities and Ford signed it into law in December.

But that law—which was known as the Presidential Recordings and Materials Preservation Act of 1974—was just the next battle in a war that would drag on for an astonishing quarter-century. Among the highlights of this contest was Nixon's constitutional challenge to the 1974 law, which the former president lost in the Supreme Court by a vote of 7 to 2. In 1978, Congress passed the Presidential Records Act, which ended the tradition of presidents owning their papers. (This law was central to the 2023 indictment of former president Donald Trump in connection with his retention of classified documents at his Mar-a-Lago estate after he left office.) The 1978 law, however, only applied to future presidents and thus did not cover the continuing dispute over the Nixon material, which amounted to roughly 42 million documents and 950 tapes. In 1991, a federal district court in Washington ruled that the material was not Nixon's private property, but that decision was overturned by the D.C. Circuit in 1992. That judgment, in turn, led to years of negotiation between Nixon (and eventually his estate) and the federal government over the disposition of the material. In the end, Nixon won; the papers and tapes belonged to him, and the federal government had to buy them back. The saga finally ended in 2000 when the federal government paid Nixon's estate $18 million for the papers and tapes, which are now available for public view and listening at the National Archives facility in College Park, Maryland, and online. (The Nixon family, still represented by Jack Miller and his firm, had originally demanded $200 million.) The largest share of the money went to Nixon's presidential library, which holds his post-presidential papers, in Yorba Linda, California.

Nixon's life followed a similar trajectory to that of his papers, a gradual return to public respectability, if not his former eminence. As his health improved, he began restoring his personal finances, which were in shambles when he resigned. Nixon returned to prosperity with a $2.5 million advance for his memoir, a $600,000 deal for a series of television interviews with David Frost, and the sale of his Key Biscayne estate to a group of his friends. In 1979, Nixon moved back to New York City, where he had spent his wilderness years, between his loss in the 1962 California governor's race and his 1968 election as president. Once again in robust health, Nixon traveled the world, returning several times to China, where he was treated as a beloved dignitary. Nixon lectured widely and wrote several more books. Watergate and his resignation remained central to his legacy, but so, too, were his accomplishments in foreign policy. Nixon died on April 22, 1994, at the age of eighty-one.

————

Nixon got what he wanted from the pardon, but Ford, it quickly became clear, did not. Instead of allowing the nation to move beyond Watergate, the pardon made his presidency a hostage of it. Ford saw this himself. The relatively few Watergate questions at Ford's August 28 press conference had prompted him to decide on the pardon; the idea was to make sure that he wouldn't have to spend the rest of his presidency answering questions about Nixon. But by the time of his next press conference, on September 16, the week after the pardon, virtually all the questions were about Nixon and the pardon. With admirable candor, Ford admitted that he was surprised by the intensity of the reaction to the pardon. Asked whether the pardon had, as he intended, bound up the nation's wounds, Ford offered a rueful smile and said, "I must say that the decision has created more antagonism than I intended." Also at the press conference, he noted the link in his mind between the pardon for Nixon and the amnesty for those who avoided the Vietnam draft. "The connection between those two cases," he said, "is the effort that I made in the one, to heal the wounds involving the charges against Mr. Nixon, and my honest and conscientious effort to heal the wounds for those who had deserted military service or dodged the draft."

Ford continued to try to connect his twin gestures of healing—toward Nixon and toward the Vietnam resisters. In the week after the pardon, Ford established a clemency review board, which was to evaluate the fitness of applicants for "earned reentry" into American society.[3] The board was a politically balanced group, led by former senator Charles Goodell, who was an opponent of the war, and it included liberals such as Vernon Jordan, then the president of the Urban League. In the end, though, Ford's plan pleased almost no one. Liberals noted that the strictures were such that only about a fifth of those eligible applied for the amnesty. And conservatives objected to any amnesty at all for draft dodgers. In a broader sense, too, Ford's attempted linkage between the two gestures offered a useful lesson about presidents' pardon power. The public doesn't evaluate pardons as a collective package but rather on their individual merits. The justification for each pardon must stand or fall on its own.

Announcing the pardon in the middle of the midterm election campaign poisoned an already deadly atmosphere for Republicans. Democrats won a historic landslide in 1974, gaining forty-nine seats in the House of Representatives and four in the Senate, to expand their majorities in both bodies. What was more, the election introduced the "Watergate Babies," ninety-three new legislators, nearly all Democrats, many of whom were young and aggressive. Over the final two years of his term, Ford issued dozens of vetoes, but Congress still produced a raft of liberal legislation on such issues as campaign finance and ethics, public access to government information, and antitrust law. Ford spent his entire presidency on the defensive against a hostile Congress.

It became part of the folklore associated with the pardon that it cost Ford the 1976 election, just as Ford's friend Tip O'Neill thought it would when he first heard about it. In fact, that conclusion is less than certain. At least as important as the pardon was the Republican primary challenge to Ford from Ronald Reagan, who finished his second term as governor of California at the end of 1974. Though Reagan was later famous for his "eleventh commandment"—"thou shall not speak ill of any fellow Republican"—Reagan sabotaged Ford's campaign to an extraordinary degree. Even though Ford clearly had enough delegates to win the nomination, Reagan carried his campaign against the president all the way through to the convention in Kansas City, which was unprecedented in the history of the Republican Party.[4] Ford entered the general election as an unelected incumbent who was leading a battered and divided Republican Party.

The pardon also figured less in the general election than many believe. As is usually the case, the economy was a major factor for the incumbent, and inflation and unemployment remained high. Jimmy Carter, who emerged from the obscurity of a single term as governor of Georgia to win the Democratic nomination, made honesty in government a central part of his platform. "I'll never lie to you," he promised, which was certainly intended as a reaction to Watergate. But Carter rarely talked about Ford's pardon of Nixon during the campaign; for example, Carter didn't mention it once during his acceptance speech at the Democratic convention. Ford and Carter debated three times, and the pardon came up only in a single question in one debate. Throughout the campaign, Carter led in the polls, but Ford closed the gap toward the end, and the election turned out to be very close. Carter won 50.1 percent of the popular vote, with 297 electoral votes, and Ford won 48.0 percent, with 240 electoral votes. A shift to Ford of 18,000 votes in Ohio and Hawaii would have flipped the result.

In such a close election, any number of factors might have changed the outcome. In retrospect, though, the folklore may be more important than the facts. To this day, it's widely believed that the pardon of Richard Nixon cost Gerald Ford the 1976 election.

CHAPTER 26

All Roads Lead to, and from, Willie Horton

THE PRESIDENTS WHO FOLLOWED GERALD FORD DREW clear lessons from his pardon of Nixon. The drama and disruption that followed the pardon on September 8, 1974, reinforced the idea that pardons were, above all, political acts. As a result, presidents recognized that they had to align their acts of clemency with the broader goals of their administrations. But several of these subsequent presidents faced a dilemma. They wanted to grant some pardons that did not come with political benefits; indeed, these presidents knew that the acts of clemency would be embarrassing, even toxic. So, they came up with what seemed like a solution: trying to bury unpopular pardons in the lame-duck final weeks of their presidencies.

Like Trump in 2024, Carter in 1976 was the rare presidential candidate who made a campaign promise about clemency. Hundreds of thousands of American men refused to serve in the Vietnam War; many lived as fugitives in the United States while 100,000 others fled to Canada. Ford had begun the process of reintegrating these men into American life with his plan for "earned reentry" into the United States. But the great majority of Democrats wanted the next president to do more. Carter had mixed feelings on the subject. As a Navy veteran, he didn't identify with those who broke the law and refused to serve. But Carter also had a strong religious belief in forgiveness and, more practically, a desire to appeal to the liberal wing of his party, which regarded him with skepticism.

As a candidate, Carter decided to make a bold stand—and a firm promise. Like Ford, Carter decided to make his announcement in front of a veterans group, to demonstrate political courage. On August 24, 1976, he spoke to the American Legion in Seattle. "I do not favor—and I want you to listen carefully because I don't want you to misunderstand me—I do not favor a blanket amnesty," he said. "But for those who violated Selective Service laws, I intend to grant a blanket pardon. To me there's a difference. Amnesty means what you did was right; a pardon means what you did, right or wrong, is forgiven. So, a pardon yes, amnesty no." Unlike Ford's speech to the veterans when he announced his earned reentry plan, which was greeted with stony silence, Carter's was vigorously booed.[1] Here, Carter learned what Ford found out with his attempts to invoke the *Burdick* case's holding that acceptance of a pardon is tantamount to a confession. Legalistic parsing of pardons rarely works; pardons are nothing more, and nothing less, than presidential free passes.

Still, Carter stuck with his determination to pardon all the draft evaders. He did so on January 21, 1977, his first full day in office. He granted "a full, complete and unconditional pardon" to all persons who violated, or who "may have committed" any violation of, the draft laws during the Vietnam era. Unlike Ford's "earned" program, Carter imposed no requirement on those who received the pardon.

The pardon to the Vietnam resisters was controversial, but the political impact was muted. Polls showed a rough split of opinion on Carter's action. But Carter had made clear what he was going to do, so his opponents were not surprised, and his supporters were not betrayed. It was, in all, a model of how a president should handle a controversial pardon—with candor and openness. His pardon wound up benefiting about 200,000 people, including about 50,000 of those who went to Canada. (About 50,000 others who fled to Canada decided to remain there as residents.)

As for Carter's other acts of clemency, they reflected a dominant political theme of the last half-century. Through earlier periods of

American history, crime was largely seen as a local issue, to be addressed by mayors and their chiefs of police. But Richard Nixon capitalized on the increases in crime in the 1960s and 1970s by effectively nationalizing the issue. "Law and order" was a powerful message in Nixon's two victories, and the national obsession with the issue outlasted Nixon's time in office. This shift in mood about crime affected how all later presidents exercised the pardon power. For the previous decade or so before Carter, the use of presidential clemency had been fairly consistent, with Johnson, Nixon, and Ford granting 31 percent, 36 percent, and 27 percent of requests respectively, but the proportion dropped to 21 percent with Carter.[2] In all, Carter gave 563 pardons and commutations (besides the Vietnam resisters), which was just somewhat larger than the 404 by Ford, who served half as long. Carter's record reflected a pattern that continued long after his presidency. As concerns about crime grew, the number of presidential pardons declined.

For the most part, Carter took his cues from the recommendations of the Justice Department's pardon attorney, but he did make some clemency decisions on his own. Judge Sirica had sentenced Gordon Liddy to twenty years for his role in Watergate, but Carter commuted his sentence after he served four-and-a-half years. Carter said he did so because Liddy would otherwise have served a great deal more time than other Watergate figures. (The commutation of Liddy's sentence also served as a reminder that, thanks to Ford's pardon, Nixon himself faced no criminal consequences at all.) Carter also commuted the sentences of four Puerto Rican nationalists who had been involved in terrorist activities, including an assassination attempt against President Harry Truman, which killed a police officer, in the 1950s. All had served decades in prison by that point, and their release was a cause célèbre among some Democratic politicians. Thanks to a lobbying campaign which included Ronald Reagan, Carter's future political opponent, Carter commuted the sentence of Patricia Hearst, the heiress who was kidnapped in 1974 and then committed a bank robbery with her captors. Carter's order freed her after twenty-two months in prison, eight months before her scheduled release.

One of Carter's final pardons, and probably his least defensible, was issued on the day before he left office. (As will become apparent, last-minute pardons in presidential terms have a dismal history.) Carter pardoned Peter Yarrow, the folksinger who was part of Peter, Paul and Mary. In 1970, Yarrow had been convicted and served three months in prison for "taking improper" liberties with a fourteen-year-old girl who came to his hotel room for an autograph. This appears to be the only presidential pardon in history for a sex crime against a child. (There later turned out to be a series of further accusations against Yarrow for sexual abuse of minors.) But the pardon to Yarrow received little attention because it took place just hours before the American hostages in Iran were released and Ronald Reagan was sworn in as president.

———————

Reagan wanted to show that, as a Republican outsider in Washington, he felt no guilt or burden for Watergate and the associated abuses of the Nixon era. For Reagan, the FBI remained a pillar of respectability, not a vector of civil liberties abuse. To make that point, on April 15, 1981, just three months into his presidency, Reagan pardoned Mark Felt and Edward S. Miller, two senior FBI officials who had been convicted of ordering illegal break-ins in national security investigations. In his statement accompanying the pardon, Reagan drew a pointed contrast to Carter's early pardons. "Four years ago, thousands of draft evaders and others who violated the Selective Service law were unconditionally pardoned by my predecessor," he said. "America was generous to those who refused to serve their country in the Vietnam war. We can be no less generous to two men who acted on high principle to bring an end to the terrorism that was threatening our nation." (Decades later, Felt revealed that he had been "Deep Throat," the secret source for Bob Woodward in his Watergate coverage.)

Reagan made several more pardons which were also intended to score political points. Junior Johnson was a NASCAR race driver who was enormously popular with Reagan's base. In 1956, Johnson had spent a year in jail for moonshining. Reagan pardoned him in 1986. Eugenio Martínez was one of the Watergate burglars who had been born in Cuba and spent most of his life in anti-Castro activities, including with the CIA. After he completed his fifteen-month prison term, Reagan pardoned him in 1983. Yankees owner George Steinbrenner had been charged by the Watergate special prosecutor with making illegal campaign contributions to Nixon. More than a decade before the pardon, Steinbrenner had pleaded guilty and paid a small fine. This pardon had limited practical effect, but it was a classic example of inequitable clemency. Because Steinbrenner was wealthy and prominent, he received a gift denied to others who were similarly situated.

But the real change in the Reagan presidency was revealed in the pardons he didn't grant. He gave clemency to just 12 percent of those who applied, which was a decline even from Carter's reduced rate. At the same time, Reagan embraced and signed the Sentencing Reform Act of 1984, which made a series of dramatic changes in federal law enforcement. Most importantly, the law abolished parole for federal crimes. Henceforth, all sentences would be for a specific length of time, with only the possibility of a 15 percent reduction for good behavior in prison. The law also established mandatory sentencing guidelines for all federal crimes, so that sentences would be consistent across regions and judges. (In later years, because of Supreme Court decisions, the guidelines became discretionary rather than mandatory.) In a separate law, also signed by Reagan, Congress established higher mandatory minimum sentences for a variety of drug crimes.

With all these changes, Reagan inaugurated the era of mass incarceration. The population of federal prisons went from 26,000 in 1981 to 57,000 in 1989, and the transformation of the law in the 1980s led to the doubling again of federal prisoners by 1997. (Approximately 90 percent of people in prison and jail are under state jurisdiction and state incarceration levels also soared in this period.) The increase in the federal prison population makes the decline in the number of pardons Reagan issued all the more striking. In 1910, parole was introduced to the federal system, and the number of pardons went down, because there was now a different and better pressure valve to allow for the release of deserving prisoners. But unlike in 1910, there was no increase in pardons to make up for the end of parole;

the opposite, in fact. Granting less clemency was a way for Reagan to show he was tough on crime. Reagan issued just 406 pardons and commutations in eight years, which was about the same number as Ford issued in two-and-a-half.[3]

Even before George H. W. Bush won the race to succeed Reagan, Bush did his predecessor one better. Reagan let few criminals out of prison; Bush demonstrated what could happen to a political rival when the wrong criminal was released on his watch. The legacy of Bush's tactic in the 1988 campaign endures to this day.

On October 26, 1974, Willie Horton and two associates robbed and killed a seventeen-year-old gas station attendant in Lawrence, Massachusetts. Horton was convicted of first-degree murder and sentenced to life in prison without the possibility of parole. Still, on June 6, 1986, Horton was released as part of a weekend furlough program, and he failed to return to prison. Ten months later, in Oxon Hill, Maryland, Horton assaulted a man named Clifford Barnes in his home, tied him up and stabbed him. When Angela Miller, Barnes's fiancée, arrived, Horton raped her twice. He then fled in Barnes's car and was captured after a shootout with police. Horton was sentenced to two consecutive life terms in Maryland, where he remains in custody.[4]

Michael Dukakis, Bush's Democratic opponent, was not the governor of Massachusetts when the furlough program began, but he was in charge when Horton was released. In addition, Dukakis had vetoed an attempt to prevent murderers from receiving furloughs. Bush and his surrogates used the Horton case, including in a notorious television commercial, to portray Dukakis as weak on crime. It was devastating. And the "Willie Horton effect," as it was sometimes called, transcended the 1998 election. As Senator Dick Durbin, an Illinois Democrat, later observed, "The ghost of Willie Horton has loomed over any conversation about sentencing reform for over thirty years."[5]

Horton received a furlough—a short-term release from prison—but his effect applied to pardons and commutations as well. Horton raised the stakes for any president who considered granting early release for anyone in prison or even for any ex-offender. If the recipient of clemency went on to commit a crime, the political consequences for the grantor could be calamitous, as they were for Dukakis. The safer course was simply to deny clemency, and that was the pattern in subsequent years. Bush himself took this cautious route and was even stingier than Reagan. In four years, Bush granted just seventy-four pardons and three commutations.

Because Bush was so parsimonious with clemency, that made his final act in office especially disgraceful. Bush himself had modest involvement in the Iran-contra affair that took place under Reagan's presidency, when Bush was vice president. White House aides to Reagan arranged for the sale of missiles to the Islamic government of Iran, which was under an arms embargo, in hopes of prompting the release of American hostages in the Middle East. The government officials then used some of the proceeds of those sales to assist the contras in Nicaragua, who were fighting the left-wing government there. At the time, Congress had banned American military aid to the contras. A criminal investigation, led by Lawrence E. Walsh, whose title was independent counsel, went on for the entirety of Bush's presidency.[6] Walsh's investigation led to several convictions and guilty pleas. Five days before the 1992 election, Walsh honored a court-imposed deadline and filed a superseding indictment—that is, a revised set of charges—against Caspar Weinberger, the former secretary of defense, for perjury and obstruction of justice. Unlike the first indictment, this one mentioned Bush's role in the Iran-contra matter, and the charges caused a furor, which some, apparently including Bush himself, believed contributed to his loss to Bill Clinton.

On Christmas Eve in 1992, as Bush played out the last days of his presidency, he took his revenge against Walsh. He pardoned Weinberger, shortly before his trial began, as well as four other Reagan administration officials who had been convicted or pleaded guilty to charges in Walsh's investigation. They were Robert McFarlane, who was the White House national security advisor, Elliott Abrams, who was an assistant secretary of state, and Clair George, a top CIA official. Bush also pardoned Duane Clarridge, another CIA official, whose trial was scheduled to start in March 1993.

In his statement about the pardons, Bush said Walsh's investigation represented "a profoundly troubling development in the political and legal climate of our country: the criminalization of policy differences." In fact, the charges against all these men had nothing to do with "policy differences," but rather involved lying to and obstructing investigations, which are common grounds for federal prosecutions. Bush's pardons were like the Ford pardon of Nixon in miniature—a grant of mercy to privileged characters who escaped justice because of their connections to the powerful.

CHAPTER 27

The Atrophy and Rebirth of the Pardon Power

IN 1993, BILL CLINTON'S FIRST YEAR AS PRESIDENT, HE IS-
sued no pardons and no commutations. He did the same in 1994.
This behavior was on brand. Clinton belonged to a generation of
Democrats who refused to concede the mantle of law and order to
Republicans. (So did then-Senator Joe Biden, who is four years older
than Clinton.) Especially in the early 1990s, when crime was still at
historic highs, Clinton devoted much of his presidency to putting
people in prison, not getting them out. There would be no "Willie
Hortons" under Bill Clinton. In a way, this, too, was a legacy of Ford's
pardon of Nixon. If granting pardons sent a political message, not
granting them made a point as well.

Even with Democratic majorities in the Senate and House, Clinton had enormous difficulty passing legislation in his first term. A
much heralded plan to reform health care, led by Hillary Clinton,
went nowhere. The one area where Clinton could win bipartisan cooperation in Congress was crime. In 1994, Clinton signed the Violent Crime Control and Law Enforcement Act—known as the Crime
Bill—which Biden sponsored in the Senate. The 356-page law provided federal money for the hiring of 100,000 new police officers,
$9.7 billion for the construction of new prisons, and an expansion
of crimes eligible for the death penalty. (The Oklahoma City bombing, which took 168 lives, happened on April 19, 1995, and Timothy

McVeigh, who committed the bombing, was later executed under the new provisions of the Crime Bill.)[1]

Some parts of the Crime Bill reflected more traditional liberal priorities. It banned the manufacture of semiautomatic firearms— assault weapons—for ten years. (The ban was not renewed in 2004.) In a section that was principally written by Biden, the Violence Against Women Act authorized $1.6 billion to prevent and investigate crimes against women. But the overall trajectory was pro–law enforcement and pro-incarceration. That was also true of another law Clinton signed, the Antiterrorism and Effective Death Penalty Act of 1996, which increased penalties for terrorism and created new legal barriers for defendants challenging sentences of death. In fairness to Clinton's record on these issues, it should be noted that crime trended significantly downward during his eight years in office, though the reasons for the decline are disputed. What's clear is that Clinton's record on clemency reflected his political priorities. After granting fifty-three pardons and three commutations in 1995, he again granted none in 1996 and 1997. In 1998 and 1999, the number ticked up modestly—a total of fifty-five pardons and twelve commutations.

Things changed in 2000, Clinton's final year in office. He started thinking more generously about his opportunity to grant clemency. In part, this may have reflected a measure of empathy because by this point he himself had been the subject of a long-running criminal investigation led by Ken Starr, the independent counsel. Clinton also came to realize that he had granted far fewer pardons than even his recent predecessors, and he saw that he had the chance to undo some injustices in the system. As he wrote in his memoir, "My philosophy on pardons and commutations of sentences . . . was conservative when it came to shortening sentences and liberal in granting pardons for nonviolent offenses once people had served their sentences and spent a reasonable amount of time afterward as law-abiding citizens, if for no other reason than to give them their voting rights back."[2]

So, if Clinton was "liberal" in granting some kinds of pardons, why had he still granted so few? He had an answer: because of the incompetence, sloth, and caution of the Office of the Pardon Attorney in the Justice Department. "The Justice Department's pardon office knew that

they couldn't get heat for delaying cases or for recommending denials,"
Clinton later wrote, "a constitutional function vested in the President
was slowly being transferred into the bowels of the Justice Department."

In a way, Clinton had a point. There is a paradox, even an outright conflict of interest, with the principal responsibility for pardons
being lodged in the Justice Department. The department's prosecutors brought the cases from which the convicts sought relief; and the
regulations for the pardon process required that the prosecutors in
each case be consulted about the wisdom of clemency. It's no surprise
that prosecutors rarely endorse the undoing of their own work. As
Margaret Colgate Love, a former pardon attorney in the Justice Department, later wrote, "By the time President Clinton entered office
in 1993, the pardon program at Justice had lost whatever independence and integrity it once enjoyed within the Department, and was
functioning primarily to ratify the results achieved by prosecutors."[3]
The pro–law enforcement, pro-incarceration spirit of the era had
taken root at the Justice Department.

But Clinton was the president. If he thought that his Justice Department was failing, he could have done something about it. Instead, he basically ignored his clemency power until the middle of
2000, when his staff began pressing the Justice Department for more
recommendations for clemency. At that point, in classic bureaucratic
fashion, the pardon attorney's office stalled—and then, remarkably,
stopped making recommendations altogether. Frustrated by the
pressure from the White House, Roger Adams, the pardon attorney,
in October 2000 told applicants for clemency to take their cases directly to the president.[4]

Chaos ensued. The White House counsel staff didn't have the
resources to evaluate the hundreds of requests that poured in due
to the Justice Department's abdication. Neither did Clinton himself,
who was preoccupied with a disputed presidential election to succeed
him and with his own last-ditch effort to achieve peace in the Middle
East. Still, friends and former aides reached out to Clinton in hopes
of winning pardons for themselves or their clients. Finally, on his last
day in office, Clinton issued 140 acts of clemency, which brought the
total for his eight years to 457, a total similar to Reagan's two terms.

Some of the final-day pardons went to plainly deserving convicts, including several "so-called 'girlfriend' cases," as Clinton put it, which were narcotics prosecutions of women brought as leverage against their more culpable male partners. He did some score-settling with independent counsels, pardoning Susan McDougal, an Arkansas associate who had been relentlessly pursued by Starr, and Archie Schaffer, who faced draconian punishment from a different independent counsel. At least one pardon was simply odd. In response to personal appeals from Jimmy and Rosalynn Carter, Clinton pardoned Patricia Hearst, whose prison sentence Carter had commuted two decades earlier. That made Hearst the only person in American history to have a sentence commuted by one president and be pardoned by another.[5]

But other acts of clemency issued that day were simply indefensible—classic illustrations of the perils of last-minute, lame-duck pardons. For instance, Clinton pardoned his brother, Roger, who had served a short prison sentence after being convicted in 1985 of conspiracy to distribute cocaine and distribution of cocaine. There was no explanation for this pardon except nepotism. Worse yet was the pardon of Marc Rich, a billionaire commodities trader. In 1983, in Manhattan federal court, Rich and his partner Pincus Green were charged with sixty-five counts, including racketeering, income tax evasion, wire fraud, and violating the arms embargo with Iran. Rather than face trial, both men fled to Switzerland and never returned to the United States. Clinton could not have been ignorant of Rich's status; he had been on the FBI's Ten Most Wanted list and "fugitive financier" was practically his official title. In the final days of Clinton's presidency, Clinton was the subject of an extensive lobbying campaign to pardon both men. It was led by Jack Quinn, Clinton's former White House counsel, but the more consequential advocacy came from Ehud Barak, the Israeli prime minister, who was grateful for Rich's contributions to Israel and the Middle East peace process. (Denise Rich, Marc's ex-wife, had also been a major political and financial supporter of Clinton's campaigns.) In the days before he left office, Clinton was presented with detailed arguments that Rich and Green were not guilty of the charged crimes, but the crucial fact remained that they had run away from United States rather than face their days in court. For good reason, the controversy over the Rich pardon clouded Clinton's final days in office.

———————

George W. Bush watched the unseemly conclusion of his predecessor's term with disdain. As a result, he nearly checked out of the clemency business altogether. Like Clinton, Bush issued no pardons or commutations in his first two years in office; but unlike Clinton, Bush never picked up the pace. He issued just nineteen pardons and two commutations in his second two years. In finished his second term with just 189 pardons and eleven commutations. This stinginess fit with Bush's tough-on-crime political persona.

Nevertheless, Bush's final weeks in office were consumed with a battle over a single act of clemency. I. Lewis "Scooter" Libby was Vice President Dick Cheney's national security advisor and then his chief of staff. In 2007, Libby was convicted of perjury and obstructing the investigation of the leak of a covert CIA officer's identity by other government officials. Libby was sentenced to thirty months in prison. In a rare departure from his usual practice, Bush issued a commutation of Libby's sentence before he had to report to prison. That wasn't enough for Cheney. As their terms in office wound down, the vice president pressured Bush to grant Libby a full pardon. Cheney was relentless, Bush resistant, and their relationship, once close, was irrevocably sundered.

A passage in Bush's memoir didn't name Cheney but seemed directed at him:

> One of the biggest surprises of my presidency was the flood of pardon requests at the end. I could not believe the number of people who pulled me aside to suggest that a friend or former colleague deserved a pardon. At first I was frustrated. Then I was disgusted. I came to see the massive injustice in the system. If you had connections to the president, you could insert your case into the last-minute frenzy. Otherwise, you had to wait for the Justice Department to conduct a review and make a recommendation. In my final weeks in office, I resolved that I would not pardon anyone who went outside the formal channels.[6]

Bush was so aggrieved by the final rush for pardons that he raised it with his successor, Barack Obama, as the two men made the traditional car ride to the inauguration on January 20, 2009. "On the ride up Pennsylvania Avenue on Inauguration Day, I told Barack Obama about my frustrations with the pardon system. I gave him a suggestion: announce a pardon policy early on, and stick to it."[7]

———

Obama didn't follow Bush's advice, but he did follow his example—and Clinton's. Obama issued almost no pardons or clemencies during his first term. He granted none in his first two years and twenty-two pardons and one commutation in his second two. It's easy for presidents to push clemency to the back of their agendas. Other matters seem (and are) more pressing. Bush had terrorism, Obama a faltering economy. Political caution is another factor. The risk of another "Willie Horton" can be eliminated by releasing no one at all.

But Obama made a significant change in 2014. By this point, crime had been declining for many years, and the movement against mass incarceration was accelerating. So, at Obama's behest, the Justice Department launched what it called the Clemency Project. Concerned that too many low-level drug offenders were in federal prisons, Obama established a process to review their sentences. It was a cumbersome operation. Prisoners would send in requests for reductions, the Justice Department would conduct an initial screening, and then send eligible cases out to private attorneys who had volunteered to assist the applicants.[8] In short order, 35,000 inmates applied, and the project was overwhelmed. Many of the attorneys, while well intentioned, knew little about federal sentencing and could not make useful evaluations of their clients' cases. Once submitted, the applications went through as many as twelve layers of review before they went to the president. At each stage, of course, a bias toward caution led to a predisposition for denial. In the end, over the course of the Clemency Project, Obama granted 1,715 commutations and 212 pardons. He rejected 25,000 petitions and failed to act on 9,400 more.

It took considerable political courage for Obama to undertake such a project at all, especially since the individual applicants were already in prison. It's much safer for presidents to pardon those whose convictions were many years in the past, as were their days in custody, if they served any at all. By ordering the release of hundreds of inmates, Obama was taking the risk that one of them would go on a crime spree and turn into "Willie Horton." Fortunately, none did. Obama's record was formidable, especially compared to his predecessors. He issued more commutations than the past twelve presidents combined. And Obama's acts of clemency produced no sweet deals for insiders, no special dispensations for the rich, no scandals.

When Biden, Obama's vice president, became president in 2021, he took a similar initial approach to clemency. In the first three-and-a-half years of his presidency, Biden issued only twenty-five pardons and 131 acts of clemency. But Biden's tough-on-crime instincts constrained him from going as far as Obama did. Biden did make two dramatic announcements about pardons. On December 22, 2023, he said that he was planning to pardon everyone who had been prosecuted for simple possession of marijuana on federal lands and in the District of Columbia. On June 26, 2024, he announced that he was going to pardon members of the armed services who had in previous years been subjected to courts-martial for being gay or lesbian. But unlike Obama's Clemency Project, Biden's actions were mostly symbolic. Though thousands of people were eligible for these pardons, few took advantage of Biden's offers: about two hundred for marijuana and not even a hundred for the courts-martial.

Then, on December 1, 2024, Biden pardoned his son Hunter—after the president and his aides repeatedly promised that he would do no such thing. In June, a jury had found Hunter guilty of three felony counts relating to lies about his drug use in his application to own a firearm in Delaware. Then, in September, he pleaded guilty to nine federal tax charges in California. He was due to be sentenced in both cases later in December. But the pardon from his father wiped out that possibility and gifted Hunter a clean record, as if he had never been charged.

President Biden justified his action on the ground that Hunter had been "selectively, and unfairly, prosecuted. . . . No reasonable person who looks at the facts of Hunter's cases can reach any other conclusion than Hunter was singled out only because he is my son—and that is wrong." There is something to this argument. The president's political adversaries have long been obsessed with trying to prove that Joe Biden was somehow involved with Hunter's misdeeds, most of which appear to have stemmed from his long-term addiction to drugs. Despite years of pursuit, including a spurious impeachment investigation, Biden's critics never came close to proving that the president had anything to do with his son's criminal behavior, or that Joe Biden benefited in any way from it. Still, the fact remains that Hunter Biden stood convicted of twelve crimes—and he was, in fact, guilty of all of them. Prosecutors played hardball with Hunter, which is something that prosecutors sometimes, even often, do. But those other guilty defendants didn't have the President of the United States to bail them out. To be sure, too, Trump's oft-stated plans to take revenge against his political enemies in his second term spurred Biden's decision, especially with the expansive nature of the pardon, which covers all possible crimes from 2014 to 2024. (The only comparably broad pardon was the one that Ford granted Nixon.) Joe Biden's love for his son, as well as his anger about Hunter's treatment, was understandable, but this consummate act of nepotism stained the record of the Biden presidency.

Later in December 2024, Biden appeared to recognize that his pardon for his son might look more defensible if he finally began to extend the same kind of grace to others. He pardoned thirty-nine people and gave commutations to about 1,500 more who had already been released to home confinement during the Covid pandemic. He was still being pressed by advocates to take more dramatic steps— including lowering the sentences involving crack, when there was a dramatic disparity compared to those involving powdered cocaine, and commuting to life in prison the sentences of those on federal death row. In Biden's final days in office, then, the question was whether his bequest to his son began, for him at least, a transformational approach to clemency.

One of the lesser evils of Biden's pardon of his son was that it suggested a rough parallel to the clemency record of the man who served between Obama and Biden—and who will return to the White House after Biden. But when it came to pardons, Donald Trump in his first term was, as in so many other areas, unlike any other president in American history.

CHAPTER 28

The First-Term
Trump Pardons

OVER HIS FIRST FOUR YEARS IN OFFICE, TRUMP ISSUED 143 pardons and 94 commutations, and this total of 237 acts of clemency ranked on the low side by modern standards. Rather than the absolute number of pardons, what was striking was the way Trump issued them, and to whom. Trump basically ignored the Office of the Pardon Attorney; only twenty-five, or 11 percent of the total, came through the Justice Department process, much lower than his predecessors. More than any recent president, Trump handled pardons and commutations himself. Often without any input even from his White House staff, Trump turned clemency into the crudest political currency, which he used, for the most part, to reward dozens of undeserving cronies, allies, and crooks. Trump's pardons were rooted in nepotism, favoritism, self-dealing, and vengeance.

At the same time, Trump did more to liberate unjustly incarcerated people—and to reduce mass incarceration—than any other president. It's a strange story.

———

From the beginning, Trump saw clemency as currency to spend for his own benefit. Trump's reasons would be familiar to the seventeenth-century parliamentarians in England who limited the king's power to prevent just such abuses. "Mercy" was low among Trump's motivations. Unlike Alexander Hamilton, Trump cared little whether justice was too "sanguinary and cruel." Rather, to Trump, the pardon power was just another tool to advance his self-interest.

Even more than Nixon, Trump recognized that the possibility of pardons—the *dangling* of pardons—could be an important line of defense in an unfolding presidential scandal. Indeed, Trump put Nixon to shame in shamelessness. In the famous White House conversation of March 21, 1973, Nixon and John Dean recognized that the public would rebel at the prospect of a preemptive pardon of Howard Hunt, who was an important witness in the Watergate scandal. "Hunt's now demanding clemency or he's going to blow," Dean said. "And, politically, it'd be impossible for, you know, you to do it." Nixon agreed: "That's right." Dean continued, "I'm not sure that you'll ever be able to deliver on clemency. It may be just too hot." Trump had no such internal or external censor, and he paid no price for his candor.

Trump's wielding of the pardon power may have been criminal. Robert Mueller, the special counsel, led an investigation of Trump's ties to the Russian government in advance of the 2016 election. As in any presidential scandal, a central issue was whether lower-level figures would cooperate with the prosecutor and testify against the president. Two of Mueller's most important potential witnesses were Michael Flynn, Trump's first national security advisor, and Paul Manafort, Trump's campaign chair. Early in Mueller's investigation, on December 1, 2017, Flynn pleaded guilty to lying to the FBI, and Manafort was later indicted and convicted in a multimillion-dollar fraud in connection with his campaign activities. Trump repeatedly suggested in public that he might pardon Flynn and Manafort, which amounted to encouragement for them to stay silent and loyal to him.

After Flynn pleaded guilty, Trump was asked about the possibility of a pardon for him. "I don't want to talk about pardons for Michael Flynn yet," he said. "We'll see what happens. Let's see. I can say this: When you look at what's gone on with the FBI and with the Justice Department, people are very, very angry." After Manafort was charged, Trump was asked about a pardon for him and said, "No, I don't want to talk about that. . . . But look, I do want to see people treated fairly. That's what it's all about." Hours later, Manafort's bail was revoked and the president posted on Twitter (now X), "Wow, what a tough sentence for Paul Manafort, who has represented Ronald Reagan, Bob Dole and many other top political people and campaigns. Didn't know Manafort was the head of the Mob. What about [James] Comey [former director of the FBI] and Crooked Hillary and all the others? Very unfair!" (Shortly after Manafort was indicted, Rudolph Giuliani, who was then Trump's lawyer, said, "When the whole thing is over, things might get cleaned up with some presidential pardons.")

Mueller operated under the Department of Justice policy that prohibited indictments of sitting presidents; as a result, Mueller could never bring a case that would test whether Trump committed crimes by hinting that pardons might be in the works. Still, Mueller investigated the question of whether Trump's discussions of pardons for Flynn and Manafort amounted to criminal obstruction of justice. In a way, Trump's brazenness worked in his favor. His dangling of pardons took place in public, and most criminals choose to conceal, rather than broadcast, their unlawful intent. (Certainly, that was how Nixon operated.)

But in his final report, Mueller concluded that Trump's public behavior might nevertheless still have violated the criminal law. "Many of the President's acts directed at witnesses, including discouragement of cooperation with the government and suggestions of possible future pardons, occurred in public view," he wrote. "While it may be more difficult to establish that public-facing acts were motivated by a corrupt intent, the President's power to influence actions, persons, and events is enhanced by his unique ability to attract attention through use of mass communications. And no principle of law excludes public acts from the scope of obstruction statutes." At a minimum, then, Trump's public behavior regarding pardons edged close to the line of criminality, if not over it.

––––––––

Trump's first pardon set the tone for many that followed. Joe Arpaio was the longtime elected sheriff of Arizona's Maricopa County, which includes Phoenix. He was a notorious anti-Hispanic bigot, with a special interest in creating harsh and demeaning prison conditions, especially for undocumented immigrants. Arpaio was also a leading spokesman, as Trump was, for the lie that Barack Obama was not born in the United States and thus ineligible to be president. In 2017, Arpaio was convicted of criminal contempt for failing to follow court orders to stop racial profiling. While Arpaio's case was on appeal, on August 25, 2017, Trump pardoned him, declaring in a tweet that Arpaio was an "American patriot," who "kept Arizona safe!" Like virtually all of Trump's pardon recipients, Arpaio had shown no remorse for his crimes; their brazenness matched his own. Later, at a rally in Arizona during the 2024 campaign, Trump saluted Arpaio, who was in the audience. "You are a legend!" Trump said.

Trump followed the Arpaio pardon with one for Scooter Libby, the onetime aide to former Vice President Cheney, who had been convicted of perjury and obstruction of justice in 2007. President George W. Bush's refusal to grant this pardon had sundered his relationship with Cheney, so Trump's pardon was a way of twitting Bush, with whom Trump had a fraught relationship. Trump also pardoned Dinesh D'Souza, a right-wing provocateur who had earlier been convicted of making fraudulent campaign contributions to a Republican Senate candidate in New York, as well as Conrad Black, a Canadian former newspaper publisher and author who had been convicted in a multimillion-dollar fraud. Black had endeared himself to Trump by writing a fawning biography, *Donald J. Trump: A President Like No Other*. Not only did these pardons arrive at the White House outside the Justice Department process, but the recipients also flouted the government's usual conditions for pardons, especially "acceptance of responsibility, remorse and atonement." Far from apologizing, they gloried in their criminal conduct. These initial pardons drew praise from Trump's base and outraged reactions from Democrats, which seemed to be their principal purpose.

At the same time, Trump's affection for his fellow celebrities pushed him in a different direction. The key figure was Kim Kardashian. When Trump was president, the reality television star was attempting to become a lawyer through a process called apprenticeship rather than by going to law school. During her studies, Kardashian became interested in prison reform and clemency, and she used her massive social media following to call attention to the case of Alice Marie Johnson, a sixty-five-year-old woman who was serving a life sentence for a nonviolent drug offense. At the time, too, Kardashian was married to the rapper Kanye West, who had been a Trump supporter.

Trump noticed Kardashian's social media posts and invited her to visit the Oval Office on May 30, 2018, where they were joined by Jared Kushner, Trump's son-in-law and a close adviser. Kushner had his own interest in criminal justice reform, because his father, Charles, had been convicted of making illegal campaign contributions, tax evasion, and witness tampering in a bizarre case that took place in New Jersey in 2005. The core allegation against Charles Kushner was that he had hired a prostitute to seduce his brother-in-law, who was cooperating in the investigation of him. Charles arranged for the tryst to be recorded, with the tape then sent to his sister. After his conviction, Charles was sentenced to two years and served fourteen months, while Jared was in college. Thanks to Kardashian's lobbying, Trump quickly commuted the sentence of Alice Johnson, who was twenty years into her life sentence. (Later, after seeing Johnson's speech at the 2020 Republican convention, he pardoned her.)

Kardashian and Kushner pushed Trump to pursue the issue of excessive prison terms, and they persuaded him to go beyond simply pardoning a handful of sympathetic people, like Johnson. An odd political alliance was born. Some prominent Democrats, like Senator Cory Booker, of New Jersey, welcomed Trump's interest in the issue, as did some libertarian Republicans, like Senator Mike Lee, of Utah, as well as other Republicans who were concerned about the soaring costs of mass incarceration. Religious leaders, drawn from both the evangelical Christian and Orthodox Jewish communities, weighed in. Somehow these disparate actors joined forces, and Congress passed the First Step Act in December 2018. The law, which Trump signed, represented the federal government's first step away from the era of mass incarceration which had begun in earnest under Reagan. The act reduced some mandatory minimum sentences, expanded judges' discretion to sentence below mandatory minimums, and allowed inmates to file motions for reduced sentences on "com-passionate" grounds. One year after the law was signed, the federal prison population had dropped by five thousand, and it continued to decline in later years. By mid-2024, more than 33,000 federal inmates were released under the reforms of the First Step Act, a number many times greater than Obama's commutations.

After crime increased in the wake of the Covid pandemic, and even after it turned downward again in 2023 and 2024, Trump prac-tically disowned the First Step Act, to the extent that he mentioned it at all. In his campaign for president in 2024, Trump preferred instead to return to the customary Republican position of denouncing Dem-ocrats as weak on crime. But the fact remained that with the First Step Act, Trump did what, as a general matter, his opponents wanted and his supporters opposed. He engineered a historic criminal justice reform which will echo through the system for many years and free more people than any president could plausibly pardon or commute in a single term. To all appearances, Trump regrets doing so, but it's an important legacy of his first term.

As far as pardons and commutations were concerned, Trump raced to the bottom. "Mercy," in the conventional sense, had little to do with Trump's actions in those final days. They were all, at their core, about Trump himself—deposits and withdrawals in his favor bank. They were tokens of gratitude, expressions of vengeance, payments for future consideration, and acts of political provocation. As in other areas of his presidency, there were so many scandals with pardons and commutations in this period that it was difficult for the public to fasten on a single one. The sheer number of outrageous pardons served as a kind of insulation against critical public attention to any one of them. (One reason that Bill Clinton's pardon of Marc Rich drew so much notice was because of its singularity.) Pardons and commutations were a central part of Trump's final days in office of his first term, but they were overshadowed by an even greater scandal that was unfolding at the same time—his attempt to overturn his loss of the presidential election to Joe Biden.

In the months before Trump left office, he paid off a handful of political debts. He pardoned Michael Milken, the financier who had been convicted of securities fraud, after a lobbying effort from Sheldon Adelson, the billionaire casino owner who was one of Trump's most generous supporters. Trump also pardoned Bernie Kerik, the former New York City police commissioner who had been convicted of a variety of corruption charges. Kerik was by that point a Fox News contributor and an outspoken Trump partisan.

But the gold rush for pardons began in earnest after Election Day, 2020. Those who wanted something from Trump, especially pardons, recognized that he was on his way out of the White House, and they figured it was their last chance. (They assumed, incorrectly as it turned out, that Trump would never return.) The recipients in this period started with Charles Kushner, who got a pardon simply because he was Jared's father. Trump also used pardons to nurse his grievance against Robert Mueller, the special counsel who had investigated Trump's ties to Russia. Trump followed through with the pardons that he had dangled to prospective witnesses against him. He used pardons to undo every conviction that Mueller obtained. This group included Flynn as well as George Papadopoulos and Alex van der Zwaan, who were all convicted of lying to investigators. Trump pardoned his old friend Roger Stone, whose sentence he had earlier commuted, in another false statement case, as well as Manafort in his fraud case. Though Steve Bannon, Trump's former chief White House strategist, was indicted for fraud by federal prosecutors in New York (not by Mueller), Trump regarded the indictment as an affront. So, Trump pardoned Bannon, too. By granting these pardons, Trump guaranteed that federal prosecutors would never have leverage to compel these witnesses to testify against him.

Another group of pardons served as thank-yous to Republican House members who had been Trump's most loyal supporters in Congress. They asked for clemency for several former colleagues who had been prosecuted for corruption in office (some of it egregious), and Trump delivered. Among those receiving clemency were Duke Cunningham, of California, who was convicted of taking $2 million in bribes, among other crimes; Duncan Hunter, also of California, who pocketed thousands of dollars of campaign contributions and spent it on extramarital affairs; Rick Renzi, of Arizona, who was convicted of racketeering and extortion; Robin Hayes, of North Carolina, who lied to investigators in a bribery investigation; Chris Collins, of New York, who pleaded guilty to insider trading and false statements; and Steve Stockman, of Texas, whose commutation meant he was released after serving only two years of a ten-year sentence for stealing upward of $1 million. There was, of course, no contrition or acceptance of responsibility from any of them.

In a political gesture, Trump pardoned several military officials who were accused of war crimes in Iraq and Afghanistan. For example, Lieutenant Clint Lorance was serving a nineteen-year prison sentence for ordering the murder of two unarmed Afghan villagers. Navy SEAL Eddie Gallagher was charged with shooting at civilians for entertainment, including an Iraqi schoolgirl and an elderly man. He was accused of fatally stabbing a seventeen-year-old prisoner and then photographing himself with the corpse. (He was convicted of lesser charges.) Major Mathew L. Golsteyn was awaiting trial for premeditated murder of a Taliban bomb-making suspect. Trump pardoned them all and later brought Lorance and Golsteyn onstage at one of his political fund-raisers.[1]

By far the largest number of pardons in Trump's final days went to white-collar criminals. Many of them had spent tens or even hundreds of thousands of dollars on lawyers and lobbyists to reach out to Trump (and Jared Kushner). Matt Schlapp, a conservative activist and lobbyist, was paid $750,000 to seek a pardon for a Georgia man convicted of securities fraud. (Schlapp failed.) Brett Tolman, a former U.S. attorney in Utah, received six-figure payments for successfully lobbying for pardons, including the one to Charles Kushner.[2] Lawyers who had represented Trump himself—including John Dowd and Alan Dershowitz, the former Harvard Law School professor— were especially busy with clemency seekers. The Aleph Institute describes itself as a nonprofit advocacy group for members of the Orthodox Jewish community who are impacted by the criminal justice system—"the vast majority of whom are indigent." But Aleph and related entities won clemency for at least twenty-seven people who were wealthy, including some of its own contributors.[3]

Again, the sheer number of undeserving recipients defused the impact of any single pardon. Several defrauded Medicare and Medicaid of millions of dollars, including by victimizing patients with unnecessary procedures. Others evaded millions in taxes. Several were convicted of insider trading. Matching the bribe recipients who were pardoned, Trump pardoned some who paid bribes to politicians. One stole trade secrets from Google. A close friend of Jared Kushner's was convicted of stalking a woman who had rejected his sexual advances. One ran a $100 million gambling ring out of his apartment in Trump Tower, in New York. Another stole $16 million from a bank. An individual with close ties to the White House who was a defendant in the "Varsity Blues" case, where wealthy parents bribed selective colleges to admit their children, was pardoned. (Other defendants in the same investigation were not.) The ex-husband of Jeanine Pirro, a Fox News commentator who was a leading advocate for Trump's false claims that he won the 2020 election, was pardoned for tax evasion.

Perhaps not surprisingly, given the last-minute rush to the White House for clemencies and the absence of scrutiny from the Justice Department, some of Trump's beneficiaries quickly found themselves in legal trouble again. At least seven recipients of clemency from Trump have been arrested again, including three for domestic violence. Jonathan Braun was serving ten years for being a large-scale marijuana dealer. He was also a predatory lender with a history of using violence. Jared Kushner arranged for Braun's clemency and release from prison on Trump's last day in office. In August 2024, Braun was arrested again for assaulting his seventy-five-year-old father-in-law, who was attempting to protect his daughter, whom Braun had attacked twice in the previous month.[4] He was also charged with larceny for failing to pay $160 in bridge tolls while driving a Lamborghini and Ferrari, which both lacked license plates, about forty times. Eliyahu Weinstein was serving twenty-four years for fraud when he received a commutation from Trump; Weinstein was then charged in 2023 in another fraud that allegedly cheated 150 people out of $35 million. Trump pardoned Jesse Benton after a conviction in a campaign finance scheme from the 2012 election. In 2023, Benton was sentenced to eighteen months in prison for another campaign finance violation, this time for facilitating a contribution from a Russian to Trump's 2016 campaign.[5]

Most chilling of all was the commutation that Trump granted on his final day in office to Jaime Davidson, a major upstate New York drug dealer who had been convicted in the 1990 murder of an undercover federal agent.[6] According to the evidence in the case, Davidson recruited three men to rob Wallie Howard Jr., who was working undercover, of $42,000 that he planned to use to buy four pounds of cocaine. Although Davidson did not fire the shot that killed Howard, he gave the gunman the weapon that was used, and thus he was charged and convicted in the murder. Davidson was sentenced to life in prison without the possibility of parole. Later, in seeking clemency, Davidson was represented by a husband-and-wife team who also represented several Trump Organization employees, including Donald Trump Jr. President Trump granted the commutation without consulting the prosecutors in Davidson's case, who were horrified when they found out he would be released. "If you ask me for a list of people who nobody should give a presidential commutation to," the prosecutor said later, "Davidson would pretty much be at the top of the list." In April 2023, after his release from prison, Davidson was arrested for attempting to strangle his wife during a domestic dispute. When his case went to trial, he was acquitted of two felonies but convicted of misdemeanor battery and sentenced to three months in prison. As of late 2024, a federal judge was weighing whether to return Davidson to prison for violating his conditions of supervised release.

In his victorious campaign for president in 2024, Trump promised a new, and even more extraordinary, wave of pardons in his next term.

*Senator Edward Kennedy and Caroline Kennedy present
President Ford with the Profile in Courage Award on May 21, 2001.*
PHOTOGRAPHER: JOEY LIBBY/COPYRIGHT JOHN F. KENNEDY LIBRARY
FOUNDATION/JOHN F. KENNEDY LIBRARY FOUNDATION COLLECTION,
JOHN F. KENNEDY PRESIDENTIAL LIBRARY AND MUSEUM, BOSTON

Time Clarifies

THE FAMILY OF PRESIDENT JOHN F. KENNEDY CREATED the Profile in Courage Award "to recognize and celebrate the quality of political courage that he admired most." The award annually recognizes a public official "whose actions demonstrate the qualities of politically courageous leadership in the spirit of *Profiles in Courage*," JFK's 1956 book about eight senators who risked their careers by embracing unpopular positions. In a ceremony at the Kennedy Library in Boston on May 21, 2001, the award went to President Gerald R. Ford, and Senator Ted Kennedy made the presentation.

"At a time of national turmoil, America was fortunate that it was Gerald Ford who took the helm of the storm-tossed ship of state," Kennedy said. "Unlike many of us at the time, President Ford recognized that the nation had to move forward and could not do so if there was a continuing effort to prosecute President Nixon. So President Ford made a courageous decision, one that historians now say cost him his office, and he pardoned Richard Nixon. I was one of those who spoke against his action then. But time has a way of clarifying past events, and now we see that President Ford was right. His courage and dedication to our country made it possible for us to begin the process of healing and put the tragedy of Watergate behind us. He eminently deserves this award, and we are proud of his achievement."

At the age of eighty-seven, Ford still had a barrel chest and steady gait, and his voice was clear as he accepted the award. The moment moved him greatly. "I would be less than candid, indeed less than

human, if I didn't tell you how grateful—how profoundly grateful—
Betty and I are for this recognition," he said. Ford later told friends
that the award from his old political adversary ranked among the
greatest moments of his life. Ford died on December 26, 2006, at the
age of ninety-three.

The historical revisionism about Ford's pardon of Nixon has continued apace. Bob Woodward, the preeminent journalist of the Watergate era, also changed his mind. In a chapter of a book on political
courage, Woodward recalled that his colleague Carl Bernstein had
startled him on that Sunday morning in 1974 with news of the pardon. "The son of a bitch pardoned the son of a bitch," Bernstein said.
But based on further research and several conversations with Ford
himself, Woodward concluded, "Ford was wise to act. What at first
and perhaps for many years looked like a decision to protect Nixon
was instead designed to protect the nation. . . . So he isn't a son of a
bitch. I was wrong."[1]

Approval of the pardon has almost evolved into the conventional
wisdom. In the oral argument of *Trump v. United States*, Justice Brett
Kavanaugh mentioned the pardon and said, almost in passing, it was
"hugely unpopular, probably why he lost in '76 . . . now looked upon
as one of the better decisions in presidential history, I think, by most
people."

In some ways, it's understandable that the public verdict on the
pardon has shifted in recent years. The popularity of all presidents
tends to increase the further removed they are from office, and that's
certainly been true of Ford and even Nixon. In addition, Ford's decency and honesty, which were genuine and always part of his appeal,
have stood out even more clearly, as several of his successors have
been seen as lacking those qualities. Ford's reputation has also been
aided by the collapse of the most serious accusation against him—
that he made a deal to trade the pardon for the presidency. And as our
politics have become more rancorous, there is obvious appeal to the
idea that a presidential decision—here, a pardon—could bring down
the temperature.

Ford did believe that the pardon would help him, and thus the
country, move on from Watergate and Nixon. Ford had sympathy

for Nixon as an individual, but the pardon was rooted more in Ford's view of the nation's interest rather than just Nixon's well-being. Ford thought all Americans would benefit if the pardon allowed him to focus on broader challenges than the fate (and papers) of his predecessor. No politician's motivations are ever pure, but Ford's at least were sound.

But Ford's pardon of Nixon was wrong in 1974, and it's wrong now. The power to grant clemency—to issue pardons or commutations—exists in tension with the checks and balances in the rest of the Constitution. In the absence of these restraints, presidents must take special care to grant pardons only when the machinery of justice has failed and the normal processes must be overruled. As Alexander Hamilton recognized two-and-a-half centuries ago, clemency can ease a national crisis if it is offered to an entire class of people to allow them and the nation a fresh start, which is what happened after the Whiskey Rebellion and the Civil War. But when it comes to individuals, Hamilton saw that pardons were nothing more, and nothing less, than gifts to ease individual suffering. Ford misunderstood what the public saw right away about the pardon—and about all pardons: that it was a gift to Nixon.

Nixon did not deserve that gift, especially since he never offered a word of meaningful contrition. The pardon was just a free pass handed from one powerful man to another. That was bad enough on its own, given the magnitude of Nixon's misuse of the powers of the presidency, but it was also unjust because his subordinates were at that very moment heading to trial for the crimes they committed with and for Nixon himself. The *Burdick* case was forgotten fifty years ago, and it's been forgotten again since, and for good reason. True, the Court's words remain in effect: a pardon "carries an imputation of guilt; acceptance a confession of it." But Ford's hope that the existence of this legal precedent somehow translated into a genuine admission of guilt by Nixon has always been preposterous.

But what of Ford's principal justification for the pardon—that it was a healing gesture for the country? It wasn't—and it didn't. Of course, since Nixon was never brought to trial, it is impossible to know how the public would have reacted if he had been. But with

the pardon, Ford created as much partisan vitriol as a trial would
have done. So, the pardon was both a moral failure—it was the wrong
thing to do—and a practical one—it didn't accomplish its goals. The
pardon poisoned Ford's relationship with the Democratic majorities in the House and Senate, and the Democrats' margins grew in
the 1974 midterms because of voters' revulsion at the pardon. Even
though he was a man of Congress himself, Ford, with the pardon,
sundered the relationships that were most important to his success as
a president. He also damaged, even if he didn't ruin, his chances for
election in his own right in 1976.

And it was all unnecessary. If Ford had reached out beyond his
tiny circle of advisers—especially Haig, the Nixon spy in his camp—
Ford would have learned that Jaworski had no intention of prosecuting Nixon. To protect an undeserving and ungrateful beneficiary,
and to prevent an outcome that was never going to happen anyway,
Ford wrecked his time in office. And, for good measure, the pardon
remains the only thing most people remember about Ford's presidency.

The story of Ford's misadventure with the Nixon pardon offers a
useful warning at a moment when the nation awaits the next X-ray
into the presidential soul—and the most extravagant misuse of presidential clemency in American history.

————————

On the afternoon of January 6, 2021, Donald Trump watched on television from the White House as his supporters rioted at the Capitol. The first breach of the building took place at 2:13 p.m., when
Dominic Pezzola, a member of the far-right militant group called the
Proud Boys, smashed a window on the Senate side of the building.
He and others began hunting down Vice President Mike Pence, who
had rebuffed Trump's demands that he betray his office and refuse to
certify Biden's victory. Ignoring pleas by his staff and others to direct
the rioters to stand down, Trump at 2:24 p.m. posted on Twitter (now
X): "Mike Pence didn't have the courage to do what should have been
done to protect our Country and our Constitution, giving States a
chance to certify a corrected set of facts, not the fraudulent or inaccu-

rate ones which they were asked to previously certify. USA demands the truth!" Emboldened by Trump's tweet, thousands more protesters then crashed through windows and doors, trampled the police in their way, and stormed into the building with baseball bats, stun guns, bear spray, and pepper spray. They caused millions of dollars in damage and injured 140 police officers. (Five later died.)

As Trump watched the events of the day unfold, he had an immediate thought. According to the people who were with him at the White House, he wanted to issue a "blanket pardon" to all those at the Capitol on January 6th.[2]

In the years that followed, Trump has been consistent in that view, especially after he also faced criminal charges (later dismissed) as a result of his actions on that day. He was accused of conducting a "criminal scheme" to overturn the results of the 2020 election principally by putting forward a slate of "fake electors" on January 6th. Trump saw each rioter as he saw himself; as a martyr, victim, and true casualty of the day's events. At his first rally after declaring his candidacy for reelection in 2024, in Waco, Texas, he played "Justice for All," a rendition of the National Anthem featuring the voices of the "J6 Prison Choir," who were incarcerated defendants in January 6th prosecutions. (They sang in prison into a cell phone.) The sound quality was poor, but Trump played it often at his rallies.

Over the course of the 2024 campaign, Trump's promises to the January 6th defendants became more expansive, his rhetoric on their behalf more heated. At first those arrested were "political prisoners"; then they became "hostages." He wrote on Truth Social that one of his "first acts as your next President" would be to "Free the January 6 Hostages being wrongfully imprisoned!" On May 10, 2023, at a CNN town hall in New Hampshire, Trump said he would pardon a "large portion" of those arrested on January 6th. "I am inclined to pardon many of them. I can't say for sure every single one, because a couple of them, probably they got out of control."[3] Later, he seemed to call for freeing all the prisoners. In June 2024, the Supreme Court rejected a legal theory that undergirded the convictions of some January 6th defendants, though most were also convicted of other crimes as well. In response to the ruling, Trump said at a rally in Virginia, "Free the [January 6th] hostages now. They should free them now for what they've gone through."[4]

In some speeches, he called for financial compensation for the January 6th convicts as well as pardons. "I mean full pardons with an apology to many," he said in one radio interview. "I am financially supporting people that are incredible," Trump said. "It's a disgrace what they've done to them. What they've done to these people is disgraceful."[5] Actually, Trump does not appear to have spent any of his own money to help the January 6th defendants, but his political action committee did contribute $10,000 to the Patriot Freedom Project, which advocates for those charged in the riot.[6]

Given the number and gravity of Justice Department prosecutions of January 6th defendants, Trump's task in granting clemency to so many people will be complex. As of November 2024, federal prosecutors have brought charges against 1,561 people in connection with their actions at the Capitol.[7] About 1,230 have been convicted so far—980 through guilty pleas and 250 after trial. (There have been two acquittals, and more than 200 defendants are still awaiting trial.) About half of the convictions were to felonies, half to misdemeanors. Roughly 750 were sentenced to prison, and perhaps half of them have completed their sentences. Ten members of the Proud Boys and the Oath Keepers, another violent right-wing group, were convicted of seditious conspiracy—that is, that they tried to "overthrow, put down or to destroy by force" the U.S. government. Stewart Rhodes, the head of the Oath Keepers, was sentenced to eighteen years; Enrique Tarrio, of the Proud Boys, got twenty-two years. The FBI is still searching for hundreds more rioters who were part of the invasion of the Capitol but have not yet been identified or arrested.

If Trump were inclined to limit the controversy over the pardons, he could pardon only the thousand or so defendants who have either completed their sentences or were never sentenced to prison in the first place. A pardon would mean that they had clean records, so they could vote and own firearms, which Trump would be sure to celebrate. But Trump never expressed any hesitation or ambivalence about his position, so it seems more likely that he would do what he promised from the beginning and what the Constitution allows: issue a "blanket pardon" to all of the January 6th defendants. Presumably, such a pardon would apply to the several hundred defendants who are still in prison, almost all of whom were convicted of crimes of violence, mostly against police officers; to those defendants awaiting trial; and to those who are still at large.

Unlike Ford and his advisers in 1974, Trump will not agonize about the *Burdick* case; he will not worry that acceptance of a pardon amounts to a confession of guilt. Likewise, Trump will neither seek nor even desire statements of contrition from the recipients. In this way, Trump already understands the pardon process better than Ford did. Trump knows that pardons are gifts with no strings attached, and that's exactly what he wants to bestow on his fellow January 6th defendants. Such is Trump's identification with the rioters at the Capitol that he began, late in the 2024 campaign, to speak of them as "we." Asked at a Univision town hall on October 16 about those arrested on January 6th, he said, "We didn't have guns." When he pardons them, Trump will, in effect, pardon himself.

But Trump now has no reason to issue an actual pardon to himself. In November 2024, after Trump again won the presidency, Jack Smith dismissed the two federal cases against him. Smith did so "without prejudice," meaning that, in theory, Trump could be prosecuted again. But Trump's Justice Department can just make the dismissal "with prejudice" and thus final. At Trump's direction, the FBI will end its hunt for the remaining January 6th rioters. The two pending state prosecutions against Trump, which are not subject to a federal pardon, will linger for a time and then, in all likelihood, meet their doom. Based on the authority of the Supreme Court's ruling in *Trump v. United States*, which was decided after these indictments were issued, the trial or appeals courts will void Trump's conviction in New York and prevent a trial in Georgia. Trump will completely avoid criminal accountability.

Instead, the only legal legacy of January 6th will be any pardons that Trump issues, and these will reflect the worst of his predecessors' exercise of this power. Trump will engage in the same kind of political preening as Reagan did in pardoning the FBI officials. Trump will display the same petty vengeance as George H. W. Bush showed in pardoning the Iran-contra defendants. Trump will ignore the underlying facts of his beneficiaries' cases as Clinton did with Marc Rich. Trump will use Biden's pardon of his son as a justification to pardon the January 6th defendants; like his predecessor, Trump will assert that the excesses of prosecutors compelled him to action. It's tempting to see Ford's pardon of Nixon as different from what Trump will do because the character and values of the two men pose such a contrast. Ford made the wrong decision, but he did so out of a love of country and a largeness of spirit; Trump is moved, as always, by narcissism and pettiness.

But despite the differences between the two presidents, the similarities between the pardon of 1974 and the expected pardons of 2025 are greater than their differences. A bad pardon for an honorable reason is still a bad pardon—and that's what Ford's pardon of Nixon was. Trump's pardons of the January 6th defendants will be bad pardons for bad reasons. But when it comes to evaluating pardons, presidential intent is irrelevant; what matters only is the result, that is, who has received the gift of mercy. Ford rewarded the greatest abuse of presidential power in history at that time. Trump will reward a different kind of abuse—the use of mob power—in the most serious threat to democratic rule since the Civil War. At this point, both Ford and Trump are beyond the reach of the law or the electorate. Together they face the only verdict still outstanding—that of history.

Author's Note

This book is principally based on approximately fifty interviews with the participants; oral histories and documents in various archives; and the voluminous secondary literature on Gerald Ford, Richard Nixon, and Watergate. Citations to secondary sources appear in the Notes.

I am especially grateful to my friends at the Gerald R. Ford Presidential Library in Ann Arbor. The library is extremely well organized, with much of the material now digitized. In addition to documents and photographs from the Ford presidency, the library has an extensive collection of interviews for oral histories. Trevor Armbrister conducted dozens of interviews, including many with Ford himself, to assist Ford in writing his memoirs, and those transcripts were especially valuable. All the photographs (except the one from the Kennedy Library) come from the Ford Library's collection, and they were all taken by the great David Hume Kennerly. David is not only a legendary photographer, but a thoughtful and wise observer of President Ford and his family. At the Ford Library, I express my thanks to Stacy Davis, Elizabeth Estabrook, Sean McConnell, and Joel Westphal.

I was also fortunate to be able to use the resources of the following. The Richard Nixon Presidential Library & Museum in Yorba Linda, California; the National Archives in College Park, Maryland (records of the Watergate Special Prosecution Force and Nixon White House tapes); the Library of Congress (Alexander Haig papers); the Miller Center at the University of Virginia in Charlottesville, Virginia (Gerald Ford presidency material); Baylor University in Waco, Texas (Leon Jaworski oral history); Clemson University in Clemson, South Carolina (Fred Buzhardt papers); and Texas State University in San Marcos (*Texas Monthly* archives). As a journalist, I especially enjoyed the opportunity to examine the archives of two of my heroes, Carl Bernstein and Bob Woodward, at the Harry Ransom Center at the University of Texas in Austin. Those records document in real time the interviews and research that led to *All the President's Men*, *The Final Days*, and *Shadow*; it was a privilege to see how these legends did their work. I also owe special thanks to the children of Benton Becker, who shared with me an unpublished biography of their father, who died in 2015.

A word about the Nixon tapes. Thanks largely to the initiative of the late Professor Stanley Kutler, virtually all the secret recordings that were made at the White House during the Nixon presidency are now public. They are available at the National Archives in College Park as well as online. However, the recordings at the Archives do not come with transcripts, and that makes them very difficult to search. A number of scholars have produced and published transcripts on their own, but it's still hit-and-miss. I am grateful to Professor Timothy Naftali for serving as my guide to the transcripts and for his scholarship on the Nixon era. Thanks also to my friend John Dean, who is not only a protagonist in this story but an important historian of the era as well.

My education on the history of clemency was assisted in great part by Professors Rachel Barkow and Mark Osler. Margaret Love, a former pardon attorney in the Justice Department, was also a generous guide. In 1999, Ken Gormley, who is now the president of Duquesne University, organized a conference in Pittsburgh on Ford's pardon of Nixon. That meeting, which was covered by C-SPAN, was especially useful to me because it included Jack Miller's most expansive discussion of his role. (Miller died in 2009.)

I am privileged again to be published by Simon & Schuster. (Along the way, I was pleased to discover that many of the most important books on this era were also published by S&S.) Mindy Marqués, my editor, was a sure and steady guide. My thanks also to Johanna Li, Larry Hughes, Fred Chase, Lisa Healy, Rachael DeShano, and the boss, Jonathan Karp. I am very fortunate that Kathy Robbins is my literary agent. Adam J. Toobin, Esq. (again) and Professor John Q.

Barrett (again and again) offered perceptive readings of the manuscript. Thank you also to Ron Bernstein.

Among the many blessings in my life are our children, Ellen and Adam, who have had the good fortune (and good judgment) to marry Eric Dodd and Noopur Sen, to whom I am pleased to dedicate this book. For the tenth straight time, Amy McIntosh edited and improved every word of this book, but that's nothing compared to how much she's improved my life.

New York City
December 2024

Notes

CHAPTER 1: NIXON'S LOST INSURANCE

1. Richard Nixon, *RN: The Memoirs of Richard Nixon* (New York: Grosset & Dunlap, 1978), p. 925.
2. Nixon, *RN*, p. 925.
3. James Cannon, *Time and Chance: Gerald Ford's Appointment with History* (New York: HarperCollins, 1994), p. 275.
4. Richard Reeves, *A Ford, Not a Lincoln* (New York: Harcourt Brace Jovanovich, 1975), p. 17.

CHAPTER 2: THE BENIGN PREROGATIVE

1. This history is largely drawn from William F. Duker, "The President's Power to Pardon: A Constitutional History," 18 *William & Mary Law Review* 475 (1977); Jeffrey Crouch, *The Presidential Pardon Power* (Lawrence: University Press of Kansas, 2009); John D. Ferrick, "The Pardoning Power of Article II of the Constitution," *New York State Law Journal*, January 1975; and Kim Wehle, *Pardon Power: How the Pardon System Works—and Why* (Norwalk, CT: Wordhall Press, 2024).
2. Duker, "The President's Power to Pardon," p. 509 n. 174.
3. Margaret Colgate Love, "The Twilight of the Pardon Power," 100 *Journal of Criminal Law & Criminology* 1169, 1178–79 (2010).
4. Love, "The Twilight of the Pardon Power," p. 1176.
5. Rachel E. Barkow and Mark Osler, "Clemency," 7 *Annual Review of Criminology* 311 (2024).
6. Love, "The Twilight of the Pardon Power," p. 1188.
7. See James D. Robenalt, "100 Years Ago, a President Forgave His Opponent's Alleged Subversion," *Washington Post*, January 6, 2022, https://www.washingtonpost.com/history/2022/01/06/warren-harding-eugene-debs/; and Ronald Radosh, "Presidential Pardons and the Spirit of Clemency," *The Bulwark*, July 14, 2020, https://www.thebulwark.com/p/presidential-pardons-and-the-spirit-of-clemency.

8. To Holmes's later regret, he wrote the opinion upholding Debs's conviction, https://supreme.justia.com/cases/federal/us/249/211/.

CHAPTER 3: THE VP'S JOB

1. Thomas DeFrank, "The Things It Carried," *Smithsonian*, July 2008, https://www.smithsonianmag.com/air-space-magazine/the-things-it-carried-45246668/.

2. Gerald R. Ford, *A Time to Heal: The Autobiography of Gerald R. Ford* (New York: Harper & Row, 1979), p. 85.

3. Dick Cheney, Gerald R. Ford Oral History Project, Gerald R. Ford Foundation, p. 15, https://geraldrfordfoundation.org/centennial/oralhistory/dick-cheney/.

4. James Cannon, *Time and Chance: Gerald Ford's Appointment with History* (New York: HarperCollins, 1994), p. 92.

5. Ford, *A Time to Heal*, p. 85.

6. Ford, *A Time to Heal*, p. 118.

7. Robert T. Hartmann, *Palace Politics: An Inside Account of the Ford Years* (New York: McGraw-Hill, 1980), p. 2.

8. Hartmann, *Palace Politics*, p. 26.

9. Alexander M. Haig, *Inner Circles: How America Changed the World. A Memoir* (New York: Warner Books, 1992), p. 480.

10. Cannon, *Time and Chance*, p. 264.

11. Richard Norton Smith, *An Ordinary Man: The Surprising Life and Historic Presidency of Gerald R. Ford* (New York: HarperCollins, 2023), Ch. 14.

12. Hartmann, *Palace Politics*, p. 82.

13. Ford, *A Time to Heal*, p. 115.

14. Cannon, *Time and Chance*, p. 263.

15. Ford, *A Time to Heal*, p. 122.

16. Ford, *A Time to Heal*, p. 127.

17. Jim Windolf, "Remembering a Wild Night at the 1975 White House Prom," *Vanity Fair*, May 29, 2015, https://www.vanityfair.com/culture/2015/05/susan-ford-1975-white-house-prom. See also Betty Ford, *The Times of My Life* (New York: Harper & Row, 1978), pp. 152–54. See generally Jeffrey Toobin, *American Heiress: The Wild Saga of the Kidnapping, Crimes and Trial of Patty Hearst* (New York: Doubleday, 2016).

CHAPTER 4: "A TOTAL PARDON"

1. The best canvas of the possible answers to those questions can be found in Garrett M. Graff, *Watergate: A New History* (New York: Avid Reader Press, 2022), pp. 170–78.

2. The tape of this conversation and the others discussed here were first uncovered by Professor Timothy Naftali. See Timothy Naftali, "Trump's Pardons Make the Unimaginable Real," *The Atlantic*, December 23, 2020,

https://www.theatlantic.com/ideas/archive/2020/12/how-abuse-presidential
-pardon/617473/.
3. Graff, *Watergate*, p. 304.
4. Naftali, "Trump's Pardons Make the Unimaginable Real."
5. John Dean, *Blind Ambition: A White House Memoir* (New York: Simon & Schuster, 1976), p. 259.
6. Ford, *A Time to Heal*, p. 117.
7. Ford, *A Time to Heal*, p. 120.

CHAPTER 5: TO CHARGE *LE GRAND FROMAGE*

1. Graff, *Watergate*, pp. 520–22.
2. Richard Ben-Veniste and George Frampton Jr., *Stonewall: The Real Story of the Watergate Prosecution* (New York: Simon & Schuster, 1977), p. 187.
3. James Doyle, *Not Above the Law: The Battles of Watergate Prosecutors Cox and Jaworski* (New York: William Morrow, 1977), pp. 240–41.
4. Leon Jaworski, *The Right and the Power: The Prosecution of Watergate* (New York: Reader's Digest Press, 1976), p. 87.
5. Jaworski, *The Right and the Power*, pp. 45–48.
6. Jaworski, *The Right and the Power*, p. 99.
7. Doyle, *Not Above the Law*, p. 266.
8. The documents in this section are all linked in this thoughtful discussion of the issue in Walter Dellinger, "Indicting a President Is Not Foreclosed: The Complex History," *Lawfare*, June 18, 2018, https://www.lawfaremedia.org/article/indicting-president-not-foreclosed-complex-history.

CHAPTER 6: BOTH SIDES OF WEST EXEC

1. Cannon, *Time and Chance*, pp. 270–72.
2. Nixon, *RN*, pp. 974–95.

CHAPTER 7: EXPLETIVE DELETED

1. Nixon, *RN*, pp. 970–71, 975.
2. H. R. Haldeman, "The Decision to Record Presidential Conversations," *Prologue Magazine*, Summer 1988, https://www.archives.gov/publications/prologue/1988/summer/haldeman.html.
3. Leonard Garment, *Crazy Rhythm* (New York: Times Books, 1997), p. 264.
4. Raymond Price, *With Nixon* (New York: Viking, 1977), p. 251.
5. Price, *With Nixon*, p. 251; Stanley I. Kutler, *The Wars of Watergate: The Last Crisis of Richard Nixon* (New York: Alfred A. Knopf, 1990), pp. 446–47.
6. Kutler, *The Wars of Watergate*, p. 452.
7. Jaworski, *The Right and the Power*, pp. 147–48.

CHAPTER 8: SUPREME STAKES

1. Quoted in Naftali, "Trump's Pardons Make the Unimaginable Real."
2. Nixon, *RN*, p. 1000; Kutler, *The Wars of Watergate*, pp. 217–19.
3. Nixon, *RN*, p. 1000.
4. Doyle, *Not Above the Law*, p. 331.
5. Doyle, *Not Above the Law*, pp. 334–35. See also Robert Draper, "Colonel of Truth: How My Grandfather, Leon Jaworski, Saved America," *Texas Monthly*, November 2003, https://www.texasmonthly.com/articles/colonel-of-truth/.

CHAPTER 9: THE VISE CLOSES

1. Michael Dobbs, *King Richard: Nixon and Watergate: An American Tragedy* (New York: Alfred A. Knopf, 2021), pp. 27–28; Graff, *Watergate*, p. xxix.
2. Stephen Ambrose, *Nixon: Ruin and Recovery, 1973–1990* (New York: Simon & Schuster, 1991), pp. 353–55.
3. Ambrose, *Nixon: Ruin and Recovery*, p. 374.
4. Graff, *Watergate*, pp. 77–78.
5. Michael Giorgione, *Inside Camp David: The Private World of the Presidential Retreat* (New York: Little, Brown, 2017), pp. 34–43.
6. Nixon, *RN*, pp. 1045–46.
7. Ford, *A Time to Heal*, p. 122.
8. Ford, *A Time to Heal*, p. 123.
9. Nixon, *RN*, p. 1048.
10. Haig, *Inner Circles*, p. 472.
11. Timothy Naftali, "Richard Nixon," in *Impeachment: An American History* (New York: Modern Library, 2018), pp. 144–45.
12. Nixon, *RN*, p. 902.
13. Cannon, *Time and Change*, p. 282.
14. Bob Woodward and Scott Armstrong, *The Brethren: Inside the Supreme Court* (New York: Simon & Schuster, 1979), p. 309.

CHAPTER 10: PARDONS AND SELF-PARDONS

1. Thomas M. DeFrank, *Write It When I'm Gone* (New York: G. P. Putnam's Sons, 2007), pp. 11–14; https://geraldrfordfoundation.org/centennial-docs/oralhistory/wp-content/uploads/2013/05/Tom-DeFrank.pdf.
2. Ford, *A Time to Heal*, pp. 24–25; Smith, *An Ordinary Man*, pp. 335–36.
3. Hartmann, *Palace Politics*, pp. 165–66.
4. Henry Kissinger, *Years of Upheaval* (Boston: Little, Brown, 1982), pp. 1195–96.
5. Smith, *An Ordinary Man*, p. 322.

6. Walter Pincus, "Origin of Pardon Idea in Question," *Washington Post*, February 1, 1976, p. A2.

7. The conversation was first disclosed in Cannon, *Time and Chance*, pp. 286–87.

8. See, for example, Grant Tudor and Justin Florence, "The Self-Pardon Question Is Coming," *Lawfare*, June 12, 2024, https://www.lawfaremedia.org/article/the-self-pardon-question-is-coming?utm_source=substack&utm_medium=email; Gary J. Schmitt, "Could Donald Trump Pardon Himself," American Enterprise Institute, Public Seminar, October 4, 2023, https://www.aei.org/op-eds/could-donald-trump-pardon-himself/; Frank O. Bowman III, "Presidential Pardons and the Problem of Immunity," 23 *Journal of Legislation and Public Policy*, 425, 45–71 (2020); Garrett Epps, "The Self-Pardoning President," *The Atlantic*, January 13, 2019, https://www.theatlantic.com/politics/archive/2019/01/can-president-pardon-himself/579757/#; and Brian C. Kalt, "Pardon Me? The Constitutional Case Against Presidential Self-Pardons," 106 *Yale Law Journal* 779 (1996).

9. https://www.justice.gov/file/147746/dl?inline=.

10. *Ex parte Garland*, 71 U.S. 333 (1866); *United States v. Noonan*, 906 F.2d 953 (3rd Cir. 1990).

11. Antonin Scalia, "Common-Law Courts in a Civil-Law System: The Role of United States Federal Courts in Interpreting the Constitution and Laws," Tanner Lectures on Human Values, Princeton University (1995), https://tannerlectures.utah.edu/_resources/documents/a-to-z/s/scalia97.pdf.

CHAPTER 11: THE SIXTH OPTION

1. Haig, *Inner Circles*, pp. 479–80.

2. Haig, *Inner Circles*, p. 481. See also Bob Woodward and Carl Bernstein, *The Final Days* (New York: Simon & Schuster, 1976), pp. 325–26.

3. Haig, *Inner Circles*, pp. 480–84; Smith, *An Ordinary Man*, p. 323; Hartmann, *Palace Politics*, pp. 126–28.

4. Cannon, *Time and Chance*, pp. 290–91. The papers that Buzhardt prepared do not exist in Ford's presidential library and appear to have been lost in the day-to-day shuffle of events.

5. Bob Woodward, Speech to the National Press Foundation, February 19, 2020, https://www.youtube.com/watch?v=xNZPnseRmaE.

6. Hartmann, *Palace Politics*, pp. 130–32.

7. Cannon, *Time and Chance*, pp. 298–99.

8. Ford, *A Time to Heal*, pp. 9–10.

9. In Ford's memoir, he writes that Haig called him late that night. It was almost certainly that Ford called Haig at that time. Other accounts suggest it was Ford who made the call, and it makes more sense that Ford did. Ford, *A Time to Heal*, pp. 9–10.

10. Cannon, *Time and Chance*, p. 301.
11. Hartmann, *Palace Politics*, pp. 136–37.
12. Harmann, *Palace Politics*, p. 137.
13. Ford, *A Time to Heal*, p. 13.
14. Bob Woodward, *Shadow: Five Presidents and the Legacy of Watergate* (New York: Simon & Schuster, 1999), p. 11.
15. See, for example, Seymour M. Hersh, "The Pardon," *The Atlantic*, August 1983.

CHAPTER 12: PARTY IN INTEREST

1. Haig, *Inner Circles*, p. 487.
2. Nixon, *RN*, p. 1060.
3. Nixon, *RN*, p. 1060.
4. Haig, *Inner Circles*, p. 489.
5. Kissinger, *Years of Upheaval*, p. 1200.
6. Haig, *Inner Circles*, p. 491.
7. Kissinger, *Years of Upheaval*, p. 1203.
8. Ford, *A Time to Heal*, p. 20.
9. Ford, *A Time to Heal*, p. 24.

CHAPTER 13: THE SUN SETS ON NIXON

1. Hartmann, *Palace Politics*, p. 156.
2. Woodward and Bernstein, *The Final Days*, p. 415.
3. H. R. Haldeman and Joseph Dimona, *The Ends of Power* (New York: W. H. Allen, 1978), pp. 360–70; Woodward and Bernstein, *The Final Days*, p. 407.
4. Haldeman and Dimona, *The Ends of Power*, p. 368.
5. Haig, *Inner Circles*, p. 494.
6. Nixon, *RN*, p. 1079.
7. Jaworski, *The Right and the Power*, pp. 217–19; Haig, *Inner Circles*, pp. 500–501.
8. Haig, *Inner Circles*, p. 500.
9. Cannon, *Time and Chance*, p. 337.
10. Smith, *An Ordinary Man*, p. 344.

CHAPTER 14: NIGHTMARE'S END

1. Haig, *Inner Circles*, p. 517.
2. Cannon, *Time and Chance*, pp. 352–53.
3. Robert Sam Anson, *Exile: The Unquiet Oblivion of Richard Nixon* (New York: Simon & Schuster, 1984), p. 23.
4. Smith, *An Ordinary Man*, p. 360.
5. William Gulley with Mary Ellen Reese, *Breaking Cover* (New York: Simon & Schuster, 1980), p. 229.

CHAPTER 15: FORD SETTLES IN

1. Doyle, *Not Above the Law*, p. 346.
2. Jaworski, *The Right and the Power*, p. 225.
3. Doyle, *Not Above the Law*, p. 348.
4. Ford, *A Time to Heal*, 141.
5. Hartmann, *Palace Politics*, pp. 142–43.
6. Barry Werth, *31 Days: The Crisis That Gave Us the Government We Have Today* (New York: Anchor, 2006), pp. 71–72; Cannon, *Time and Chance*, pp. 360–61.
7. Smith, *An Ordinary Man*, p. 369.
8. Cannon, *Time and Chance*, p. 366.

CHAPTER 16: THE COLLAPSING FLOOR

1. James Rosen, *Scalia: Rise to Greatness, 1936–1986* (Washington, D.C.: Regnery, 2023), p. 123.
2. Smith, *An Ordinary Man*, p. 377.
3. Hartmann, *Palace Politics*, pp. 198–99.

CHAPTER 17: A LEAK-FREE DECISION

1. Cannon, *Time and Change*, p. 370.
2. See Laura Kalman, "Gerald Ford, the Nixon Pardon, and the Rise of the Right," 58 *Cleveland State Law Review* 349, 357 (2010).
3. Ford, *A Time to Heal*, pp. 158–59.
4. Hartmann, *Palace Politics*, pp. 257–60; Haig, *Inner Circles*, p. 513; Cannon, *Time and Chance*, p. 373.
5. Benton Becker, "The History of the Nixon Pardon," 30 *Cumberland Law Review* 31 (2000).

CHAPTER 18: DELIVERING THE PUMPKIN

1. Anson, *Exile*, pp. 29–20; Dobbs, *King Richard*, pp. 79–81.
2. Gulley, *Breaking Cover*, p. 229.
3. Anson, *Exile*, p. 31.
4. Jaworski, *The Right and the Power*, p. 222.

CHAPTER 19: THE PROSECUTION CAVES

1. Jaworski, *The Right and the Power*, p. 226.
2. Doyle, *Not Above the Law*, p. 367.
3. Werth, *31 Days*, pp. 280–82; Anson, *Exile*, pp. 50–51.
4. Werth, *31 Days*, p. 281.

5. Jaworski, *The Right and the Power*, p. 241.
6. Jaworski, *The Right and the Power*, pp. 231–32.

CHAPTER 20: FROM NIXON TO TRUMP

1. Trump was also charged in three other criminal cases. In New York state court, he was indicted for and later convicted of creating false business records to cover up his payments to Stormy Daniels, a porn actress; the case largely concerned his behavior before he became president. He was also charged in federal court in Florida with misuse of classified information after he left the presidency. (In July 2024, federal district judge Aileen Cannon dismissed the case on the ground that Jack Smith, the special counsel, was improperly appointed; while the government's appeal was pending, the Department of Justice dismissed the case.) Finally, Trump was charged in Georgia state court with corrupt attempts to overturn his loss in that state's election in 2020. That case is pending. With Trump returning to the presidency in 2025, all of the cases against him are likely to end in dismissals.
2. Hartmann, *Palace Politics*, p. 262; Werth, *31 Days*, p. 293.

CHAPTER 21: SHOWDOWN AT CASA PACIFICA

1. Werth, *31 Days*, pp. 296–98.
2. Werth, *31 Days*, pp. 297–98.
3. See, for example, Richard Nixon, *In the Arena* (New York: Simon & Schuster, 1990), p. 21.

CHAPTER 22: THE LAST CUFF LINKS

1. Ford, *A Time to Heal*, pp. 172–73.
2. Werth, *31 Days*, p. 310.

CHAPTER 23: "WE HAVE ALL PLAYED A PART"

1. Hartmann, *Palace Politics*, p. 266.
2. Werth, *31 Days*, pp. 216–17.
3. Jerald F. terHorst, *Gerald Ford and the Future of the Presidency* (New York: The Third Press, 1974), pp. 226–27.
4. Werth, *31 Days*, p. 319.

CHAPTER 24: THE LEGACY OF THE PARDON

1. Scott Kaufman, *Ambition, Pragmatism and Party* (Lawrence: University Press of Kansas, 2017), p. 190; Douglas Brinkley, *Gerald R. Ford* (New York: Times Books, 2007), p. 68.

2. Ford, *A Time to Heal*, pp. 178–79

3. Haig, *Inner Circles*, pp. 516–17.

4. Haig, *Inner Circles*, p. 518.

CHAPTER 25: FORD'S BURDEN

1. Julie Nixon Eisenhower, *Pat Nixon: The Untold Story* (New York: Simon & Schuster, 1986), pp. 432–35; Anson, *Exile*, pp. 60–62; Ambrose, *Nixon: Ruin and Recovery*, pp. 465–66.

2. Cannon, *Time and Chance*, p. 386.

3. Smith, *An Ordinary Man*, p. 404.

4. Rick Perlstein, *Reaganland: America's Right Turn, 1976–1980* (New York: Simon & Schuster, 2020), pp. 3–4.

CHAPTER 26: ALL ROADS LEAD TO, AND FROM, WILLIE HORTON

1. Graham G. Dodds, *Mass Pardons in America: Rebellion, Presidential Amnesty, and Reconciliation* (New York: Columbia University Press, 2021), p. 166.

2. Rachel Barkow, "Clemency and the Presidential Administration of Criminal Law," 90 *New York University Law Review* 802, 816 (2015).

3. Barkow, "Clemency and the Presidential Administration of Criminal Law," p. 826.

4. See Beth Schwartzapfel and Bill Keller, "Willie Horton Revisited," The Marshall Project, May 13, 2015, https://www.themarshallproject.org/2015/05/13/willie-horton-revisited.

5. Schwartzapfel and Keller, "Willie Horton Revisited."

6. See Jeffrey Toobin, *Opening Arguments: A Young Lawyer's First Case—United States v. Oliver North* (New York: Viking, 1991).

CHAPTER 27: THE ATROPHY AND REBIRTH OF THE PARDON POWER

1. See Jeffrey Toobin, *Homegrown: Timothy McVeigh and the Rise of Right-Wing Extremism* (New York: Simon & Schuster, 2023), p. 97.

2. Bill Clinton, *My Life: The Presidential Years* (New York: Vintage, 2005), p. 628.

3. Margaret Colgate Love, "The Pardon Paradox: Lessons of Clinton's Last Pardons," 32 *Capitol Law Review* 185, 193 (2002).

4. Love, "The Twilight of the Pardon Power," pp. 1169, 1200.

5. See Toobin, *American Heiress*, pp. 337–40.

6. George W. Bush, *Decision Points* (New York: Crown, 2010), p. 104.

7. Bush, *Decision Points*, p. 105.

8. Mark Osler, "Fewer Hands, More Mercy: A Plea for a Better Federal Clemency System," 41 *Vermont Law Review* 465, 485–87 (2017).

CHAPTER 28: THE FIRST-TERM TRUMP PARDONS

1. Maggie Haberman, "Trump Brings 2 Officers He Cleared of War Crimes Onstage at Fund-Raiser," *New York Times*, December 8, 2019, https://www.nytimes.com/2019/12/08/us/politics/trump-war-crimes-pardons.html.

2. Karl Evers-Hillstrom, "Trump-Tied Lobbyists Paid Massive Sums to Push Pardons," *Open Secrets*, January 22, 2021, https://www.opensecrets.org/news/2021/01/trump-tied-lobbyists-paid-massive-sums/; Michael S. Schmidt and Kenneth P. Vogel, "Prospect of Pardons in Final Days Fuels Market to Buy Access to Trump," *New York Times*, March 21, 2021, https://www.nytimes.com/2021/01/17/us/politics/trump-pardons.html.

3. Kenneth P. Vogel and Nicholas Confessore, "Access, Influence and Pardons: How a Set of Allies Shaped Trump's Choices," *New York Times*, March 21, 2021, https://www.nytimes.com/2021/03/21/us/politics/trump-pardons.html; Kenneth P. Vogel and Eric Lipton, "Another Trump Clemency Recipient Faces Domestic Violence-Related Charges," *New York Times*, October 14, 2024, https://www.nytimes.com/2024/10/14/us/politics/philip-esformes-trump-clemency-recipient-new-charges.html.

4. Michael S. Schmidt and Maggie Haberman, "Trump Clemency Recipient Accused of Assaulting Wife and Father-in-Law," *New York Times*, August 21, 2024, https://www.nytimes.com/2024/08/21/us/politics/jonathan-braun-assault.html?searchResultPosition=1; Dan Mangan, "Trump Clemency Recipient's Arrest Draws Attention of Judge in Old Drug Case," CNBC, August 26, 2024, https://www.cnbc.com/2024/08/26/trump-clemency-recipient-jonathan-braun-judge.html.

5. Michael S. Schmidt and Maggie Haberman, "A Trump Clemency Recipient Is Convicted of Domestic Violence," *New York Times*, September 3, 2024, https://www.nytimes.com/2024/09/03/us/politics/trump-clemency-jaime-davidson.html?searchResultPosition=1.

6. Judd Legum, "Murderer Whose Life Sentence Was Commuted by Trump Convicted of Domestic Violence," *Popular Information*, September 3, 2024, https://popular.info/p/murderer-whose-life-sentence-was.

EPILOGUE: TIME CLARIFIES

1. Bob Woodward, "Gerald R. Ford," in Caroline Kennedy, ed, *Profiles in Courage for Our Time* (New York: Hyperion, 2002), pp. 310, 314.

2. This account is drawn from the report of the United States House Select Committee to Investigate the January 6th Attack on the United States Capitol, which was released on December 22, 2022. See especially Chapter 7, https://january6th-benniethompson.house.gov/.

3. Amanda Terkel, "Trump Says He Would Pardon a 'Large Portion' of Jan. 6

Rioters," NBC News, May 10, 2023, https://www.nbcnews.com/politics /donald-trump/trump-says-pardon-large-portion-jan-6-rioters-rcna83873.

4. Irie Sentner, "Trump Calls for Those Arrested for Jan. 6 to Be Freed Imme-diately," *Politico*, June 28, 2024, https://www.politico.com/news/2024/06/28 /trump-jan-6-attack-free-arrested-00165900.

5. Mariana Alfaro, "Trump Vows Pardons, Government Apology to Capitol Rioters if Elected," *Washington Post*, September 1, 2022, https://www.washing tonpost.com/national-security/2022/09/01/trump-jan-6-rioters-pardon/.

6. Shelby Talcott, "'Welcome to the Family': How Donald Trump Learned to Love the January 6 Movement," Semafor, March 19, 2024, https://www .semafor.com/article/03/18/2024/donald-trump-january-6.

7. Under Biden, the Justice Department maintained a regularly updated webpage about the progress of the January 6th investigation. It's unlikely to remain when Trump returns to office. https://www.justice.gov/usao-dc/46-months -jan-6-attack-us-capitol#_ftn1.

Index

About the Author

Jeffrey Toobin is one of the most recognized and admired legal journalists in the country. On television, in bestselling books, and in magazines and podcasts, he has covered all of the most dramatic legal controversies of the past three decades. *The Pardon: The Politics of Presidential Mercy* is his tenth book.

Toobin has been a leading figure in coverage of the Supreme Court while at CNN and at ABC News, where he won an Emmy Award, as well as during his tenure as a staff writer for *The New Yorker*. Both *The Oath: The Obama White House and the Supreme Court* and *The Nine: Inside the Secret World of the Supreme Court* were *New York Times* bestsellers. *The Nine* was awarded the 2008 J. Anthony Lukas Prize for Nonfiction.

Toobin's work has also been the basis for major television events. *The Run of His Life: The People v. O. J. Simpson* was the basis for the acclaimed ten-part limited series, *American Crime Story*, starring John Travolta and Cuba Gooding Jr., and FX Network featured a limited series based on *A Vast Conspiracy: The Real Story of the Sex Scandal that Nearly Brought Down a President*.

Toobin has written several other critically acclaimed books, including *Too Close to Call: The Thirty-Six Day Battle to Decide the 2000 Election*. *True Crimes and Misdemeanors: The Investigation of Donald Trump* became an immediate *New York Times* bestseller, as did his previous book, *American Heiress: The Wild Saga of the Kidnapping, Crimes and Trial of Patty Hearst*.

Previously, Toobin served as an assistant U.S. attorney in Brooklyn. He also served as an associate counsel in the Office of Independent Counsel Lawrence E. Walsh, an experience that provided the basis for his first book, *Opening Arguments: A Young Lawyer's First Case—United States v. Oliver North.*

Toobin earned his bachelor's degree from Harvard College and graduated magna cum laude from Harvard Law School, where he was an editor of the Harvard Law Review. He lives with his family in New York City.

Also by
JEFFREY TOOBIN

"The most AUTHORITATIVE and COMPELLING history
of the 1995 Oklahoma City bombing to date....
A GRIPPING READ." —The Associated Press

Available wherever books are sold.